Trois Etoiles

The Member for Paris

A Tale of the Second Empire Vol. 1

Trois Etoiles

The Member for Paris
A Tale of the Second Empire Vol. 1

ISBN/EAN: 9783741179129

Manufactured in Europe, USA, Canada, Australia, Japa

Cover: Foto ©ninafisch / pixelio.de

Manufactured and distributed by brebook publishing software (www.brebook.com)

Trois Etoiles

The Member for Paris

COLLECTION
OF
BRITISH AUTHORS

TAUCHNITZ EDITION.

VOL. 1183.

THE MEMBER FOR PARIS BY TROIS-ETOILES.

IN TWO VOLUMES.

VOL. I.

"A force de marcher l'homme erre, l'esprit doute,
Tous laissent quelquechose aux buissons de la route,
Les troupeaux leur toison et l'homme sa vertu."
                                        VICTOR HUGO.

THE MEMBER FOR PARIS:

A TALE OF THE SECOND EMPIRE.

BY

TROIS-ETOILES.

COPYRIGHT EDITION.

IN TWO VOLUMES.—VOL. I.

LEIPZIG

BERNHARD TAUCHNITZ

1871.

The Right of Translation is reserved.

CONTENTS

OF VOLUME I.

		Page
CHAPTER I.	Ce fut un Deuil dans le Pays	7
— II.	Honest Gerold	29
— III.	Vox Populi Vox Dei	65
— IV.	Anno Domini M.DCCC.LIV	74
— V.	Bourgeois Politics	84
— VI.	A First Brief	118
— VII.	A First Speech	125
— VIII.	Sweets and Bitters of Popularity	157
— IX.	Horace starts in Journalism	169
— X.	New Friends, New Habits	186
— XI.	Love and War	198
— XII.	M. Macrobe offers Money	216
— XIII.	M. Pochemolle's Request	227
— XIV.	M. Macrobe inserts the thin End of the Wedge	239
— XV.	How Empires are governed	254
— XVI.	Mademoiselle Angélique	271
— XVII.	"The Future Madame Filoselle" . . .	283
— XVIII.	M. Macrobe "at Home"	291
— XIX.	Young Candour, Old Subtlety	304

THE MEMBER FOR PARIS.

CHAPTER I.

Ce fut un Deuil dans le Pays.

HAUTBOURG on the Loire is a venerable old town, which played an important part in French history some six or seven hundred years ago, when gentlemen wore plate-armour and cut each other's throats by way of pastime. If we may trust the legend, it originally formed part of the fief of a mighty Count Alaric, who, being a disloyal subject and in league with the devil, thrashed his king, Louis le Gros, in a field adjoining the town, which Providence and the municipal council between them have since appointed for a brick-kiln. If you turn to Froissart you will find that a Count de Hautbourg fought behind John II. at Poictiers, and was in the train of that ill-starred monarch when he rode through London on a tall horse, having his vanquisher, the Black Prince, beside him on a small one. Three centuries and a half later another Count de Hautbourg turned up in the Bastille, where he had been put for being a Jansenist; and in 1793 a certain Raoul-Aimé, Marquis of Hautbourg and Clairefontaine, was heard of on the guillotine, where he perished, it seems, with remarkable good grace and equanimity. I am not going to weary you with a long account of what the Hautbourgs did in exile during the Republic and the reign of Napoleon; but if you are versed in contemporary history you must have read all about that Marquis of H. and C., who accompanied Louis XVIII. to Hartwell, married in England Mary-Anne Sophia, daughter of Ezekiel Guineaman, Esquire, and died, under the Restoration, a duke, a peer of France, and a secretary of state. To him succeeded his eldest son, who was also a peer of France, but never a minister, and who figured as one of the leaders of that "anti-dynastic" opposition, which made the life of poor Louis Philippe so extremely unpleasant to him. This nobleman being in Paris, in 1851, at the time when Monsieur Bonaparte, as he called him, effected his *coup-d'état*, was so unfortunate as to take a walk in the afternoon of the 3rd December, at the precise moment when the emissaries of the said Monsieur B. were most intent upon their work. Finding himself suddenly face to face with a troop of M. de Goyon's horse, whose mission it was to clear the streets, he made an attempt to fly—the first attempt of the kind, be it said incidentally, that he had ever made in his life. But well-mounted dragoons are not always so easy to fly from. You will remember that on this occasion the brave defenders of order had been liberally plied with wine, and had received instructions not to spare anybody who stood in their way. These instructions they obeyed; and so it befell that the noble scion of the Hautbourgs, who entertained about the same feelings towards democracy as he did towards pitch, came, thanks to the grim irony of fate, by the death of a democrat. For, when the slain were picked up on the evening of that glorious day which slew a republic and founded a dynasty, the Legitimist duke was found lying side by side with a subversive sweep, a costermonger of socialist tendencies, and a small boy, three foot high, who must have been wicked beyond his years, seeing that out of his bleeding, perverse little hand was snatched a red toy-flag emblazoned with the heinous words, *Vive la Liberté!*

Some three years after this, that is, in the year 1854, the time at which this narrative commences, the domain and castle of Clairefontaine, about two miles distant from Hautbourg, had not yet been visited by their new master. The estate, which during five-and-thirty years had teemed with splendour, animation, and festivity, now looked as if a sudden blight had fallen upon it. Grass had begun to sprout over the stately avenue, a good mile long, which led from the lodge-gates of the manor-house to its principal entrance. The shutters of the castle were all closed and barred. The stables, in which the last Duke of Hautbourg had stalled six-and-twenty horses, were deserted. The handsome little Gothic chapel, one of the sights of the country, in which it was reported that Fénélon had once preached, and in which it was a certified fact that his Majesty King Charles X. had been several times to mass during the visit he paid to the first Duke in 1827, was become a home for spiders; and—worse sign than all—the monumental fountain standing in the centre of the state court-yard—fountain built on the designs of the famous sculptor Pierre Puget, and covering a spring from which the manor drew its name of Clairefontaine—was overgrown with moss, thus revealing that its dolphins and naiads had long ceased to dash spray out of their open mouths and horned conchs into the porphyry basin under them. Had it not been for the unsightly ruins of an unfinished summer-house, which had evidently been begun in the late Duke's time, and abandoned to the mercies of wind and rain at his death, one would have fancied it was full a hundred years since anybody had trod those leaf-strewn alleys and silent chambers. Now and then in the very early morning, or in the evening towards sunset, an old crone was to be seen painfully mowing with a hand-sickle the long grass on the lawn, or gathering peaches, apricots, and cherries in the orchard, or picking lapfuls of roses and pinks from what had once been the flower-garden; but she partook more of the phantom than of the human being. If questioned, she would tell you that she was the lodge-keeper, and that she gathered the fruit and flowers to prevent them being wasted. She was a rather dismal old woman, with a querulous intonation of voice, but—like all French people of either sex—she was ready enough to talk, and would spin her quavering yarns by the hour when interrogated civilly. "She had no idea," she said, "when the new Duke was coming; she believed he lived in foreign parts. Somebody had told her that he was an odd gentleman—not mad, Monsieur, she didn't mean that, but queer-like in his ways. No one had ever seen him at Clairefontaine since he was a little bit of a boy just so high; no, he hadn't even come to M. le Duc's funeral, which was thought strange and had made folks about the country talk a little, though our Holy Virgin forbid that she should find anything to say concerning a gentleman who was a Hautbourg and certainly had good reasons for all he did. But you see, sir, despite her being an old woman, she couldn't help hearing what people said, and them as talked said that Monsieur the new Duke had not been very well off before, and that it was peculiar he shouldn't have come to the burial of a relation whose death had brought him a million francs a year. Ay, Monsieur, it was full a million, if not more. All the land from Hautbourg to Clairefontaine, from Clairefontaine to Boisfroment and Clairebourg, and from Clairebourg to Sainte-Sophie, belonged to the estate. To judge of the size one should have seen all the tenants assembled, some three or four hundred, on horseback, as she had seen them when Monseigneur the late Duke came of age, and when 'Monsieur le Roi Charles Dix' arrived on a visit with Monsieur le Duc d'Angoulême and Monseigneur le Duc de Quelen, Archbishop of Paris. Ah, that was a sight to see, that was! but, mon Dieu, those times were far gone, and men were no longer now what they were then. In those days she was a young woman, and her husband, who was head gamekeeper, had loaded his Majesty's own gun when there was a battue in the preserves. He was paralyzed now, her husband, but he had been 'a brave;' he had served as sergeant in the Prince of Condé's army at Coblentz along with the first Duke, who was Marquis then; and he had lived in Monseigneur's household upwards of forty years. There was no head gamekeeper now, in fact no gamekeeper at all, and the estate was managed by a new agent, M. Claude." Was he a kind man, this Monsieur Claude?—"Oh, yes, sir; she couldn't but say he was kind enough; he was a quiet-spoken gentleman from Paris, and never hard to the tenants. But, after all, Monsieur—" and here the old woman's voice would wax more querulous and whimpering—"it wasn't the same as having M. le Duc here. The country had been all dead like for the last three years, and she had heard tell that if this went on much longer half the folks up at the town yonder would be ruined. You see, sir, they used to live on Monseigneur, they did, and the new Duke's keeping away was no more nor less than taking the bread out of their mouths."

This account, gloomy and piteous as it might sound, was yet cheerful in comparison to what one heard in the town itself. There the closing of the Château of Clairefontaine and the protracted absence of the new Duke were viewed as public calamities; and one had only to walk along the tortuous old streets and mark the dejected faces of the shopkeepers, to guess that unless M. le Duc put in an appearance very shortly the old woman's prediction about the *gazelle* was not unlikely to be realized. As we said at starting, Hautbourg was a venerable town, but it had had its day, and it could no longer afford to do without patronage. On each side of the main-street, which was called *La Rue de Clairefontaine*, the sign-boards and devices over the shops (for sign-boards are as much in vogue in French provincial towns as they were in England 150 years ago) testified abundantly that, spite of revolutions and noble principles of equality, the relations between borough and manor-house were as feudal as they had ever been at the best of times. Over the crockery-dealer's was the picture of a young person standing beside a bubbling fountain and handing a mugful of water to a knight in plate-armour, with underneath the words: *Au Chevalier de la Claire fontaine.* Over the ironmonger's was another knight in plate-armour, dispensing what appeared to be shovels and tongs to his menials, and exhorting them to be "*toujours prêts*," which was the motto of the Hautbourgs. Over the pork-butcher's was a Hautbourg slaying a wild-boar; over the gun-smith's a fourth Hautbourg firing off a culverin, and so on. Of course the chief inn was the Hôtel de Clairefontaine, and its rival over the way the Hôtel Monseigneur; and equally of course there was in the midst of the market-place an equestrian statue of the Hautbourg of Crécy, with a long homage in Latin to the valour of that warrior.*

The Dukes of Hautbourg had always done their very best to foster in the borough a spirit of dependency, and with the greater success as the town, having no manufactures to support it, and being situated neither on a river, nor in the vicinity of a large canal, nor on the trunk line of an important railway, possessed none of the elements of modern vitality, and would probably have dwindled away into a village had it not been for the great family at Clairefontaine. It was to this family the town owed everything. Its schools, its free library, its museum of stuffed birds, its restored church, filled with furbished brasses and stained-glass windows; its restored gate, out of which the Count Alaric had proceeded when he went to beat Louis VII., and on which still bristled a spike, where it was assured this same Count used to spit the heads of his subjects who were behind-hand with their taxes;** its quaint fountain and horse-trough

---

* This statue was erected at the Restoration, the original one standing before 1789 having been melted down under the Republic, one and indivisible, to coin pence with.

** I ought to mention that there were some who insisted this was only the remnant of an ancient weather-cock, but there are unbelieving people everywhere.

in the street near the cattle-market, its red-brick almshouses and free dispensary,—all these institutions had been built, founded, or renovated with Clairefontaine money. Furthermore, the late Duke, with a view to keeping up his territorial influence, had spent annually some four hundred thousand francs in the town. All the necessaries of life in the way of furniture, food, and clothing, both for himself and servants, and many luxuries also, which a less politic nobleman might have bought in Paris, this far-sighted landlord purchased at Hautbourg. He even went the length of wearing in Paris coats cut by the Hautbourg tailor, and of suffering none but the Hautbourg doctor to attend him in illness—acts of courage these which entailed their reward, for I honestly believe the two facts combined did more for the popularity of the Duke, and for the self-esteem of the borough, than if Monseigneur had caused Hautbourg to be raised to the rank of a firstclass prefecture, and had brought a cardinal-archbishop to reside there. But this was not all. The establishment at Clairefontaine was not only an ever-flowing source of profit in itself; it also acted as a great central planet around which gravitated a number of satellites, in the shape of smaller country-houses, occupied by the lesser nobility and gentry of the department. So long as the hospitable doors of the castle remained open these lesser gentry abounded. Harvest festivals, archery-meetings, hunting-parties, masked balls, and charity fairs, followed each other in unbroken, eddying succession. Not a small purse but endeavoured to vie with the big purse; hall played the suit of castle, and villa returned the lead of hall: the whole summer and autumn season was a carnival, and the direct result

CE FUT UN DEUIL DANS LE PAYS.   15

appeared in this, that the trading men of Hautbourg
grew fat, their wives and children waxed ruddy, and
the borough in general 'wore a sleek and prosperous·
look, such as speaks of plenty, and savings in the
funds.

All this, however, was a thing of the past now.
The eclipse of the great planet had involved that of
the satellites, and Hautbourg was fallen of a sudden
from its snug position of ease into penury, the more
hard to bear as it had been unexpected. The Hautbourg of 1854 was but the ghost of the Hautbourg of
1851. Can you fancy Capua ravaged by a pestilence,
Pompeii become bankrupt, or Herculaneum abandoned
just previous to its interment? There was not a carriage
to be seen in that neatly-paved serpentine Rue de
Clairefontaine, in which, of a fine autumn afternoon
in the good times of the late Duke, the local quid-
nuncs had often counted as many as a couple of dozen
vehicles, come in for shopping, and drawn up in a
long *queue* outside MM. Blanchemelle and Camisole's,
the linen-drapers, or Madame Bavolet's, the *modiste*
from Paris. MM. Blanchemelle and Camisole and
Madame Bavolet had always prided themselves upon
keeping pace step for step with the fashions of the
capital, and it was certainly to their credit that their
bills were, if anything, rather heavier than those of the
Rue de la Paix; but, alas! where were they and the
fashions now? MM. B. and C. were advertising cotton-
checks cheap, and a humble placard in Madame Bavolet's window informed you that bonnets were to be had
within "first style" for fifteen francs! It is curious
what a single blow with a dragoon's sword can do.
The unsuspecting pimple-nosed trooper who cut down

Monsieur le Duc, had at the same stroke ripped open the money-bags of a whole borough, dispersed the denizens of some score of mansions, and mowed away the prosperity of twenty square miles as completely as if it had been so much grass. I need not tell you how popular he was, this pimple-nosed trooper, in Hautbourg; but I think he would have spent a pleasant quarter of an hour if the municipal council could have had the dealing with him for fifteen minutes in private. Nevertheless, I am bound to say there was some one against whom public opinion was yet more incensed than against *him*, and that was the new landlord—the new Duke of Hautbourg. After all, the dragoon had acted in ignorance; he was a brute, who was paid to do his work; and as for the Monsieur Bonaparte who had paid him, why, you see, he had become Emperor since, and so the less discussion about him the better. But what was to be said for a man who had come into a million francs a year, a colossal estate, a magnificent name, and who yet hid away in some hole-and-corner foreign town, and never condescended to show himself? I ask you, what was the good of being a Duke, if one did not stand forth and show oneself? The law ought to put a stop to dukes who did not show themselves. Their being suffered to hold land was a nonsense; it was immoral, and the sooner they were compelled by statute either to relinquish their money or to spend it like gentlemen, the better it would be for everybody. Such were the discourses that were uttered in Hautbourg; and if you would like to hear what else was said about the new and mysterious owner of Clairefontaine, you have only to step in and listen to the conversation held one evening after a very sorry market-day at the *table-d'hôte* of the chief hotel in the place.

It was at that critical moment in the repast when the boiled beef has been removed, and when the company are waiting, silent, to see what is coming next.

Farmer Toulmouche, wizen and small—a fine specimen of a French farmer nourished on lean pork and red wine—poured himself out half a tumbler of *ordinaire*, diluted it with water, and mournfully ventured upon an observation.

"I never see such a market-day in all my life," he said. "This very day three years ago I sold twenty beeves—no more nor less. To-day I sold never a one."

"Nor I," dismally echoed Farmer Truchepoule, an agriculturist of rather bigger calibre. "Never a one."

"Oh! don't let's talk of past times," protested M. Scarpin, the local bootmaker, dejectedly. He had come to dine at *table-d'hôte* to raise his spirits a little, for trade had not been very brisk at home that day, and Madame Scarpin, according to the wont of lovely woman, had made him bear the penalty of it.

"No, don't let's talk of past times," assented M. Ballanchu, the seedsman, with a sigh; but he instantly added, "When I think of that Duke skulking away like this, and allowing everything here to go to rack and ruin, *par tous les cinq cent mille diables*, it makes my blood boil."

M. Ballanchu was a fat man, and when his blood boiled, after an invocation to the five hundred thousand devils, his countenance reddened and was ferocious to behold.

"Of what duke are you speaking?" asked young M. Filoselle, the commercial traveller, whetting his knife against his fork with a view to the roast veal which Madelon, the servant wench, was just then bringing in. This was only M. Filoselle's second visit to Hautbourg. On both occasions he had found a prodigious difficulty in screwing orders out of the "beggarly" town, and he saw no reason whatever for standing on ceremony.

"Why, the Duke of Hautbourg, to be sure," answered M. Ballanchu, in astonishment; "whom else should I mean?"

"Ah, yes, I remember," proceeded M. Filoselle, trying the edge of his knife on his thumb. "You did nothing but talk about him last time I was here. Well, hasn't he turned up yet?"

This levity disgusted M. Scarpin, the bootmaker, who communicated to his neighbour, M. Hochepain, the tax-gatherer, that those Parisians were growing more and more bumptious every year. Unfortunately, this remark was lost upon M. Hochepain, for, besides being deaf, he was at that moment immersed in profound speculation as to who would get the veal kidney.

It was Farmer Follavoine, the replica picture of Farmer Toulmouche, who undertook to answer the traveller.

"Turned up!" he rejoined bitterly. "No, and never likely to. Why should he turn up? His agent collects his rents for him regular; and so long as them's all right, I don't suppose he's going to care much whether us here goes to the deuce or not."

"I know I shouldn't—not two pins," remarked M. Filoselle, pleasantly.

"Do you take stuffing?" called out M. Duval, the landlord, from his end of the table.

"I should think he did—he takes everything," ejaculated the stout Madelon: the person alluded to being M. Hochepain, the tax-gatherer.

"If I were you," said M. Filoselle, shaking the pepper-pot over his plate, which was by this time full of roast, and grinning approval at Madelon's sally— "If I were you, I shouldn't sit down and pull faces all the year round, as you seem to be doing. If you want to see your Duke back again, why don't you—Madelon, my angel, the bread—why don't you draw up a petition and have it off to him with a deputation?"

"What good would that do?" asked M. Scarpin contemptuously.

"Not much, I am afraid, mon pauvre M. Scarpin, if it was you who headed the deputation: for your Duke might think the jaundice had broken out here, and people who are rich don't like the jaundice. But if you sent somebody with a more cheerful face on his shoulders, something might come of it. After all, though," pursued the collected M. Filoselle, "it depends on what sort of a man your Duke is. In my experience there are dukes and dukes. I once knew a duke who was no higher than Madelon's waist there, *par exemple;* he wasn't so stout. We travelled together on board a steamboat going down the Rhine—you don't know the Rhine, M. Scarpin? it's a splendid river, *couleur café au lait*, with a bordering of sugar-loaves on each side. The duke was standing abaft blowing away at a cigar. Said I to him 'Monsieur le Duc, it is the mission of great men to patronize the arts and manufactures. I am travelling for three world-famed houses: one in the drapery way, another in the musical instrument line, and the third in the wine business. I also take subscriptions and advertisements for two newspapers, one democratic, the other conservative. If you will honour me with an order for a flute, and put down your name as subscriber to one of the papers, you will encourage native industry and promote the development of journalism.'

"'Monsieur,' he replied drily, 'I am not a great man. I don't play the flute, and I think that journalism is a great deal too much developed as it is,' and with this he turned on his heel. *Ah diable!* that's what I call a sharp duke; and if yours is like him, I agree with you, it wouldn't be much use petitioning. But . . ."

"Go to, saucy *farceur* from Paris!" interrupted M. Ballanchu wrathfully. "You're all of you alike with that cursed habit of sniggering at everything. I tell you it's not a matter to laugh at, that a whole town should be going on to ruin, because a crotchety old man, who has had all the good blood in him poisoned by that infernal city of yours, chooses to hide away and hoard up the gold he ought never to have inherited. I tell you, we country-folk whom you Parisians turn up your snub-noses at, are a precious sight better than you; do you hear that, young whippersnapper? Bad luck to you, one and all!"

"Hear, hear," chorussed Farmers Toulmouche, Truchepoule, and Follavoine, who had an unmitigated contempt for Parisians. They had never seen Paris, either of them, and didn't wish to.

M. Filoselle was not the least abashed. He had just finished his veal, and was occupied in mopping up the gravy in his plate with some bread-crumb. This operation completed to his satisfaction, he raised his eyes towards his interlocutor, and said, "Monsieur the Seedsman, my birthplace is not Paris but Dijon; I first saw the light in the city renowned for its mustard, and I beg you to observe that my nose is of the aquiline order of architecture. As for the old gentleman with the crotchets, who had his good blood poisoned in Paris, I should like to hear something more about him, for he must be an interesting phenomenon to study."

M. Ballanchu growled.

"Come, come," interposed M. Duval, the host, in a spirit of conciliation, for he had tact enough to see that his fellow-townsman, finding himself unequal to a wordy war, might have recourse to some other means of asserting rustic supremacy—"Come, come, gentlemen, don't let us have M. le Duc interfering with our dinner. He's done us enough harm without that."

"I should think he had, confounded radical!" grumbled M. Ballanchu, still eying M. Filoselle threateningly.

"Radical?" echoed the commercial traveller, catching up the word, and laughing from ear to ear. "There, my good Monsieur Seedsman, didn't I tell you he must be a phenomenon, this old man. *Peste!* you don't suppose it's every province in France that begets radical dukes."

"No, and a good job too," roared M. Ballanchu. "And this one would never have been what he is if his nephew had had five minutes' time before dying to disinherit him. Clairefontaine wasn't made for such as he—a wrong-headed, obstinate, canting Jacobin."

There was a stiff old half-pay officer of the name of Duroseau dining at the *table-d'hôte*. He had been too much absorbed as yet by the process of mastication, to take any part in the conversation. (His teeth were false, and he was obliged to eat slowly to prevent them coming out.) But now, having laid down his knife and fork, and noticing the puzzled look on the commercial traveller's face, he said gruffly,—"Young man, you must have heard of the ex-deputy, Manuel Gerold?"

"Of course I have, captain; he was one of the first speakers in the old Assembly under the Republic and poor King Pear.* I heard him speak once in the House of Representatives. Thunder! Monsieur Ballanchu, your voice was nothing to his. But what of him, captain?"

"Well, young man, it's he who is now Duke of Hautbourg."

M. Filoselle, who had not been brought up at court, and ignored a good many maxims of dinner-table etiquette, gave a prolonged whistle.

M. Duroseau went on, not sorry to have taken the "forward young jackanapes" aback.

"At the time when you saw Monsieur Manuel Gerold, under the late King's reign" (Captain Duroseau laid an emphasis on the words *late King*. He

---

* Le Roi Poire, literally, King Pear—his Majesty King Louis Philippe. The sobriquet was much in vogue between 1830 and 1848: it was an allusion to the shape of his Majesty's head. Happy the king whose enemies can find no worse nickname for him than King Pear.

was not a Bonapartist; he had fought under the Dukes of Orleans, Nemours, and Aumale in Africa, and would have been glad to cut off M. Filoselle's ears for calling Louis Philippe King Pear)—"At the time, I say, when you saw M. Gerold his proper title was Count de Clairebourg; but he has always been a Republican, and never called himself otherwise than by the family name—Gerold. He is the uncle of the Duke who was killed by—by—ahem!—in 1851. He was locked up at the *coup-d'état*, but let out as soon as it was found that he was his nephew's heir. At present he is living in Brussels."

Captain Duroseau, having delivered himself of this concise biographical summary, deemed he had contributed his ample share towards the general fund of conversation, and turned his attention towards a piece of Gruyère cheese.

"*Tiens, tiens,*" muttered the commercial traveller, who had become a little pensive, "that tall man with the grey hair and the eyes like lanterns, who set me all aglow when he let fall those words about liberty and justice—that man is Duke of Hautbourg! And you call him a canting Jacobin, M. Ballanchu. Do you know what we called him in Paris? We had surnamed him *l'honnête Gerold.*"

"He was a Republican, sir," said Captain Duroseau, looking up from his cheese. The captain admired honesty as much as any man, but he would not allow that it could exist amongst Republicans.

"I don't care that—what you called him in Paris," retorted the seedsman, snapping his fingers energetically. "I only know this much, that it was a bad day for us all down here in Hautbourg when the property up at Clairefontaine yonder fell into the hands of a man who had such cursed mean notions as to how a landlord should spend his money. Let a man be what he likes, say I, so long as he's poor; but when he's rich, and a duke, why then let him show people what a nobleman is, and throw radicalism and all that pack of nonsense to them as have need of it."

This sentiment seemed so perfectly in accordance with the spirit of practical wisdom, that the three farmers, the bootmaker, the host, and the tax-gatherer, burst into a cordial "Ay, ay, well said." Of course, the tax-gatherer had not heard a word, but his idea was that somebody's health had been proposed, and as the seedsman followed up his remarks by draining his glass dry, he, the tax-gatherer, did likewise. The only two who did not join in the applause, were the half-pay captain and the commercial traveller. The former muttered drily that he did not see what change of fortune had got to do with change of politics, and the latter simply asked:—"Does this M. Gerold, this new Duke of Hautbourg, do nothing for the poor of your town?"

"Poor, sir! who cares two figs for the poor?" replied M. Ballanchu, always foremost in the van. "Who ever said a word about the poor, I should like to know? Do you suppose because a man sends ostentatiously twenty thousand francs a year to be distributed amongst a parcel of cripples and old women, I and my fellow-tradesmen are any the better for it? Perhaps you think I can pay for my dinner by telling our host there that M. le Duc has put a thousand napoleons into the poor-box? Ask M. Duval."

This sarcasm, emitted in a tone of derisive scorn, obtained an immense success. M. Duval thought it was one of the most delicate flights of wit he had heard for many a long day, and inwardly blamed himself for the unjust estimate he had formed of M. Ballanchu's mental powers. As for the three farmers, Toulmouche, Truchepoule, and Follavoine, they reflected that this seedsman was assuredly a strong head, who would one of these days do something in politics.

A little jealous of his compeer's triumph, M. Scarpin, the bootmaker, felt the moment had come for reaping some glory in his turn.

"Now-a-days," said he, "the poor are a great deal too rich; they take the bread off the plate of their betters...."

"Alas! and only leave one the veal!" exclaimed M. Filoselle. "You see," he added, pathetically, "we have lighted upon degenerate times. What with radical dukes and wealthy paupers, there is no knowing where we should all go, were it not for the honest sentiments of such men as M. the Seedsman. M. Ballanchu, I admire your theories; M. Scarpin—paragon of bootmakers!—I shall make a note of your observation. But tell me—for I have yet to learn—why your depraved Jacobin lives at Brussels. That part of the mystery has not been explained yet." And the commercial traveller turned towards Captain Duroseau.

"I don't know, sir," replied the old officer, curtly; "M. de Hautbourg's business doesn't concern me." The fact is, in spite of himself, the worthy captain looked upon a duke rather in the light of a superior officer; and he was not best pleased to hear him discussed with so much familiarity by a company of clod-hoppers" and "counter-jumpers."

"When a man lives at Brussels," exclaimed M. Ballanchu, in a sapient tone, "I say there must be something in it. I know more of Brussels than M. le Duc thinks for. People don't go and live at Brussels unless they have a reason."

"No, that they don't," assented M. Scarpin, mysteriously.

"Then you mean to say——?" insinuated M. Filoselle.

"I mean to say nothing, sir," responded M. Ballanchu, sternly. "Only, I'm a man of business, I am; and, unless I have proof positive that a man has a good motive for doing anything, I make it my rule to believe the contrary. This M. le Duc is not exiled by the Government, he has plenty of money and a house waiting here for him. Why doesn't he come to it? If you can tell me that, I shall be ready to listen to you; but, until you do, you will allow me to have my own opinion." And saying this, M. Ballanchu folded his napkin and pushed his chair from the table.

"Yes, yes," muttered M. Scarpin, likewise laying down his napkin, and shaking his head. "There's something not clear in all this. Why was the Duke kept at such distance by his nephew and brother in past days? Why was he never asked to Clairefontaine? Why did nobody never hear nothing of him until, when it was found that Monsieur the late Duke having left no will, it was he who was to come into the property? Why does he hide away now without daring to show himself?"

The seedsman, the bootmaker, the three farmers, and the host exchanged meaning glances. To tell the truth, they were a little alarmed at their own perspica-

. Without having the least idea what it was they
)ected, each yet felt as though his preternatural
teness had put him on the scent of a tragic state
ret. The most solemn-looking, however, was the
·gatherer. As he had not caught a single syllable
vhat was said, his countenance was more mysteri-
ly profound than that of any of the others.

The captain, who disliked tattling, and who, be-
:s, had finished his cheese, rose and took up his
to go; M. Filoselle followed his example; and this
the signal for a general break-up of the party.
the commercial traveller, who, perhaps, was used
having the last word, had not the good sense to
re; maintaining that silence which is known to be
;old. Picking up his carpet-bag in a corner of the
m, he exclaimed with enthusiasm: "O charming
n! remarkable alike for its boiled beef and for the
ial instincts of its inhabitants, it pains my heart to
'e thee. But say, Ballanchu, we shall meet again;
l, perchance, next time I come thou wilt purchase
me an instrument of music whereon to pipe the
ises of that duke whom now thou abusest; for
uld he put in an appearance here, O friend! and
uldst thou have the luck to make his acquaintance,
link thou wilt soon discover that, spite of his living
Brussels" (here M. Filoselle judged well to put a
dent distance betwixt him and the seedsman) "he
weighs in honesty both thee and me—ay, and the
of us, not to speak of the tax-gatherer."

"Talk for yourself, you parrot-voiced puppy,"
ittered the red-faced M. Ballanchu. "And the day
uy anything of thee, write it down in a book that

I've got more money than I want, and have ceased to care about being swindled."

"*Vive l'esprit!*" retorted the undaunted M. Filoselle. "There is but one Duke, and Ballanchu shall be his seedsman. M. Duval, I charge you take care of that man; he is so sharp that I foresee he will cut himself." And with this Parthian shot, M. Filoselle chucked Madelon, the serving-maid, under the chin, threw her a twenty-sou piece, made his obeisance to the company, and vanished.

"*Que le diable l'emporte!*" shouted the seedsman, shaking his fist after him. "And as for that 'honest Gerold' of thine, I fancy thou and he would make a pretty pair." To which observation the whole company for the third time cried assent, M. Hochepain this once joining like the rest; for, having caught the two words "pretty pair," he concluded they must refer to a couple of cauliflowers which had figured at the board, and so remarked in confidence to the irate seedsman:

"Yes, a pretty pair truly, but not quite boiled enough."

* * * * *

This dinner and this conversation took place at the Hôtel de Clairefontaine towards the end of September in the year 1854. A week afterwards, day for day, some stir was caused in the hotel by what was no longer a diurnal occurrence, the arrival of three travellers. They had come by the mid-day train, purposed dining, and would, perhaps, stay a night. One of them was an old man of about seventy, the other two looked like his sons.

CHAPTER II.

Honest Gerold.

Un sacrifice fier charme une âme hautaine :
La gloire en est présente et la douleur lointaine.

As stood to reason, they were given the best rooms
[t]he hotel; indeed, there was good choice, and to
[spar]e, for the house was empty. Mdlle. Madelon
[sho]wed them into the yellow drawing-room on the
[first] floor overlooking the market-place, and lost no
[time] in telling them that the two pictures on the wall
[faci]ng them as they went in were portraits of Mon-
[seig]neur the late Duke of Hautbourg and his father—
[the] owners of this house, if you please, gentlemen."
[Tha]t, over the fireplace, with the periwig, was Monsieur
[the M]arquis, who had been beheaded by Monsieur
[Rob]espierre; and that in the corner there, with the
[rob]e in brown holland, was another member of the
[Hau]tbourg family, Monseigneur Jean de Clairebourg,
[Bish]op of Marvault, a holy man, who had done a
[grea]t deal of good by burning some Protestants.
[Mdl]le. Madelon had recited all this so often that she
[kne]w it by heart. She used at one time to turn a
[pret]ty penny by pointing out to travellers the identical
[bed] in which Monseigneur the first Duke of Hautbourg
[had] slept on the night of his return from emigration
[in 1]814, before they had had time to prepare his room
[for] him at the castle. Unfortunately, she had rather
[ove]rdone this, for, finding it paid, and that people

liked to sleep in Monseigneur's bed, she had ended by pointing out every couch in the house as having been occupied by his Grace, and had even unwarily put a gentleman of the Filoselle type, who came thrice to the hotel, each time in a different bed, warranted slept in by the great noble. On going away the third time the gentleman had inquired drily whether emigration had not imparted somewhat erratic habits to Monseigneur, since he spent his nights going about from bed to bed.

The oldest of the three strangers listened very kindly to the girl's prattle, and the two younger ones seemed amused by it. They were three as handsome faces as any admirer of manly beauty could have hoped to meet. The veteran carried himself erect, and had something in his gait that revealed the old soldier. His hair and beard were both long, however —longer than old soldiers generally allow themselves; for the hair, which was of dazzling white, fell to the shoulders, and the beard half covered the chest. What chiefly attracted one in this old man was the expression of his eyes, which was singularly eloquent and gentle. They beamed upon one, those eyes; and one felt, under their quiet, steady gaze, that they could never have quailed before anybody. The voice, too, had a rare accent of benevolence; it was the voice of a man who thought well of human nature and had met on his path more good characters than bad ones.

The two younger men were sufficiently alike to make it discernible at a glance that they were brothers. The elder looked three or four and twenty; the other was probably a couple of years his junior. Both had the same eyes—at least very nearly the same—as the old man, and their faces were like his, bright, open, and intelligent. Of the two, it was, perhaps, the younger who was the strongest, and he also looked the graver; the elder was slighter of build, more graceful, and certainly more inclined to laugh, for scarcely a minute passed but saw his pleasant features lighted up by a smile. Both were very well dressed—not a common merit in France, where young men are the worst dressers in Christendom:—but as traits of character can be gathered from little facts, it may as well be mentioned that, whilst the younger wore a plain black silk cravat tied in a knot, the elder had a black satin scarf, with a cameo pin in it, and, moreover, wore a gold ring.

Between the three men seemed to exist that cordial, trustful familiarity bred of deepest love on the one hand, and of fullest affection, respect and confidence on the other.

Mdlle. Madelon, though not given to enthusiasm, thought within herself that they were three as nice gentlemen as she had seen for a long while; and proceeded to testify this sentiment by dusting some of the chairs—an operation which she often neglected where less comely strangers were concerned. Having done this, and opened the windows to show "Messieurs" the market-place and the statue of the Poictiers hero prancing in the middle, she announced that Monsieur Duval would doubtless be up presently to offer his respects; and, sure enough, the words were scarcely out of her mouth, before that gentleman appeared in person.

He was very obsequious, carried a napkin on his arm as if his house were chock full and he had done nothing but wait at table all day; and expressed a hope that the gentlemen were lodged to their liking.

"Perfectly, M. Duval, thank you," said the old man, politely. "But we shall not have occasion to make much use of your comfortable rooms, for my sons and I will be out all day. It is one o'clock now; I think we shall hardly be home before seven; may we rely upon you to get us dinner for that hour?"

"Monsieur may place his entire confidence in me," replied M. Duval, bowing. (Allow me to notice here how fond Frenchmen are of phrases with the word confidence. An English inn-keeper would have answered, "Dinner will be on the table punctually at seven, sir.")

The travellers having seen their rooms and entrusted their bags to Mdlle. Madelon, had no further reason for staying in-doors, and so followed M. Duval downstairs. The worthy host entertained them with warm praises of himself and his house all the way, and was once more renewing to them his assurance about the confidence and the dinner, when he remembered, just as the strangers were crossing the entrance-hall, that he had forgotten to ask for their names. The French police are always very anxious to know the names of strangers who stop at hotels, and the instructions given to inn-keepers on this subject are peremptory. No name, no lodging. Besides, M. Duval was curious on his own account to know whom he was harbouring. Everything about these well-looking, gentlemanlike travellers pointed to the presumption that they were not haphazard folk.

"I beg your pardon, Messieurs," he cried, "would

you have any objection to put your names on the register?"

The old man appeared a little annoyed, but he said nothing to show it, and followed M. Duval into the parlour, where the host began bustling about to find a new quill pen, and then laid out on the table that imposing folio register, which has to be inspected by M. le Commissaire every three days. The pages were marked out in columns, and the traveller was requested by printed queries at the top to supply information as to the few following particulars:—*Name and Christian Name, Age, Birthplace, Profession or Trade, Motives of present Journey, Name of place last visited, Name of place to be visited next, Nature of the Certificates of Identity in the Traveller's possession;* and lest the traveller should after this feel that he had not said enough and be disposed to communicate more about himself and his intentions, there was a ninth column headed *Observations*. The white-haired stranger took the pen from M. Duval, and in a clear large hand silently filled up the blank spaces both for himself and his two sons; the host keeping at a discreet distance apart the while. When the formality had been gone through, however, M. Duval made a point of deploring the troublesome inquisitiveness of the police, who put gentlemen to so much trouble; and so followed the strangers to the door, very hearty in his apologies as he was in everything. As soon as they had left the house he returned to the parlour. "Now," said he, "let us see;" but he had hardly cast his eyes on the register and the bold handwriting, still wet, han he gave a scarefied start crying: "Mon Dieu! it's not possible—no—yet, by heavens! it is though."

And with one bound he was at the street-door again, his face all aglow with excitement, trying if he could perceive the travellers. But they were already out of sight. They had turned the corner of the market-place and were gone down the street towards the high-road leading to Clairefontaine.

M. Duval was fain to come in again, but he did not remain indoors long; and before an hour was over, the whole town of Hautbourg was in as great a state of excitement as he was.

The road to Clairefontaine was a fine one, and must have borne an animated appearance during the reign of that irrepressible late Duke who was so continually cropping up in the conversations of the Haut-bourgeois. An enterprising builder had, however, done his best to spoil it by converting a part of it into a suburb of the borough. He had erected on each side of it a number of lath-and-plaster trifles decorated with the pretentious name of *châlets* and even of *châtelets*, but which looked about as much like the real thing as a child's house of toy-bricks looks like Windsor Castle. There are few things so ghastly as new ruins, and these *châlets*, castlets, villas, or whatever else they may be called, were all in ruins, not from age, but from want of care. Imagine a band of school-girls decked out smart for a holiday in pink and white, but caught in a good drenching deluge of rain at the day's outset and standing piteously in the sun an hour afterwards to dry themselves—such was pretty much the idea suggested by the excoriated white plaster on the walls, the washed-out red tiles, and the shutters denuded of almost every vestige of paint. In point of fact, the houses had never been inhabited, and the builder had gone where many other good builders go—into the Bankruptcy Court.

The three men walked along, chatting pleasantly, or, to speak with more accuracy, the two younger ones chatted whilst the elder listened. He seemed to have grown a little grave and preoccupied, and this gravity rather increased than diminished every minute; but he smiled at the bright humour of the eldest of his sons, who, teeming with wit and spirits, found something to say of every object, animate and inanimate, on the road; and he nodded kindly whenever the youngest, less brilliant but more thoughtful, capped his brother's witticisms by some quaint remark, arguing gentleness of mood and quiet, scholarly perception.

"Where are you taking us to, father?" asked the eldest, smiling; "I begin to think this mysterious pilgrimage of ours is to end on a ruin: everything we pass is dilapidated. Look at that public-house."

"Our pilgrimage is drawing to its close, Horace," answered the old man, returning the smile; but he added with some anxiety in his tone, "Do you really think the country looks dilapidated? We have met no beggars yet, and I generally make that my test. As to ruined public-houses, why, you know, I do not feel much sympathy for them."

Horace looked around a moment, as if trying to detect a beggar, and, not succeeding, answered, "I really think one only sees beggars in free lands. I have met plenty in Belgium, and when we went to England last year I saw nothing else; but here——"

"Here one has gendarmes instead," broke in the younger brother, quietly; and he pointed to a booted representative of Law and Order, who was, in truth, the fifth or sixth they had met that afternoon.

They had walked about a mile and a half, and, at this juncture, reached a point where four roads met. A young girl was coming towards them with a basket of eggs on her arm. The old man, who appeared doubtful as to which road to take, raised his hat and said, "Will you kindly tell us the way to Clairefontaine, Mademoiselle?"

"There to the left, Monsieur," she answered; "it's not above ten minutes' walk. See the sign-post."

They had not noticed the sign-post. It said: *Clairefontaine*, ¼ kilomètre; *Clairebourg*, 2 kilomètres; *Boisgency*, 3¼ kilomètres; *Sainte Sophie*, 5 kilomètres.

"Clairefontaine!" muttered the elder brother, and he proceeded to quote what seemed to him appropriate:—"*Fons Bandusiæ, splendidior vitro, cras donaberis hædo.* Are we bent on sacrifice, father?" he added, laughing.

The old man laid a hand on his shoulder. "You shall answer that question for me yourself, my dear boy, when we come back this evening," he replied, with a gravity which surprised his two sons. "Perhaps, indeed, Clairefontaine is to be our Bandusian Fount," he continued, gently, "and maybe there will be a sacrifice there. I accept your omen."

The party walked on in silence for the next few minutes—the father still grave, the sons both wondering—until a turning in the road brought them abruptly in view of the lodge-gates of Clairefontaine, with the princely avenue of elms beyond, and the turreted mansion, half palace, half castle, closing the prospect grandly in the distance. The old man's face seemed to light up with quick emotion, and the two young men gave a murmur of admiration. Certes, it was a splendid sight. Clairefontaine House in its lonely majesty, bathed in the purple rays of the autumn sun, and surrounded by its cortége of stately trees, still looked like a queen in the midst of her court.

"What a thing is wealth," sighed Horace. "And to think that the owner of this paradise is perhaps some Crœsus who finds the country slow, and spends three-fourths of his time in Paris cooped up in a set of rooms scarcely bigger than that lodge yonder."

"You will have the opportunity of inspecting your paradise at leisure," answered his father, "for this is the end of our journey." And the gate being now reached, he pulled the bell-chain hanging on one side of it.

Out hobbled the old crone whose acquaintance we have already made. She was used to the applications of visitors desirous of seeing the grounds, and the more of such came the better she liked it; for a visitor, generally represented at least a forty-sou piece. These, however, were not ordinary applicants, as she soon found. When the three strangers had been admitted within the massive bronze gates, forged all over with scutcheons and ducal coronets, the elder drew a letter from his pocket and handed it to her.

"It's from Monsieur Claude, the agent," he said.

The old woman fumbled in her apron for a pair of horn-rimmed spectacles, put them on with a shaking hand, broke the seal of the letter, and read these lines:—

"Madame Maboule,—

"You will please to show the bearer of this all over the castle, the rooms, stables, picture-gallery, or, should he prefer visiting the house alone, you will give him the keys.

"J. Claude."

"Oh, Monsieur, then, is the gentleman whom Monsieur Claude was speaking about the other day?" exclaimed Madame Maboule, throwing a searching but respectful glance at the strangers. "He said a gentleman was coming as would want to see the castle—a friend of Monseigneur the new Duke's, I believe?"

The old man bent his head affirmatively; his sons opened their eyes; they appeared not to know in the least whither their father was tending, nor what was his motive in bringing them there.

Madame Maboule, dismal at her best, but more than usually so when she stood in the presence of the great, whimpered a hope that Monseigneur was quite well, and inquired whether the Messieurs would go up to the house alone, or whether she should accompany them.

There was a moment's deliberation on this point; the stranger evidently wished to save the worthy old soul the mile's walk up the avenue, but Madame Maboule protested with wheezy fortitude that the walk was nothing to her, and that the Messieurs would lose their way in the apartments if she was not there to guide them. "But perhaps," added she, with an inquiring glance at them all, "the Messieurs have been here before?"

"I was here once," answered the old man, in a hurried tone, "but it was a long time ago; things have

changed since then. I might not know my way now."
And to compensate the honest crone for the trouble
she was going to take, he slipped a *napoleon* into her
hand.

"I am sure Monsieur is very generous," was the
grateful and somewhat bewildered acknowledgment; and
the next minute the four set off in company, the old
woman leading the way, and the three gentlemen walking
slowly, not to tire her.

As nothing so much resembles one old mansion as
another old mansion; and as, moreover, the description
of abandoned drawing-rooms and bed-rooms, silent
libraries and picture-galleries, old-fashioned furniture
muffled up in chintz coverings, and old-fashioned beds
overhung with imposing dusty canopies, can scarcely
be expected to interest any save very enthusiastic ad-
mirers of bric-a-brac, we will not follow the strangers
in their inspection of the Castle of Clairefontaine, but,
leaving them to the care of Madame Maboule, wait for
them outside on the open terrace, overlooking what
had a few years before been one of the finest gardens
in the province. The walk up the avenue had taken
about three-quarters of an hour, protracted as it was
by constant halts on the part of Madame Maboule to
point out this or that feature of interest in the landscape. Here was a bench on which Monsieur the late
Duke would often sit to read his paper. There, on
that rising plot of ground, a belvedere erected by Monsieur the Marquis, who was very fond of looking at
the stars with a telescope, eighty years ago; there,
again, in that by-path, if the Messieurs would step out
of their way and see, was a marble urn erected over the
burying-place of a pet dog by Madame la Marquise, wife

of Monseigneur who was imprisoned in the Bastille by Louis XIV.—a very beautiful lady, gentlemen, and much respected by the King. But of all the objects, that which had most fascination for the old woman was a beech-tree that had been used to hang a Jacobin on. The man had led the sacking of Clairefontaine in 1793, and had retired to live in peace for the next twenty years. But in 1814, when the exiled family returned, the peasantry had dragged him out and strung him up in the night opposite the new Duke's windows—a delicate piece of attention that had greatly touched Monseigneur, and seemed both natural and proper to Madame Maboule. In the castle itself the party stayed more than a couple of hours. The old man appeared desirous that his sons should see every nook and corner of the house and miss none of its accumulated splendours. Madame Maboule lent herself readily enough to his whim. She took them from floor to floor, from room to lobby, lobby to hall, hall to chapel; turning creaking locks with her jingling keys, and explaining everything as if she was speaking about a city of the dead, and showing things that had long ceased to be understood by a modern generation. What more garrulous than an old woman who has lived five-and-sixty years on an estate, and has room for nothing else but the memory of its past glories in her venerable head? Every foot of carpet within the doors of Clairefontaine House was so much consecrated ground to Madame Maboule. She talked about her departed masters with a plaintive, wobegone, motherly sort of affection; and, throughout all her utterances, rang like the burden of a dirge—a lamentation over that new Duke whom she had never seen and whose absence she could not understand. The young men listened to her with much the same kind of silent attention which one bestows upon an aged monk showing one over a cathedral. Their father spoke very little during the whole two hours. Only once, when they were in an upper room—which, in old times, had been a nursery —he smiled a rather sad smile, and, pointing to a picture of a very young child hanging in a corner, asked who that was. "That, sir, is the present Duke of Hautbourg," answered the old woman; "it was taken nigh upon seventy years ago."

At last the inspection was over; the desolate castle had been visited from roof to basement, and the three strangers with their guide stood together on the terrace.

"Well, Emile," asked the old man of his youngest son, "what do you think of all we have just seen?" And he looked with a rather curious expression into the lad's grave, blue eyes.

"I think there is a skeleton in that house like in many poorer ones, father," replied the young man, pensively.

"What skeleton, dear boy?"

"The skeleton that prevents the new Lord of Clairefontaine from coming and living here. Do you not think, father," added he, with concern, "that there must be very bitter memories attached to some of that splendour if the new Duke of Hautbourg persists in keeping away like this?"

The father made no immediate answer, but a few moments afterwards he turned to the old lodge-keeper and said softly, "We will not trouble you to stay with us any longer, Madame Maboule. I and my sons are going to sit down for a little under yonder oak, and perhaps we shall walk about in the park for a short while afterwards."

Madame Maboule dropped a curtsey. "Very well, sir," she answered, in her usual dolorous tone. "When you want to return you have only to follow the avenue straight and I shall be down at the lodge to open the gate for you." She curtseyed for a second time and hobbled away slowly.

The three men walked towards the oak which stood in the centre of a grass-plot just beyond the outskirts of the garden and commanded a view of almost the entire park. Was it an undefined presentiment of something strange about to be told them or merely hazard that kept the young men silent as they went? anyhow, silent they were; and save but for the chirping of the birds overhead, and the muffled sound of their own footsteps in the long grass, there would have been a complete stillness all around them as far as the eye could reach. There was a wooden form running round the rough trunk of the oak, and all three sat down on it.

"Can you guess why I have brought you here?" inquired the father, addressing both his sons.

They shook their heads.

"Why, father?" they asked.

"I wish to tell you a story," he said, affectionately taking a hand of theirs in each of his as they sat on either side of him. "Should you like to be told what is the skeleton in Clairefontaine, Emile? And you, Horace, are you curious to learn how people may live cooped up in rooms no bigger than the park-lodge, and yet be more at ease than in a fine palace like this?"

Emile smiled slightly.

"Then there is a skeleton," he rejoined; and Horace added, grimly, "I was complaining that one met nothing but beggars in free countries. One may remark, also, that there seem to be a deplorable number of skeletons in rich houses. I have never been over a castle but somebody had poisoned somebody else in it, or put him down a well, or thrown him out of the window."

"Yes; but there is nothing of that kind in my story," interrupted the old man, good-naturedly. "It is not a legend of murder or mystery. It is—— Well, I can hardly call it an every-day story, but you shall hear and judge." And, seeing both young men attentive, with their eyes fixed on him, he began his recital in a quiet, simple tone—much as he would have told a fairy tale to young children.

"Once upon a time," he said, "there was a very rich nobleman, who lived in a house such as this, we will say. He was a kind-hearted, well-meaning man; but he came in troublous times, when people's minds were excited by the remembrance of many centuries of oppression, and, when at last there was a rising of the down-trodden against their masters, he paid, as we must often do here below, for the sins of some of his ancestors. Let it be recorded that he perished nobly. In dying, he left two orphan sons (their mother was dead some years before)—the elder seventeen years old, the younger nine. In the ordinary course of things, the elder must have succeeded his father, and become his brother's guardian; but there was so much exasperation against the nobility throughout the whole country, that the boys would not have been safe had

they remained in France. So both of them went into
exile. The eldest, who had assumed the family title
of marquis, became an officer in the Prince of Condé's
army at Coblentz; the younger, who was a viscount,
was taken as page of honour into the household of a
royal princess, the Countess of Provence—the same
who, a few years later, died in London, calling herself, and called by the Royalists, Queen of France. I
have no need to remind you what came eventually of
the Prince of Condé's army. The officers and soldiers
who composed it were brave men, but they were bearing arms against their country, and somehow experience
shows that victory does not remain long on the side
of those who are not in the right. After a series of
reverses they got dispersed. Some went and accepted
service in foreign armies; others—and, probably, the
wisest there—started for America, to try and build up
their fortunes once more in a new world; and others,
again, emigrated to England, where they formed a
large, but not very united, nor always very reasonable,
colony of titled refugees. Amongst those who went
to England were the young Marquis and his brother.
They had been completely ruined by the Revolution,
for it had been decreed by the Convention that those
who emigrated should forfeit their estates; so that all
the two boys had to live upon was the money raised
by means of some of the family plate and jewels,
which a devoted servant had been able to rescue from
the wreck of the property, and had contrived to
smuggle out of France. Those were hard times for
lads brought up in purple; but the two brothers would
have been ungrateful to complain, for many were
twenty times worse off than they. There were plenty

of dukes and counts who became music, fencing, language, or drawing-masters. One or two set up as small shop-keepers. There was one (he became a peer of France afterwards) who took to carpentering, and very successfully, too. Unfortunately, however, this adversity, which should have read a lesson to many of those whose lack of wisdom had been the cause of the Revolution, seemed not to profit them much, and there was little else in the refugee colony but bickerings and disputes, teacup storms and intrigues, plans for invading France and restoring the old régime, and anathemas of all sorts against the Liberal principles of the Revolution. It was this that first pained the younger of the two brothers, and, by degrees, estranged him from the Royalist cause. As he grew old enough to think for himself he could not see that the Revolution had been such a crying wrong as those of his own caste would have had him believe. Of course, the excesses of the Revolution, the blood-orgies of '93, were a wrong—a cruel wrong, and they have been dearly expiated by Republicans. But one should separate the good from the bad in pronouncing judgment;—one should draw a difference between the Revolutionists who asked only for freedom and fair laws, and who fell victims of their moderation, from the few sorry villains who— But let us speak mercifully of them, too," exclaimed the old man, humbly. "Who shall presume to judge motives: Death has passed over good and bad alike now!"

He paused for a moment, and then resumed: "The boy, the young viscount I mean, had struggled a good while with himself before daring to admit even to his own conscience that he was disposed to think

differently from those who formed his habitual society.
You see, his father had been put to death unjustly,
and it required some time before he could perceive
that it was no more just to hold the Republicans as a
body responsible for this crime than it would have
been to make his father responsible for the misdoings
of those brother noblemen of his whose follies had
driven the country into rebellion. Perhaps if the
language of the exiles in whose company he lived had
been more tolerant than it was, their conduct more
dignified, and their apparent aims more patriotic, he
would never have been brought to reason in this way,
and would have remained a royalist to the end, like
his elder brother. But, with few exceptions, the conduct of the refugees was not dignified; and if they felt
any patriotism, they seldom showed it in their schemes.
To a boy of seventeen they seemed a feeble, pre-
judiced, selfish body of men, whom misfortune had
neither chastened nor instructed; and it was impossible
not to reflect, after hearing them talk, that should they
ever recover their power they would inevitably lose it
again before long through sheer force of obstinacy and
wrongheadedness. In youth we quickly fly from one
extreme to the other, for when we lose our faith in
one set of principles we conclude that those most
diametrically opposite to them must be the right ones.
The young exile, feeling his confidence in and his admiration for the Royalist party growing less and less
every day, began gradually to take up with Republican
views. This was at the period when Bonaparte was
shaking all Europe with his Italian victories, and when
the military glory of France shone with a lustre it had
never possessed before. It was difficult not to feel

one's heart thrill at the report of battles in which Frenchmen fought and won against treble odds; and though the refugees and the English papers with them sneered at these victories and declared they were not true, yet such denials were so evidently prompted by jealousy that they rather added to than diminished the enthusiasm with which every fresh success was received by those who really loved their country. One day—this was in the year 1801—the young Viscount took a resolution. He was grown tired of an exile's life, and saw nothing to tempt him in the prospect of dangling indefinitely about the mock court of the Prince who styled himself Louis XVIII. Summoning up all his courage—and I can assure you it needed courage—he informed his brother of his intention of returning to France and enlisting in General Bonaparte's army. The Marquis had never bated a jot from his royalism, and the thought that any one of his family could ever turn Republican had not crossed his mind even in dream. He started at his brother's communication as if he had been shot. The thing seemed to him like blasphemy. A brother of his to turn renegade and serve in the ranks with those who had murdered his father! Why this was as bad as being accomplice to a parricide! He became white with dismay, seized his brother's hand, and entreated him to declare that it was all a hoax, a joke, or anything save the truth. But the younger brother held good. He had been prepared for some consternation, but he felt so sure of his own motives, he knew so well that hatred against his father's murderers burned within him as strongly as ever, that he attached little importance to the horrified expressions of his brother,

and even hoped to convert him. He pleaded his case
with all the boldness he could muster. There could
be no offence to their father's memory, he showed, in
serving their common country. It was not Robespierre
or Marat he was going to fight for—those men were
dead—he was simply going to be a French soldier;
and, in short, he adduced all the arguments which he
had uppermost in his heart, and which his conscience
has ever since—yes, ever since—assured him were
right. The Marquis, however, refused to be convinced.
Chivalrous and unbending in all points of loyalty, he
considered desertion of one's party a crime too heinous
for excuse. He was shocked: he cast his brother away
from him like a viper; and from that day up to his
death he would never consent to see him nor speak to
him again."

The old man became silent a moment. He was a
little pale; but he proceeded in an unbroken voice:
"Party spirit ran high in those days; I believe men
could hate each other more intensely than they do
now. It was a time when the words Royalist or Republican put barriers between men which no strength
of family ties could break down; and once a man had
left one camp for the other, the feud between himself
and his former friends was something deep, lasting,
and absurdly violent. In this case the younger brother
did not hate the elder, God knows! but the elder bore
an eternal grudge against the younger, and—— But
let bygones be bygones, and may those with whom
pardon lies forgive as fully as the younger brother has
forgiven. I don't want to make my story too long,"
continued the old man; "so shall only say that Fortune dealt kindly with the boy who enlisted in Bona-

parte's army. He soon rose to be an officer, was at the end of three years a captain, and might have gone much higher had he chosen to remain in the service. But in becoming a soldier under Bonaparte he had sworn allegiance to the Republic which then existed, and had not foreseen that an Empire was going to be established. When the First Consul converted himself into an Emperor, he tendered his resignation, which was not immediately accepted—for officers and men were wanted just then for the Austerlitz campaign;— but on the declaration of peace, when it was seen that he would neither accept promotion nor the legion of honour, he was allowed to retire; and so went to settle in Paris, where, by the help of pen instead of sword, he cut out for himself a new career, which was blessed, perhaps, beyond his deserts—certainly beyond his expectations. The elder brother, meanwhile, prospered in a different way. Whilst still in exile he contracted a wealthy marriage—in fact, he married the daughter of an English slave-trader—and, in course of time, came back to France with the Bourbons, was made a duke, bought back with his wife's money the family estates, which had been sold after confiscation as 'national property,' and died with many honours upon him, unwavering to the end in his allegiance to the dynasty whose ups and downs he had shared. Now what should you say," asked the old man, looking at both his sons alternately, and consulting their eyes with some signs of emotion,—"What should you say if, by a turn of fate, the elder brother's only son, having died childless, the younger brother—the Republican—had one day unexpectedly become inheritor both of the dukedom and the redeemed estates? . . . .

Try and consider," he went on in a voice that, to his sons, sounded almost pleading, so modestly appealing was it, and so earnest,—"Try and consider what was the position of this younger brother. He had never looked for this inheritance and never desired it. It came upon him through a calamity, which was itself the result of a political crime, and this alone might have afforded an honest man excuse enough for refusing the fortune, seeing that it is difficult to hate crime as we should when it has helped to make us rich. But there were other reasons. From the moment when he had parted from his brother, the Republican had, boy and man, pinned his faith to one code of principles. Rightly or wrongly, these principles did not allow of his wearing a title, and so he had discarded that of viscount, which he originally wore, for his own plain family name. It was under this name that he was generally known, and had conquered such small reputation as he possessed; and it was under this name that, by the confidence of a Radical constituency, he had been elected three or four times over to the legislature as an advocate of liberal opinions— that is, of freedom at home and of slave-abolition in the colonies; for, remember, we are speaking of a few years ago, and the abolition of slavery was one of the chief party-cries of French liberals before '48. Now, under all these circumstances," concluded the speaker slowly, "could this man who refused to wear a viscount's title with consistency assume a dukedom? or could this man, who was an opponent of slavery, accept an estate that had been bought with the money of a slave-trader?"

There was a moment's silence—it was only a single

instant—and then both sons rose together, their heads uncovered and their eyes glistening.

"No, father," faltered the youngest proudly, but he was too much moved to say more: and the eldest added, his voice gushing with admiration and enthusiasm, "But you had no need of dukedom or estate, father, to make your name illustrious."

The three men shook hands; and in that warm, silent grasp, and the few words just recorded, was the father's act of self-denial—his refusal of wealth and rank for conscience' sake—ratified by his children.

This, by the way, was the first the two young men had ever heard of their family history. They had known their father only as Manuel Gerold, a Republican, who was one of the most esteemed leaders of his party, and whose unaffected integrity and simple undeviating fidelity to principle had earned for him, at the hand of friends and foes alike, the enviable surname of "the honest Gerold."—There are certain Frenchmen who have the knack of making Republicanism peculiarly hideous, but Manuel Gerold was not one of them. The Republic, such as he dreamed it, would have been a very fine thing; unfortunately, it had this drawback, that before it could be established every man must have put away the leaven of unrighteousness and become transformed into an enlightened philanthropist devoted to schemes of intelligent benevolence. I do not think that in the worthy gentleman's projects of commonwealth any provision at all had been made for Houses of Correction—much less for such functionaries as a hangman, gendarmes, or turnkeys. He had a way of talking about schools which gave one to understand that crime was but the result of ignorance, and that if men only knew how to read, write, and count, the necessity for coercive establishments would disappear. I suppose it would have been hardly fair to remind him of the remarkable number of individuals who turn their knowledge of the three rules to account by subtracting funds from their neighbours' pockets in order to add them to their own. With all his naïveness, however, and his humane belief in the innate virtues of mankind, Manuel Gerold was no mere dreamer. He could be shrewd when he chose, and he had such a hearty scorn for all that was mean or false that he had more than once taken adversaries aback by the crude, energetic way in which he assailed abuses. There was something in him both of the soldier and of the priest. Very mild in his habitual moods, very indulgent also, and chivalrously amiable, he could light up at the recital of a wrong, and pour out words with the same startling vehemence which the hermits of old must have used when they preached the crusades. Having, as he thought, nothing to expect of his family, he had brought up both his sons to the notion that they were humble *bourgeois* who would have to fight their way through life as he had had to fight his; and it had been one of his most constant lessons to them that if a man only remain honest he must end by being prosperous. This was a deep-rooted belief with him: it was not an empty maxim. Had he been well read in his Bible—which I am sorry to say he wasn't—he would have quoted the noble lines: "I was young and now I am old, yet have I not seen the righteous forsaken nor his seed begging their bread." But being a republican Frenchman (and one who held himself for a freethinker, though he invoked God's blessing twenty times in a day) he simply quoted from his own experience, and said that he had known many men, honest and otherwise, but that he had never met with an honest man who had had cause to repent of his integrity. Educated in this precept, the boys had grown up to be, above all, manly and straightforward; they shared their father's loathing for everything that was not true and frank, and both bade fair, if nothing came amiss, to follow him step for step in his Republican opinions. France is not one of those countries where every right-minded person has a peerage on his table, so that it had been easy enough to keep them in ignorance of their father's family connections. A good many of Manuel Gerold's friends did not so much as suspect that he had any relationship to a ducal house; and as for the general public, the tendency towards self-depreciation is a failing of such decidedly limited growth amongst Frenchmen, that a man who dubs himself plain *bourgeois* is taken at his own valuation without either difficulty or questions. It should be added, now, that their father's communication did not much bewilder the young men. A few days before, Manuel Gerold, who had been living with them at Brussels ever since the *coup-d'état*, had informed them quietly that he intended taking them to France "on a business visit," and once at Clairefontaine, he had told them his secret in the abrupt and simple way just shown. But the feeling brought uppermost in their minds by the recital was not one of very great surprise or excitement. At twenty-four and twenty-one rent-rolls and dukedoms have not the same peculiar significance in our eyes which they acquire in after life. Somehow the young men thought it quite natural that their father should turn out to be a duke; just as natural that he should refuse to wear his title; and the most matter-of-course thing possible that, having inherited an estate with a slur of ill-gained money on it, he should put it away from him without hesitation. But this did not prevent their admiring and feeling proud of his disinterestedness; for noble traits have the faculty of moving us, even when we are best prepared for them.

There was a long pause, after which the father, who had been looking at his sons with great joy and tenderness, said: "And what should be done with an estate which everybody refuses?"

Emile was the first to speak.

"It has been bought with the price of human beings," he answered gravely; "let it be sold and the money employed in redeeming slaves, or in helping to abolish slavery in America."

"Yes, yes," assented his brother eagerly.

Manuel Gerold had produced a piece of folded parchment of unmistakeably legal appearance. "For the last three years," he observed, "the estate has been masterless, that is, an agent has collected the revenues and paid them into different charities; but here is a deed I have had prepared which makes over the whole property to both of you jointly; so that now the disposal of it is in your hands."

Horace took the parchment and was for tearing it up instantly: "This shall be the sacrifice of which we spoke this morning," he exclaimed, laughing, and his brother approved, adding: "Yes, let us tear it up, it can do no good with us."

"Stay one moment," interposed Manuel Gerold,

and he quoted the two lines that have been placed at the head of this chapter. They were from a new play of Ponsard's, very popular at that time. "Let me advise you to wait and not act under impulse, dear boys," he continued; "the merit of your sacrifice will be greater if it is accomplished after reflection. I did not like to speak to you of this before you were of an age to pronounce whether you thought as I did about this unlucky heritage; but I would not have you pronounce too quickly. Think whilst you may, in order that there shall never be any regret at having acted too hastily."

"But what should we think about?" asked the elder brother in a tone of surprise, and looking almost reproachfully at his father. "Can Emile or I ever think differently about this matter to what we do now?"

"Heaven grant not! my brave boy," replied the old man, smiling to reassure him; "but I was considering the satisfaction you yourselves might feel in after-life, when, looking back upon these times, you could remember that you had given up a fortune, not on the spur of a generous moment, but calmly and deliberately, like men. This is what I was going to propose to you: let the title-deed remain in your hands for a stated period—say four or five years. During that time the revenues of Clairefontaine shall be devoted to whatever charities you wish; and if at the end of the term you have kept steadfast to your resolution, then let Emile's proposal be adopted, and the whole heritage return to its true owners, the unfortunate slaves with whose freedom it was bought."

It required some little time before either of the brothers could be brought to see the advantages of this scheme; indeed it is doubtful whether they ever did see the advantage of it at all; but the younger, to please his father, whose real motives he divined, pretended conversion. Emile perceived that the true wish in Manuel Gerold's heart was that his sons should not be influenced by his presence in the decision they took; he desired that they should act for themselves when he was not there to see them, so that the merit of the sacrifice should be entirely with them:—"Very well, father," said the young man placidly, "let us wait for a while; it can make no difference."

The elder brother, however, did not give in so soon. He had opened the parchment and cast his eye mechanically over it: the deed was as formal as possible; it had been prepared before witnesses and signed, so as to be unimpeachable in a court of justice; it divided the estate into two equal parts, Clairefontaine Castle, with the domain of the same name and all the land situated in the town of Hautbourg, being the share of Horace; and the freeholds of Clairebourg, Boisgency, and Sainte Sophie, together with the family mansion in the Faubourg Saint Germain in Paris, being that of Emile. To satisfy the requirements of the law the Republican had been obliged for once in his life to sign with all his titles, and his name figured as *Manuel Armand Gerold de Clairefontaine, Duke of Hautbourg and of Clairefontaine, Marquis of Clairebourg and of Sainte Sophie, Count of Boisgency, and Baron Gerold of Hautbourg.* Horace Gerold, after looking at all this, folded up the document again and said in a tone of seriousness rather unusual to him: "I think we shall do better not to wait: our duty in this case is so plain that delay seems almost a wrong.

Besides, five years! Who knows what may happen in that time?"

"But there is no absolute necessity for your making the term five years," replied Manuel Gerold cheerfully. "Make it what you like; say two years, or three years. All I want is that you should put yourselves through an ordeal sufficient to show that you are not afraid of the temptation. For, believe me, if you remain firm in your purpose for some reasonable time, it will be an encouragement to you in many and many trials to come; it will convince you that those sacrifices which seem hardest to the world are not hard to those who have a little common patience to help them."

This settled the matter. The moment it became a question of proving that he felt no fear of wavering, Horace Gerold would have agreed to wait twenty years. He looked about him at the park, with its desolate expanses of untrimmed lawn and wild-growing trees; at the old mansion opposite him, sad and untenanted; and this prospect, the lonely beauty of which had charmed him but a few hours before, now seemed to him chill and repelling: later he felt as though he could have refused a thousand such castles one after the other, and so, putting the parchment in his pocket, he said quietly: "Let it be five years, father. This is the 20th September, 1854; on the 20th September, 1859, we will destroy this deed and make a new one. I shall remember the date."

"Amen," answered Manuel Gerold fervently.

It was now about five o'clock; and the great resolution being taken, the father and his two sons walked leisurely in the direction of the lodge-gates, where Madame Maboule had promised to be in waiting for them.

On their way they talked on the subject which naturally engrossed the young men most for the moment, the history of the Hautbourgs past and gone. Manuel Gerold spoke of the time when he had last seen that park, some sixty years before, on the night when his father was arrested as a Royalist, and he himself and his brother were spirited away through a side-door, whilst five or six hundred peasants, led on by a local ragamuffin, attacked the castle and plundered all they could find in it. He remembered the dismal coach that had come to fetch the Marquis away, the gloomy flashing of the gendarmes' swords in the torch-light, the exulting yells of the rabble at seeing the nobleman manacled like a felon, and the desperate, heroic attempt made by a few of the tenants, who loved their master, to rescue him from the hands of his captors. It was by the efforts of these tenants that the Marquis's two sons had been saved from being arrested like him. The tenants had used force, for the boys wished to go with their father, and Manuel Gerold recollected a rough, devoted farmer who had gagged him with his hand to prevent him screaming. Then there was talk of the bloody assize that had been held in the old town-hall at Hautbourg by one of Robespierre's judges; of the destruction of all the monuments and memorials that could in any way recall the great family of Clairefontaine, of the pillage of the church, and its conversion into a granary, and of the sale of Clairefontaine by the Republican Government to a Radical attorney for a few thousand francs. When the family returned at the Restoration this attorney, who had already made a colossal fortune, asked for five million francs to surrender the estate, and it was generally credited that he would have insisted upon double had he not had strong reasons for apprehending that the Duke would have him out and shoot him. "See there," continued Manuel Gerold, stopping and pointing with his stick to a moss-covered grotto, of the sort without which no great park was complete a hundred years ago. "I remember as if it was yesterday my poor father sitting there in powdered wig and ruffles, and teaching me to spell words out of the *Gazette de France* on his knee; the *Gazette* was the great paper then; it used to reach us twice a week with news from Paris, and was about the size of a pocket-handkerchief." These reminiscences of past times, called up tenderly by the father, listened to religiously by the sons, occupied the party until they reached the end of the avenue, where Madame Maboule, civil and melancholy, was standing with the gate wide open to let them pass.

"Good afternoon, gentlemen," she cried, tremulously, "and maybe, sir, if you see Monseigneur, you will tell him how glad we should all be to see him. The place looks like a church-yard now there's nobody there; it does indeed."

Manuel Gerold muttered a few kind words in returning her salutation; and, once outside the gate, turned round to take a last look at the old house and park. His face was perfectly calm, but he said in a low voice, and with an affectionate wave of the hand towards the place where he and his fathers had been born, "Good-by to Clairefontaine; it came honourably into our hands eight centuries ago; our ancestors will not reproach us for having surrendered it honourably."

With these words, the father and his sons walked away, going back, by the same road as they had come, to Hautbourg. On the way, Horace and Emile, by tacit agreement, refrained from speaking any more about Clairefontaine or the past, and their talk was entirely about the immediate future. Both brothers had graduated as licentiates of law, the elder at Paris in 1851, the younger at Liége in 1854, and it had been decided that they should go to Paris at the opening of term in October, to enter themselves at the Bar. Their visit to Clairefontaine and the things they had heard there did not in any way modify these arrangements; but the young men were anxious to induce their father to accompany them, and he had hitherto refused, alleging his intention of returning to Brussels, where most of his old Republican friends were living. They now tried again to shake his determination, but to little purpose.

"No, let me return into my voluntary exile," he said, gently. "My time is over now; if I could do any good I would come; but the Liberals of to-day have need of younger and stronger soldiers than I."

Emile and Horace both protested against this view, and the discussion was carried on until the three had reached those remarkable lath-and-plaster villas of which mention has been already made. At this point they noticed that for the last couple of hundred yards or so the people they met had eyed them curiously, and been peculiarly sedulous in the matter of hat-raising. The lath-and-plaster dwellings extended about three-quarters of a mile out of the town, and the nearer they drew to Hautbourg so much the more did the number of the passers-by increase. Every one of them without exception stared, stood aside, and uncovered his head.

"It is evident we are not *incognito*," observed Horace Gerold; "this comes of putting down one's name in hotel books." A gendarme was coming towards them at that moment; he stared, too, and ... made a military salute.

"Ah," said the Republican, that settles the point. "It is not Manuel Gerold they are bowing to, but the Duke of Hautbourg." He stopped a moment. "I had not counted upon this," he muttered. "I had hoped most of the people here were ignorant that Gerold and the Duke were one. It would not do to have a triumphal entry into the town; suppose we retrace our steps and walk about till it gets dark."

But it was too late. On looking round it was perceived a throng of people to the number of some twenty or thirty had gathered in the rear and were following at a respectful distance—not demonstrative but attentive. Simultaneously another throng, three times as big, loomed on the horizon in front. The fact is, Monsieur Duval of the Hôtel de Clairefontaine, startled out of all reticence and composure by the discovery that he was giving hospitality to none other than the famous Duke, who was both the despair and the stock subject of conversation of everybody in the borough, had spent his afternoon going about from house to house and proclaiming the stupefying piece of news that "HE, yes HE, had at last come; and was going to dine at the hotel at seven!" The intelligence in so far as regarded the dinner was not deemed of vast purport, but the other fact about "*his* having come" flew through the town like wildfire, and was speedily exaggerated into the most positive assertion that "*he* had come in company with his entire household," the footmen and butlers composing the aforesaid household being most circumstantially described. There were of course people in the crowd who soon declared themselves in a position to give particulars as to the way in which *he* had come. One had seen the open barouche and four drive up whilst everybody was at luncheon; another had especially noticed the two omnibuses behind containing the family; a third, declining to keep so important a secret to himself, avowed that he had talked with Monsieur le Duc half an hour, and that Monsieur had told him he was coming to live at Clairefontaine forthwith. Please imagine the sensation! . . .

Immediately, and as though by magic, Hautbourg had became transformed. Silk dresses, buried in lower drawers ever since the fatal "three years ago," were drawn out in hot haste; windows were thrown open and decked with glazed-calico tricolour flags, showy tablecloths, or any other artistic thing that came first to hand; children had their faces washed, much to their disgust, and were hastily sheathed in Sunday clothes; Monsieur le Curé, abruptly apprised of the news whilst he was taking his afternoon nap, rushed with the inspiration of wisdom to the cupboard where his best cassock hung, and speedily appeared in the market-place, clean-shaven, brushed, with a missal under his arm and with gloves on; as for Monsieur le Maire, Messieurs of the Municipal Council, and Monsieur the Beadle, they might have been descried, towards six o'clock, standing three deep round the door of the Hôtel de Clairefontaine, silent, august, and prepared to distinguish themselves.

But what shall be said of Monsieur Ballanchu the

seedsman, Monsieur Scarpin the boot-maker, and Monsieur Hochepain the tax-gatherer? These three, like honest tradesmen as they were, announced themselves ready to forgive and forget. Monsieur Ballanchu had bought, on credit, a new pair of double-soles from M. Scarpin, and was giving them an airing in honour of the auspicious occasion; Madame Scarpin in scarlet cap-strings was standing at her door, and had supplied herself with two pocket-handkerchiefs, one *utile*, the other *dulce*, *i.e.* fragrant with Eau-de-Cologne, to be waved when the HE and family should pass. As Madame Scarpin was not the only matron, by a hundred or so, who was standing at her door, with capstrings hoisted and pocket-handkerchief in reserve, you may readily conceive what a fine spectacle the town presented at about the time when HE was expected.

At last (it was about 6.30 P.M., and expectation had begun to assume that spasmodic form which reveals itself in treading on one another's toes and kicking each other's shins)—at last the report flew: "HE comes! HE comes!" It was quite true: there he came, a little astonished, but perfectly dignified, and walking between his two sons. All three were bareheaded, for everybody was shouting as if he or she had only five minutes more in which to shout on earth. And the hats and the handkerchiefs,—how they shook and fluttered! And the shrill piping of the children, how it rent the air, with cries of *vive Monsieur le Duc;* whilst, with a mighty thunder like that of a bull of Bashan, Monsieur Ballanchu, purple in the face, was roaring *vive le Duc de Hautbourg et Monsieur le Marquis*. Monsieur le Curé, meek and benign, stood up on tip-toe to obtain a better sight, and raised his shovel-hat high above him as if in apostolic benediction; Monsieur le Maire, Messieurs of the Municipal Council, and Monsieur the Parish Beadle, yelled as nobody had ever heard them yell before; Monsieur Duval, the hotel-keeper, had dressed himself as if for a state-ball, and was smirking radiantly on his doorstep, with Mademoiselle Madelon behind, effulgent in a clean gown, a piece of ribbon round her throat and a brooch somewhere on her bosom. To crown all, and complete the *tableau*, the local force of six policemen and twelve gendarmes were drawn up in a symmetrical semicircle, and seemed disposed to salute. You see, they had not yet received advices from Paris that this Monsieur le Duc was a "Socialist." They simply took their cue from Monsieur le Maire, and, seeing him enthusiastic, were enthusiastic, too, as became good officials.

CHAPTER III.

"Vox Populi Vox Dei."

THE cheering, saluting, and pocket-handkerchief-waving would have been all very well but for this fact —that they could have no influence whatever on the resolution of the three gentlemen whom they were intended to honour. The eldest of the three bowed very coldly and gravely; the elder of the two brothers, hailed, for the first time in his life, as "Monsieur le Marquis," appeared disposed to treat the matter as a joke; the younger brother kept as serious as his father, and, if anything, looked contempt for men who could make such servile fuss about people who were perfect strangers to them. It never struck this ingenuous youth that M. Ballanchu, whilst he bellowed with veins distended and bloodshot eyes, had five-and-twenty unpaid bills ornamenting the inside of his desk at home; and that poor M. Scarpin, for all his zeal in screaming himself hoarse, was sick at heart in fear of approaching bankruptcy.

The noise and excitement continued long after the Gerolds had entered the hotel, and had been ushered by the obsequious M. Duval into the yellow drawing-room, now blazing with wax-candles and extemporized floral decoration. In the middle of the room stood the table, spread with snowy cloth and decked with all the available silver plate in the establishment. M. Duval had even gone the length of borrowing an épergne from the local jeweller; and the local jeweller, in consenting to the loan, had merely stipulated that one of his shop-boys should be allowed to serve at table disguised as waiter, so as not to lose sight of the precious piece. It was not that he mistrusted Monsieur Duval, but in a town where everybody has become poor, you know, it is best to take one's precautions.

Monsieur Duval had flattered himself upon creating a favourable impression. He had spent ten minutes over the bow of his white tie, twenty in the hands of his neighbour the barber, who had put his hair into curl, fifteen in superintending the toilets of his subordinates, to see that they were as splendid as himself, and forty in planning and arranging with his own deft hands the adornment of the yellow drawing-room as above. It should be added that he had also invested two twenty-franc pieces in the purchase of the flowers which made such a fine show, and that the *menu* he had devised for M. le Duc's dinner was a thing unique in provincial experience.

The first words of Manuel Gerold—or of M. le Duc if you like it better—fell upon him, however, like a bucket of iced water upon a glowing fire; for, whilst the crowd were still shouting below, and whilst he, M. Duval, smiling from ear to ear, was assuring his guests that the dinner would be served up in an instant—but that meanwhile, if "Monseigneur"* would allow it, M. le Maire of the town and M. le Curé, together with

---

* Monseigneur simply means "my lord," and was used before 1789 in addressing all very great noblemen. Nowadays it is reserved for princes of the blood, and church dignitaries, archbishops, bishops, &c. Loyal tenants, however, like M. Duval, will still call their noble masters "Monseigneur."

several other of the officials, would feel honoured by being allowed to pay their respects—the Duke, after a moment's whispering with his sons, drew out his watch, and asked a little stiffly: "Monsieur Duval, at what time does the last train start for Paris to-night?"

Poor M. Duval, utterly disconcerted at this surprising question, stood stock still and looked blankly at his interlocutor.

"The last train for .... for Paris?" he stammered. "Why, surely Monseigneur does not think of going away to-night?"

At any other time Manuel Gerold would have answered kindly, and stated his intentions without reserve; but the stupid acclamations of the crowd, and the cringing, almost dog-like attitude of the persons whom he had seen during the last half-hour, had put him out of humour, so that he replied with a curtness altogether out of keeping with his usual manner.

"I cannot say what my plans are; but I beg, Monsieur Duval, that you will not call me Monseigneur any more. If you have ever heard anything about me, you must be aware that I am a Republican, and that consequently I admit no differences of rank but such as exist between men who are honest and those who are not."

As a Frenchman, M. Duval understood this speech at once. He bowed silently and staggered out of the room—professedly to fetch a time-table, virtually to hide the confusion and chagrin which were overwhelming him with a sense that all was lost and that the new Duke was indeed a Radical!

As soon as he was gone the Gerolds held a rapid conference and decided that they must go that night and not risk any interviews with mayors or vicars. There was nothing in Manuel Gerold of the charlatanry of Republicanism, and he felt not the slightest ambition to proclaim aloud to the world why it was that he forsook Clairefontaine. His sons thought as he did; the demonstrative homage of the worthy *Hautbourgeois* had too pecuniary a ring in it to cause them any elation. They had seen in their father, a few years before, carried in triumph by several thousand electors, who cheered lustily, not the name or the purse, but the man; and the present exhibition seemed to them humiliatingly mean in comparison.

M. Duval re-entered in a few minutes, woe-stricken in demeanour and freighted with a time-table. Behind him he left the door open, and on handing the table to Manuel Gerold, appeared to hesitate timidly as though he had something to ask but dared not. Outside on the landing there was a sound of whispering with slight shuffling of feet, and down below in the street, the cries *vive Monsieur le Duc! vive Monsieur le Marquis!* &c. were being uttered enthusiastically and perseveringly as ever.

Manuel Gerold took the time-table, marked the look of trepidation on the host's rueful face, and was about to ask the reason, when he was spared the trouble; for, before M. Duval had said a word, the door left ajar was thrown wide open and in sailed Monsieur le Maire, M. le Curé, as many of the Municipal Council as could squeeze in after him, M. Ballanchu the seedsman, M. Scarpin the bootmaker, M. Hochepain the tax-gatherer, and some half-dozen more *ejusdem farinæ*, inquisitive, awe-stricken, and respectful. To prevent all chances of rebuff M. le Maire had brought with him his daughter, a damsel of fifteen summers, attired in white as if for confirmation, and armed with a bouquet about a yard in circumference The whole procession advanced a couple of steps into the room and bowed like a single councillor. Then the damsel, being nudged forward by her father, stepped out reddening, and presented the bouquet.

It was to the old man she offered it. He had risen, together with Horace and Emile, and, as the child came to him, he laid a hand kindly on her head.

"To whom is it you are giving these flowers, my child?" he asked: "to Manuel Gerold, or to the Duke of Hautbourg?"

This question had not been foreseen in the full-dress rehearsal of the performance which Monsieur le Maire had gone through down below with his daughter, so the excellent magistrate immediately hastened to the rescue. He had mentally prepared a short but effective speech, treating of the importance of the nobility in the social scale, the dangers of anarchy, the Imperial dynasty, the salutary blending of liberty and order, and the price of wheat—topics all bearing more or less on the return of the new Duke. Losing his presence of mind, however, at the critical moment, he began his remarks by an allusion to the Crusades, addressing Manuel Gerold as "*Monsieur le Duc, fils illustre d'une race de Croisés.*"

The Republican at once cut him short.

"Mr. Mayor," he said gently but firmly, "I am sincerely thankful, both to yourself and your fellow-townsmen, for the friendly greeting you have given my sons and me to-day; but I should be glad to learn that this welcome of yours has not been offered under a misapprehension. If you have greeted me simply as the descendant of a family long connected with your town, then thank you most gratefully again and again; but if you have welcomed me under the belief that I was coming to assume any new character, I think it right to tell you that certain private arrangements which I am compelled to make will prevent my ever standing towards you in the same relation as did my late nephew."

Here were all the new-born hopes of Hautbourg nipped in the bud. There was a long murmur, with whispers and sighs from everybody, except M. Hochepain, the tax-gatherer, who, to the indignation of his brethren, cried energetically: "Hear, hear," under a wrong impression. He was sternly called to order by M. Ballanchu, and, whilst this little episode was being enacted in the hindmost ranks of the assemblage, near the door, M. le Curé, brushing his shovel hat nervously with the sleeve of his cassock, and beaming unutterable entreaty through the glasses of his honest spectacles, trotted forward and undertook to plead the cause of his sorrowing parishioners. He was a worthy ecclesiastic, and made the most of his point. The sense of diminished church-dues was so strong within him that he would have been eloquent in the face of a king, how much more then in the presence of the man with whom it lay to restore prosperity to the borough, and so, indirectly, to replenish the coffers of the parish church. He quoted Maccabees, the Book of Ezekiel, and the parable of the man who buried his talents in a napkin. He marshalled in array St. Thomas Aquinas, St. Augustine of Hippo, and St. John

Chrysostom. He adduced the sufferings of St. Simeon Stylites on his pillar, St. Laurence on his gridiron, and St. Andrew of Utica, who perished by fish-hooks. And all this he did with so much unction and zeal as to excite the secret envy of the Mayor, the wonder of the Municipal Council, the admiration of M. Ballanchu, and, indeed, of everybody save that unlucky M. Hochepain, who, being always out of his reckoning, and having still present to his mind the angry rebuke of the seedsman, took it upon himself to exclaim, "No, no," just when such an expression of opinion on his part was most unfelicitous. Happily, M. le Curé was too deep in his own harangue to hear, for he was just then closing with a masterly peroration, depicting the horrors of famine and the remorse which must necessarily overtake the rich man who allowed his poor brethren to die of hunger. This last form of appeal was only ventured on as an extreme resort, for, as a general rule, M. le Curé had much greater faith in the salvation of rich brethren than of poor ones. He had had occasion to notice that it was the rich who went oftenest to church and put most into the plate.

A great pity that so much eloquence should have missed its effect, but it did. Manuel Gerold's words in answer were few, but they sounded to the good priest like so many thwacks with a cane. The Republican observed that he had never contemplated letting anybody die of hunger; that his annual subscription of 20,000 francs for the poor of Hautbourg would be continued, and even added to if it were insufficient; that he would instruct the agent not to press for rent those who really could not afford to pay, and that if any person in Hautbourg had met with misfortune which it was possible to relieve by extra donations, he would do his best to help him." This said, however, he made one of those coldly polite inclinations of the head by which kings, cabinet ministers, and people who are bored, intimate their wish to end an interview. The hint was taken with dismay by the curé, with consternation by the mayor and council, with suppressed mutterings by MM. Ballanchu, Scarpin and Co., and with philosophical indifference by M. Hochepain, who, having never understood from the first why he had come upstairs, was not much surprised to find himself going down again.

Everybody bowed on backing out as on coming in, and it was the crest-fallen M. Duval who held the door open. Three-quarters of an hour after the desponding deputation had made its exit, the strangers themselves were gone. Finding that a train left for Paris soon after eight, they had galloped through M. Duval's munificent dinner, or, rather, through a quarter of it, and so stabbed the professional self-esteem of that honest innkeeper, as well as dashed down his hopes. Not even the 500-franc note with which the Republican generously paid him his bill was enough to make him forget the accumulation of so much bitterness in a single day.

Manuel Gerold and his sons set out on foot to go to the station, but though the market-place and the streets were still crowded, they were not cheered this time as they had been an hour or two before. The ill news brought down from the yellow drawing-room by M. le Maire, M. le Curé and authorities, had spread pretty fast, and as the three gentlemen appeared at the door of the hotel, first one individual, then another who had caught sight of them, proffered a cat-call or derisive whistle—(remember, darkness had set in, and it was easy to whistle without being seen). These isolated marks of disfavour were like the single squibs that are fired off at the commencement of a firework entertainment. Gradually, they increased in number, in strength, and in noise, just as the sky-rockets that come after the squibs. *"A bas les Républicains!" "A la fosse les Socialistes!" "A la lanterne les Rouges!"* Such were the amenities which this lively mob delivered. In a minute or two, the cries, cat-calls, whistles, and kind wishes had become general. Everybody—man, woman, and child—contributed his or her objurgation to the cheerful total, and the three Gerolds were eventually escorted to the station by a closely-packed rabble, screaming, yelping, hooting, and barking, *"A la fosse!" "A la lanterne!" "A la potence!* (gibbet)" &c. One gentleman, thinking probably that this exhibition of feeling was scarcely forcible enough for a practical age, snatched up a stone close to the station and threw it at the group (it struck Manuel Gerold's shoulder), exclaiming, *"Sales Proscrits, pouah!"*

"Ignoble dogs!" cried Horace Gerold, facing round, with his fists clenched in indignant scorn.

But his father gently withheld his arm. "Must we take angry men at their word?" he said. "These don't mean what they say."

"C'est égal," muttered the young man between his teeth; "this is my first lesson in democracy, and if all crowds are like this——"

"But they're not," put in his father, earnestly.

CHAPTER IV.

Anno Domini M.DCCC.LIV.

WHILST the three Gerolds are being whirled along towards Paris, each musing in the strain peculiar to him on the ups and downs of popular favour, it will not be amiss if we take a bird's-eye survey of the year 1854, which was to be a starting-point in the lives of the two young men.

In 1854, France had already been rather more than two years in the enjoyment of its Second Empire, and people who had sworn eternal fidelity to past dynasties, had had abundant time to forget that such had ever existed, that here there were three great topics of interest in the Parisian papers: the Crimean war, the sensation drama *Les Cosaques*, by MM. Arnault and Judicis; and the Cholera. Lord Raglan and Marshal St. Arnaud, Admiral Hamelin and Rear-Admiral Dundas, MM. Arnault and Judicis (afore-mentioned) and Dr. Trousseau (on account of the cholera), were seven popular men. Monsieur Jullien—who had organized some promenade concerts in London, and composed a quadrille called the *Allied Armies*, during the performance of which some warriors in red and some others in blue were to be seen emerging from behind a curtain playing a medley of *Rule Britannia* and *Partant pour la Syrie*—was also a popular man. For the first time since the invention of printing the term *braves alliés* was being advantageously substituted for that of *Milords Godam* in the current literature which treated of Englishmen, and there were pictures of French Zouaves warmly embracing Scotch Highlanders in most of the engraving-shops of the capital. The nick-name for his Majesty the Emperor Nicholas was in London "*Old Nick*," and in Paris *le Gros Colas;* there was likewise a sobriquet for Prince Menschikoff, who was styled *le Prince Thermomètre*—a somewhat mysterious joke, but which was generally understood to mean that the Russian captain's chance of thrashing *les braves Français* depended much more upon Generals Frost and Snow than upon any proficiency of his own in the science of warfare. In order to diffuse a healthy patriotism amongst the lower orders, the Imperial Government had taken care that there should be no lack of seasonable reading, and husky gentlemen patrolled the Boulevards selling songs and pamphlets in which one found many unpleasant things about Ivan the Terrible, who cut off the ears of his courtiers, and about Alexander, who sent French prisoners of war to work in the mines of Ural, and fed them on tallow-candles. For the more intellectual portion of the community who might have been sceptic about the candles, the publishers of the late M. de Custine had brought out a new edition of his famous Russian book; and for clubs and cafés, where the frivolous abound, M. Gustave Doré, then budding into fame, had prepared a comic and pictorial *Histoire de la Sainte Russie*, in which the death of every alternate Czar by poison was most graphically and instructively pourtrayed. To tell the truth, this war was a godsend, for, had there been no dead and wounded to harangue about, no Czar to cut jokes at, and no Muscovites to pummel, who knows but that the French might have turned their ever-lively attention to that new Constitution which had just been elaborated, and devoted some of their superfluous energy to knocking it to pieces? But one thing at a time is enough for Frenchmen—happily. They only pull Constitutions to bits when they have nothing else to do; and in 1854, being fully employed with other talk, they let the Constitution alone. Besides, most of the workmen who were good at knocking to pieces were out of the way. MM. Bianqui and Barbés, the heroes of the 15th May insurrection in 1848, were under lock and key. MM. Ledru Rollin and Louis Blanc were across the channel. M. Victor Hugo, majestuous and gloomy, was inspecting the ocean from the top of his Belvedere at Guernsey, and defiantly muttering verses from his *Napoleon le Petit*. MM. Thiers and Guizot, possibly not over-satisfied with the pretty day's work they had accomplished when they smashed the Orleans throne into splinters in fighting between them for the keeping of it, were indulging in solitary reflections—the one in his own home at Val Richer, the other in Germany. M. Eugène Sue, the Socialist in kid-gloves, great at depicting virtue in corduroys, was fretting away the last years of his life at Annecy; and Dr. Raspail, another revolutionary hero, who eschewed kid-gloves but believed in the panaceal properties of camphor, was smoking cigarettes of that compound in retirement at Brussels; M. Pierre Leroux, the bogey of French mass-going matrons, had disappeared, no òne knew whither, taking his materialist doctrines with him; and Generals Cavaignac, Lamoricière and Changarnier—those modern Curiatii, out-

witted and conquered by the Imperial Horatius—
were chewing the cud of bitter meditation—very
bitter—and shooting partridges to console themselves.
As for the minor operatives in the knocking-to-
pieces trade, there were eleven thousand of them
at Cayenne, two thousand at Lambessa, and five thousand in Africa. M. Frédéric Cournet, who had commanded the barricade of the Faubourg du Temple in
June '48, had lately been killed in a duel near Windsor by his brother revolutionist Barthélemy, who had
commanded the barricade of the Faubourg St. Antoine;
and Barthélemy himself was giving fencing-lessons in
London, pending the time when he should be hanged
at Newgate for murdering his landlord and a policeman. Thus opposition, liberalism, and all unpleasantness of that sort, had been happily removed. Such
Radicals as remained in Paris held their tongues, and
it was only at the Bar (where amongst others a young
barrister of twenty-eight, named M. Emile Ollivier, was
remarkable for the vehemence of his Republicanism)
that one could ever hear anything like a subversive
speech, delivered generally in defence of some miserable journalist brought up for punishment. To give a
civilized look to the new Empire and make everything
regular, there was a Corps Législatif, composed of two
hundred and sixty members, and a Senate, composed
of a hundred and twenty; who wore, the Deputies, blue
swallow-tails with silver braiding, and the Senators,
black swallow-tails with gold ditto. The cost of them
to the nation for salaries, refreshments, &c. was about
half a million sterling: they debated on an average
sixty hours a session with closed doors, not a single
reporter being suffered to disturb them; and as they

were all invariably of one mind, their deliberations were characterized by that blessed harmony which should always prevail in Christian assemblies. The daily press, in 1854, was no longer—heaven be praised!—the turbulent, unmanageable thing it had been a few years previously. There were three journals—*Patrie*, *Constitutionnel*, and *Pays*—which sang the praises of the Imperial dynasty every evening, and though it is true there were three or four more that declined to join in this concert, yet these were ill-conditioned papers, which were perpetually getting into trouble, and which M. de Persigny, the Home Minister, doctored with whip and thong, like a liberal and wise statesman as he was. As for the *Charivari* and kindred prints, they cut their capers under difficulties. Imagine a quadrille where each of the dancers has a piece of chain and a ten-pound shot riven to the ankle of his right leg. Architecturally speaking, Paris was not yet the vast Haussmannville it has become since; but the trowel-wielding Baron was just come into office, and pickaxe, hod, and brick-cart were already on the move. Every willing citizen who was not required for exterminating Russians found employment to his fill in demolishing dwelling-places. It was known amongst taxpayers that the Rue de Rivoli was going to be prolonged, so that there might be one straight line from the Place de la Concorde to that of the Bastille; that a new Tribunal of Commerce was to be built in the heart of the once pestilential Cité, where policemen of old had never ventured without quaking; that the old Théâtre Lyrique and Théâtre du Châtelet were coming down, and that new ones would soon be erected in their stead, furnished with all modern appliances of luxury and with actually room enough in the stalls for people to sit in; that M. Alphand, the new Prefect's chief engineer and *fidus Achates*, had taken the Bois de Boulogne in hand, and was bent upon transforming it into a fairy garden, which it should need only five-and-twenty million francs a year to keep in order; that the plans of five new barracks, three new boulevards, seven new mairies, four new squares, and seventeen new churches, were being prepared on a right royal scale, regardless of expense; and that to pay for all these things there would in all probability be more taxes next year. And yet such is the admirable effect of the whip and thong in subduing the human mind and making it supple, that nobody grumbled much; though M. de Rambuteau, who had been Prefect of the Seine under Louis Philippe, remembered the time when the whole city had uttered piercing cries, and groaned aloud and predicted national ruin, because he, M. de Rambuteau, had insisted upon building the wretched meagre street which bears his name. Truly a great change had come over men in the course of three years, and one could notice the effects of it everywhere. If you entered a café in the year 1854, you were no longer deafened, as in 1848, '49, and '50, by the astounding clamour of citizens discussing across a table whether Cavaignac was a greater man than Lamartine, or Lamartine a greater man than Cavaignac, or M. Odillon Barrot a greater man than either. From prudential motives the investigation of these interesting problems had been momentarily shelved. There were gentlemen to be seen in the cafés, who walked very erect, and had small eyes, and were particularly affable in conversation.

Unfortunately, it had been remarked that those who confided their political impressions to these engaging strangers were seldom long before they were summoned to explain them at greater length to M. le Juge d'Instruction at the Palais de Justice, and this had no doubt something to do with the extremely taciturn, not to say unbrotherly demeanour, which men evinced towards each other in Parisian cafés during the year '54. There was a good deal of the same sort of danger in clubs. It was not the most agreeable thing in the world to be suddenly interrupted in a mantelshelf conversation by a gentleman with a firm beak-nose and a red rosette in his button-hole, who would suddenly spring up from an opposite end of the room and say, with grim courtesy, hat in hand, "I think I heard Monsieur express an opinion adverse to the *coup-d'état*, in which I had the honour to participate. Will Monsieur be so obliging as to name a friend?" In nine cases out of ten, your adversary was one of his Majesty's officers, grateful for past favours, and hopeful by display of zeal to merit a continuance of the same. He would take you out at six o'clock A.M. to the Bois de Vincennes, and there run you through with amazing adroitness and satisfaction. Under the circumstances it was as well to avoid political topics, and to talk in a lyrical strain, either about the glories of war or the ravages of the cholera—taking care to add, however, if one selected this last subject, that the cholera was not half so fatal under the present as under preceding reigns, as was triumphantly proved by the fact that M. Casimir Péreire, Prime Minister of Louis Philippe, had died of cholera, whereas no such catastrophe had ever befallen a minister of Napoleon, nor was likely to.

ANNO DOMINI M.DCCC.LIV. 81

But let us not be unjust towards the Imperial régime. One was not entirely confined for conversation to the war and the cholera; there were other topics upon which one might venture with more or less safety. For instance, one could speak of the monster Hôtel du Louvre, which was being completed, much to the dismay of surrounding hostelries; of the barn-like building in the Champs-Elysées, which was destined for the International Exhibition of 1855, and which (this in a whisper, for fear of beak-noses) contrasted unfavourably with Sir Joseph Paxton's edifice that adorned Hyde Park in '51; of the beauty of the new Empress, Mdlle. Eugénie de Téba, and of the intention attributed to her of importing the *mantilla* at Court; of the fashions of the year—to wit, frogged coats, striped trowsers, and curly-brimmed hats for gentlemen; three-flounced dresses, hair *à l'Impératrice*, and spoon-bill bonnets for ladies; of the thin face of M. Magne, Minister of Finance, and the plump face of M. Baroche, Minister of Justice; of the beard movement raging like an epidemic in England, and the consequent depression in the razor-trade; of Mdlle. Anna Thillon, the star of the Opéra Comique, of whom the critics unanimously wrote that she looked like an angel and sang like a peacock; of Dr. Véron, deputy for Paris and editor of the *Constitutionnel*, his renowned *cordon bleu* Sophie, and his legendary shirt-collars, more stiff and formidable than the shirt-collars of any other man of letters from Dunkirk to Bayonne; of M. de Tocqueville, the witty and thoughtful, who was writing his book, *L'Ancien Régime et la Révolution*, and M. Augustin Thierry, the scholarly, who was busy at his *Histoire du Tiers État;* of the Académie Française, grave and learned body, which professed to ignore Béranger, and which, in the course of the year, mourned five of its members—Tissot, the *savant;* Antonin Jay, the founder of the *Constitutionnel;* Ancelot, the author of *Louis XI.;* Baour Lormian, the translator of *Tasso;* and the polished Marquis de Saint Aulaire, historian of the Fronde; of the price of oysters, which cost ten centimes the dozen more than in '53, and of the scarcity of truffles on the markets of Périgord; of M. Scribe the playwright, whose eternal young widows and colonels were decidedly beginning to be found stale; and of Mdme. Emile de Girardin's new comedies, *La Joie fait Peur* and *Le Chapeau d'un Horloger* (the last two she ever wrote), which all Paris was flocking to see; of Alfred de Musset, whose once brilliant genius was almost extinguished, and of Alexandre Dumas, who was as prolific in novels as ever; of Dumas the younger, whose recent success with *La Dame aux Camélias* was still in everybody's mouth, and of Mdme. Doche, who played the part of Marguerite Gautier in that drama so touchingly, that the ladies in the boxes used to sob, whilst the gentlemen in the stalls would cough, and—when nobody was looking—dash their hands across their eyes; of Italy and Italians, notably of Silvio Pellico, who was dying at Turin, broken down by his imprisonment in the Spielberg, and of Daniel Manin, ex-dictator of Venice, who was giving music-lessons in Paris; of a new sort of glove lately imported from England, called dogskin, generally voted hideous, but worn nevertheless because it was British; and of the exorbitant price of articles in Russian leather, owing to the cessation of trade with the Czar's dominions; of M. de Villèle, the celebrated Prime

Minister of Louis XVIII., who died during the year, unremembered and almost unknown, from having spent a quarter of a century in retirement (*sic transit gloria mundi!*); of M. le Comte d'Aberdeen, who was Premier in England, and Monsieur Franklin Pierce, the orator, who was President of the United States; of certain English words which were making their way bravely into the French language, such as *steeple-chass*, *lonch*, *ponch*, and *high-life*, the latter of which was pronounced as if it rhymed with *fig-leaf;* of the vintage of the year, which was good, and the crops, which were less so; of Alma and Balaclava, Inkermann and Sebastopol, with discussions as to whether one should say Se*b*as- or Se*v*as-topol; of M. de Morny's dinners and Mdme. de Persigny's suppers; of Ravel and Grassot, Bressant and Rachel; of the end of the world, which some French Dr. Cumming had announced as irrevocably fixed for the 13th of June, 1857; and of a new establishment of Turkish baths, which had been inaugurated as a novelty on the Boulevard du Temple, and which a popular journalist, M. Nestor Roqueplan, recommended as a sovereign cure to nephews who wished to get rid of their uncles.

Such, amongst others, were the topics of current talk in Paris in the year 1854, at the time when Horace and Emile Gerold came there to try their fortunes.

CHAPTER V.

Bourgeois Politics.

"WELL, I think we've about done our furnishing," said Horace to his brother, as he stepped back to look at a long row of law volumes which he had been ranging on a book-shelf.

"Yes," answered Emile; "both our studies are in order: the man has finished nailing down the carpets in the bedrooms; I don't see what else remains to be done."

"Where have you put the tin box?" asked Horace.

"Here it is," said Emile, picking up a small tin case from out of a litter of torn newspapers, bits of string, empty boxes and wood-shavings that encumbered the floor. "What's in it?"

"Don't you know?" exclaimed the elder, looking at him. "It's that title-deed; I put it there when we came from Clairefontaine six weeks ago."

"Oh!" rejoined Emile, becoming serious, and he added after a moment: "What are you going to do with it?"

"We must find a place for the thing somewhere where we shan't be seeing it every day," returned Horace, perplexed. "I heartily wish it were off our hands; I dream about it at nights. It is inconceivable that father should have wished us to keep such a thing five years."

"There's an empty drawer in your bureau," remarked Emile, not answering the latter half of his brother's observation.

Horace was holding the case in his two hands and eying it rather absently. "H'm, no," he said, at the end of a moment's reflection: "suppose *you* keep it? I shall feel quieter if it's in your charge."

The younger brother took the case without making any remark, and carried it into the next room, which was his own study. Horace heard the opening of a drawer, and the double clicking of a lock. Then Emile reappeared with a key in his hand. "If that can make you any easier," he said, "the thing's done. I've put it in my lowest drawer, left-hand side, and we need never look at it again unless you like."

Horace drew a short sigh of relief and gave a nod of thanks to Emile. After which, as the brothers wanted to set their rooms to rights, they fell to picking up the rubbish, wood-shavings, bits of string, shreds of paper, &c., and piled them into the empty deal boxes, preparatory to having these removed to a lumber-room.

It was during a November afternoon, and the two Gerolds were just installed in the lodgings they had taken, Rue St. Geneviève, in the "Latin Quarter," close to the Panthéon. Their father had some weeks since returned to Brussels; in fact he had done no more than pass through Paris, for, as he said with truth enough, the France of '54 was not a place for men who thought as he did. Manuel Gerold had no private fortune save that which had come to him at his nephew's death; but in the course of a long and laborious career as a political writer he had amassed sufficient to end his own days in ease and to start his sons in life comfortably. He could afford to give them three thousand francs a year apiece, which is a competence in Paris for young barristers who have not extravagant tastes; and, as the Council of the French Bar requires that a man shall have "a decently furnished lodging and a library of books" before he can be admitted to plead, he had spent twelve thousand francs in fitting up the chambers of Horace and Emile, so that Monsieur le Bâtonnier and his colleagues should have no fault to find. The brothers rented a set of rooms on the third floor—one of those good old sets of rooms built a hundred and fifty years ago, with thick walls, deep cupboards and roomy passages; not like those wretched card-board dwellings which M. Haussmann's architects have contrived—houses where, if the first-floor lodger plays the piano at midnight, he is heard on the sixth story, and keeps some ten or twelve batches of fellow-tenants awake. Horace and Emile had each a study and a bed-room to themselves; and for their joint use there was a kitchen and dining-room, the latter of which, however, as they seldom dined at home, they had converted into a smoking saloon. There was also a cellar for wine, wood, and coal; and if it would interest you to know what all this cost, I may tell you that their combined rent amounted to eight hundred francs, that is, double what they would have had to pay before 1848, and a third less than they would be obliged to pay in 1870.

Clubs being as yet confined in France to men who are rich and can afford to do without them, the brothers dined and breakfasted at one of those *tables-d'hôte* so numerous in the Latin Quarter, where young barristers, journalists, doctors, professors, and the better class of students resort. The board cost eighty-five francs a month, *vin ordinaire* included; and for that sum one had a very fair beefsteak or chop, an omelette, fried potatoes, and cheese at eleven, and soup, boiled beef, roast, vegetables, and dessert at six. Certainly the French are adepts in the art of giving *multum pro parvo*. It is impossible to surmise without chagrin what dinner would be given in Great Britain to any individual who expected his six courses *per diem* for sixty-eight shillings a month.

One thousand and twenty francs paid for board and 400 francs for lodging, left each brother 1,580 francs annually for firing and lighting, washing, clothes, and pocket-money. Set down the first two of these items at 100 francs (for between two coal can be eked out), the second at 150 francs, the third at 400 francs, and there remained 930 francs for the last. A young French barrister who has 37*l.* a year for pocket-money may consider himself favoured by Providence. There is no reason why he should deny himself the diurnal *demi-tasse* at his café; he can smoke cigarettes at the rate of one pound of tobacco per month (total 60 francs per annum); on festive occasions he may wear gloves and venture upon a cigar (N.B. a Londrés, price 25 centimes, as good as a London regalia if carefully selected); he may also indulge without fear in a cab, if not over-addicted to parties; and he will still have a reserve-fund for the exhilaration of beggars, the remuneration of the *concierge* who blackens his boots, makes his bed, and sweeps his room, and for an occasional summer's day excursion to Enghien or Montmorency should his fancy so lead him. Of course, theatre-going should cost him nothing. Every barrister contrives to know a few journalists, dramatic authors and actors upon whom he may depend for play-orders —especially during the dog-days.

The house in which Horace and Emile had taken up their abode was the property of a worthy draper named Pochemolle, who kept a shop on the ground floor, and was accounted somewhat a curiosity in the parish. The curiosity lay in this, that the Pochemolles, from father to son, had occupied the house where they then lived for upwards of a hundred and seventy years —a fact so rare, so phenomenal indeed, in the annals of Parisian trade, that certain of M. Pochemolle's customers, unable to grasp the notion in its entirety, had a sort of confused belief that it was M. Achille Pochemolle himself—the Pochemolle of 1854—who had flourished a hundred and seventy years on the same premises. Yet M. Achille Pochemolle was not more than fifty; and he looked by no means older than his age. He was a small, smug-faced, gooseberry-eyed man, quick in his movements, glib with his tongue, and full of the quaint shop-courtesy of eighty years ago, which he had inherited from his sire and his sire's sire along with their profound veneration for all that concerned the crown, the nobility, and the higher clergy. It was worth going a visit to the Rue Ste. Geneviève if only to see M. Pochemolle bow when he ushered out a customer or showed one in. He still kept to all the musk-scented traditions of the *grand siècle*. For him a lady, no matter how old and wrinkled, was always a *belle dame;* and heaven forbid that he should ever have driven a hard bargain with one of the gentle sex. He used to say, "*Voyez, belle dame, cette étoffe est faite pour vous embellir,*" or "*Belle dame,*

ce ruban ne peut qu'ajouter à vos graces." Ladies liked
it, and M. Pochemolle had a fine business connection
amongst ancient dowagers and spinsters of the neighbourhood; not to mention two or three nunneries, the
sisters of which, pleased to be addressed occasionally
in pretty old-world compliments, came to Monsieur
P.'s for all that was wanted in the way of linen and
drapery for their convents.

In politics M. Pochemolle was a valiant conservative of existing institutions, whatever they were, and,
under the circumstances, it might have seemed odd
that he should have consented to lodge the sons of a
notorious Republican, had it not been for this, that
he was under obligations to Manuel Gerold, and frequently acknowledged it with gratitude. As a private
first, then as a corporal, and finally as a sergeant in
the National Guard, Monsieur P—— had fired his shot
in the three insurrections of July, 1830; February, '48;
and June, '48; fighting each time on the side of order
—that is, on the side of Government; and it was in
the last of these battles that, finding himself under the
same flag as Manuel Gerold—who was for a moderate
Republic, opposed to a "Red" one—he had been
saved from certain death by the latter, who, at the
risk of his own life, had caught up Monsieur Pochemolle from under a barricade where he was lying
stunned, and carried him away to a place of safety.
The honest draper, who set a high price on his own
life, thought with wonder and admiration of this
achievement. He had sworn a lasting gratitude to his
preserver, and seemed likely not to forget his oath;
for, when Horace and Emile Gerold came with their
father to see whether M. Pochemolle had any lodgings

to let, he had gladly given them the best he had, without troubling himself about their political opinions. He even went further, for he spread it amongst his own purveyors, grocer, coal-man, and others, that his two new lodgers were young gentlemen "who might be trusted;" and, on the November afternoon, when the brothers were setting their rooms to rights, he came up to see with his own eyes whether they had everything they wanted, taking with him as his pretext a letter which the postman had just brought for Horace Gerold.

"Come in," cried the brothers, in answer to the good man's knock, and M. Pochemolle with his letter, his gooseberry eyes, and his excellent tongue ready for half-an-hour's chat, appeared in the doorway.

"A letter, gentlemen," he said; "and I've come to see whether I can be of use to you. Deary me! but these are fine rooms and improved vastly since you're in them. This is a Brussels carpet, five francs twenty-five centimes the *mètre:* I know it by the tread. Nothing can be better than those crimson curtains, solid cloth of *Elbœuf*, cost a hundred and fifty francs the pair, I'll warrant me. And that's a portrait of your most respected father over the mantelpiece?"

"Yes, smiled Horace, taking the letter and laying it on the table. "Our father has a great esteem for you, Monsieur Pochemolle."

"Not more than I have for him, sir," answered the draper heartily, and, peering into the next room, which was Emile's, he continued: "And that, no doubt, is Madame your most venerated mother?" The picture was one of a fair-haired lady, with tender expressive eyes. The brothers had scarcely known their mother;

she had died when they were both children. They nodded and kept silent.

"Ha," went on Monsieur Achille, changing the subject with ready tact. "These pictures remind me of two of mine own which I must show you downstairs. One is a print made in 1710 (a hundred and forty-four years ago), the other is more recent—1780; both represent a part of the Rue Ste. Geneviève, and you can see my shop in them, not altered a bit from what it is now, with the name Pochemolle over the doorway and the sign of *The Three Crowns*. These three crowns, you must know, were the making of our house. Ah, Messieurs, it's a fine story, and you should have heard my grandfather tell it as he had it from his own grandfather, the hero of the tale. Just about as old as you, Monsieur Horace, he was. Then my great-great-grandfather—one day he was walking along the streets, when he sees a poor woman, worn away with hunger, and two little children on her arms, make a snatch at the purse of a fine gentleman who was stepping out of a coach, and try to run off with it. The two were so near together—he and the woman—that the servants of the gentleman laid hold of him, thinking it was he that had made the snatch; the more so as the crazy thing, in her hurry to get away, had tripped up and let go the purse, which was lying at my ancestor's feet. Of course this took him breathless like, and he was just going to say what was what, when, looking at the poor creature who was crouching on the ground shaking all over, and clasping her two babies close to her, he couldn't bear giving her up, and so says he: 'Yes, gentlemen, it's I that took the purse.'

"It seems the woman gave him such a look as he

never forgot to the day when he was laid in his coffin, and he used to say that it was worth going ten times to the gallows to have eyes look at one as hers did. You see, thieving was no joke then: it meant the gibbet: and it wasn't everybody that would have run their necks into a noose for a beggar-woman they didn't know. Well, they dragged him off to prison, locked him up with chains to his legs, they did; and my grandsire made up his mind that before long they'd have him out on the Place de Grève, and do by him as I daresay he'd seen done by a many a thief and cut-throat. But the gentleman whose purse had been snatched had seen the whole thing and wasn't going to let evil come of it. He allowed the young man to lie in prison a little while, just to see, probably, how long he would hold out; but when he saw that my grandsire wouldn't budge an inch from his story, but stuck firm to it that it was he that had taken the purse, then he spoke out, and one day came to the jail with a King's order for letting the prisoner loose. He was a great nobleman was this gentleman—one of the greatest about Louis the Fourteenth's court; and when my grandsire came out of prison—it was the Châtelet; they're building a theatre over the spot now—he saw this great nobleman, who didn't bare his head to many, standing, hat in hand, beside his coach-door. '*Will you do me the honour of riding to Versailles, sir, with me?*' he said—ay, he said, '*do me the honour*,' he did —'*I wish to present you to the King.*' And sure enough to Versailles they went both together, side by side, he and the nobleman in the same coach; and at court the King gave my ancestor his hand to kiss, and the nobles between them subscribed five hundred *louis*, with which this house and the shop below were bought. And the purse which was the cause of the whole business, and which contained three crowns when it was snatched, was presented to my grandsire by the nobleman, along with a diamond ring. They're both under a glass-case in our back parlour now, and I can tell you, gentlemen, we're proud of 'em."

"Well you may be," exclaimed Emile Gerold, warmly. "There is not a nobleman could show a more splendid patent of nobility than that purse and the three crowns."

"And what became of the woman?" asked Horace Gerold.

"Our benefactor took care of her, too. He set her up in a cottage on his country estate, and I believe her sons grew up to be honest peasants. But I don't feel much for her, though," added M. Pochemolle, sagaciously; "for, after all, if the nobleman hadn't had his eyes about him when the thing happened, she'd have let my grandsire swing, which would have been a pretty end for a man that had never fingered a penny that wasn't his own, and would as soon have thought of thieving as of committing murder."

Whilst speaking M. Pochemolle strode about the rooms, continuing to inspect everything, feeling the coverings of chairs and sofas with a professional touch, digging his fists into mattresses and pillows to test their elasticity, and closely scrutinizing the wood of which tables and bureaus were made. "I don't want to be talking only about myself, gentlemen," he said bluffly; "let's talk a little about yourselves: the goings on of an old family a hundred and seventy years ago can't interest you much, though it's civil of you to listen. Hullo, what's this?"

In ferreting about, M. Pochemolle had come upon some framed pictures standing on the floor with their faces to the wall, waiting to be hung up. He took one and turned it to the light. It was a print of David's celebrated picture, *Le Serment du Jeu de Paume*.* Poor M. Pochemolle became suddenly grave.

"No, no," said he, shaking his forefinger before his face and looking reproachfully from one brother to the other. "No, no, no—don't have anything to do with 'em."

"With whom?" asked Horace, amused.

"With them there," and M. Pochemolle pointed ruefully to the grand figure of the revolutionist, Bailly, standing with hand uplifted in the foreground of the picture. "They're not fit company for gentlemen like you to associate with," he went on: "no, they ain't, indeed. And if you'd seen as much of 'em as I have, you'd wash your hands of 'em now and for altogether."

"Are you speaking of the revolutionists?" inquired Emile.

"Ay, sir, I am."

"But come, M. Pochemolle, you were a Republican yourself not so long ago," observed Horace, laughing. "It was in fighting for the Provisional Government

---

* In 1789, Louis XVI. wishing to throw impediments in the way of the sittings of the States General, who appeared to him to be voting reforms too fast, ordered the Debate Room at Versailles to be closed, under pretence of repairs. The members thereupon adjourned to the Tennis Court, and there swore a solemn oath not to cease from their work until they had drawn up a new Constitution. David's pencil has immortalised this episode.

that you received the blow on the head which gave our father the opportunity of picking up and making your acquaintance."

"Ay, Monsieur, but the blow on the head doesn't prove I was a Republican. When I was a little chap ten years old, no higher than that pair of tongs yonder, I went to the Barrière de Clichy to throw stones at the Cossacks, who were marching into Paris. Throwing stones was the most we could do, for we were too small to fire guns. Sixteen years later, when M. Lafayette and that set were overthrowing Charles X., I went out and did my best to prevent them. The National Guard was dissolved then, but I put on my uniform all the same and went to join the Regulars. I stuck to it three days, July 27, 28 and 29, along with the Royal Guards at the Tuileries; and if the Bourbons were expelled it wasn't for want of fighting on my part. In 1848 came our King Louis Philippe's turn, and I was out again, February 23, 24, 25, never closing an eye once during the three days, and seeing six-and-thirty men of my company shot down by the *Faubourgiens*. Well, we were beat, as you know; your respected father and his friends came to power, and there was nothing for it but to rally round them to prevent their being swept away in their turn by the 'Reds.' That's why I fought for them in the three days of June, but it doesn't prove I'm a Republican, for I should do just as much for the Emperor Napoleon if any one were to try and get rid of him."

"H'm, then you can boast with your hand on your heart that you have consistently opposed progress of every sort and kind, and are prepared to do so again," remarked Horace, good-humouredly, but with a small point of irony.

"Ay, sir, I can," answered M. Pochemolle simply, though not without a counter point of irony. "I can, if you think that progress and revolution mean the same thing; but I don't. Let's have order first, say I; then we'll see about the rest afterwards."

"Yet you must have some preference for one form of government over the other," ejaculated Emile, not a little scandalized at this—to him—new way of talking.

"Yes, I like anything better than a Republic," responded M. Pochemolle with deliberation. "See, gentlemen, what is it that we tradesmen most want,— peace, isn't it?—and a good strong government that 'll let us sell our wares quietly, and keep the ragamuffins from breaking our windows. Well, when your honoured father and his friends were in office, what did we have? I know they were honest men and meant well; but honesty's not enough: it's like butter without the bread: the bread's strength, and we want strength too. M. Lamartine, M. Louis Blanc, and M. Gerold made us handsome promises, and, I know, did their best to keep them; but what did it all come to? Why, in '48, we paid twice more taxes than we'd ever paid before: we were out four days a week quelling riots, and there was no more business doing than if we'd all been living in famine time. Now under the Emperor I don't say but that the taxes are high; only we can afford to pay them. Trade's been brisker these three years past, spite of the war and that, than I ever remember it before; and we don't have any rioting."

"Oh, if you look at these questions from the

counter point of view," interrupted Emile Gerold, a little contemptuously.

"Well, sir, don't we all look at things through our particular set of glasses?" rejoined the honest draper roundly. "Here are you two gentlemen come to Paris to start as lawyers, and I am bound I shall hear you both make many a fine speech before I've done with you; but don't you think that what some of you gentlemen are most eager after when you stand up to preach for freedom and all that, is the making yourselves popular names, in order that people may flock round you, and pay you well for taking their cases in hand. Leastways that's my experience of a good many barristers."

"There's no harm in wishing to become popular," remarked Emile energetically.

"No, sir; nor in wishing to sell one's goods," replied the draper with a laugh. "Only I'll tell you what's the mistake many of the popular gentlemen make: they ask for a great deal more than we want, and a great deal more than's good for us to have; then they've another trick, which is to promise a good bit more than they can ever give."

"I believe you're trying to paint yourself much blacker than you really are," interposed Horace, smiling. "You can't care for freedom so little as you say, M. Pochemolle. That you should like selling your goods is natural enough, but you are a Frenchman, and must see something else in good government but a mere question of trade profits. Isn't there any satisfaction in being a free man in a free land? Is there no humiliation in living under a Government which treats us like children, not old enough to think for ourselves? Why, now, to go no further than your own case, do you find you have lost nothing by this new state of things? Formerly you had a parliament which debated and voted freely under public control; you could hold meetings whenever you wished to discuss political concerns; you had a free press; you elected your own mayors and your own officers in the National Guard; in a word, you were accounted somebody, and played your part in the State. But now what has become of all your rights?"

"Well, there you put the question in plain terms, and I'll answer you in the same way," replied M. Pochemolle, digging both hands into his pockets, and looking cheerily at the brothers. "A few years ago, as you say, we had all those rights, and what did they profit us? Why, during eighteen mortal years, we had nothing but M. Guizot trying to turn out M. Thiers, and M. Thiers trying to turn out M. Guizot. What do you think I cared whether it was M. Guizot or the other who was in? There wasn't a pin's head to choose between them, so far as real opinions went; only for this, perhaps, that it was M. Thiers, who talked the fastest about good government, that gave us the least of it: for 'twas in his time that we almost had the war with England, and were taxed seventy millions to pay for Paris fortifications. Then there was the press. Ah! to be sure, that was free enough: there were a couple of hundred gentlemen who abused each other in the papers every evening, and ran each other through in the Bois de Boulogne of a morning. Very pleasant for those who were journalists, but as I wasn't one, that freedom didn't help me. Next, we had the right to elect our own officers in the National

Guard, and do you know what was the result? why, there wasn't a ten sous' worth of discipline among the whole lot of us. At election-time it used to be a disgraceful sight to see the officers fawning to the privates, and if one of them was above doing it, or was at all sharp in commanding, why, twenty to one voted against him; so that he had to carry the musket again, after having worn the epaulet. I know what it is: for I don't want to make myself out better than I am: I once voted against my captain, simply because he'd blown me up before company about my rifle, which wasn't properly cleaned; only I'm hanged if I didn't feel a pang when I saw him, after the election, come and take up his stand in the ranks, whilst I had become a corporal. Then there used to be eternal fallings-out between the members of the Guard who were tradesmen and those who were professional, such as doctors, lawyers, retired officers from the army, and the like. These last were for having all the officers elected out of their set; and we tradesmen, who were in a majority, used to spite them, by electing nothing but our own party. I've seen a grocer, a tailor, and a baker, all officers in one company. I don't say a grocer can't be as brave as another man; only selling candles behind a counter doesn't prepare one for commanding troops, as we found out fast enough when the Revolution came. Shall I tell you now about our free parliament? There were four hundred of 'em in it, and the amount of talking they did was prodigious. They were at it six days a week during seven months out of the year, but I'm blessed if they ever did that for us" (M. Pochemolle snapped his fingers) "besides talking. We wanted new drains for

Paris; they wouldn't give 'em us—said it cost too much. We wanted new streets—same story. We had in the Cité yonder a whole lump of courts and alleys where people could punch one another's heads out of their windows from opposite sides of the street. They bred filth and fever they did, and so swarmed with rascals, that if the police wanted to lay hold of anybody there, they had to go twenty and thirty together. You'd have thought it would have been a mercy to burn the whole place; but when it came to be a matter of knocking it down and building something new and clean instead, everybody cried, 'Oh, no,' and 'Where's the money to come from?' And, I tell you, I was as bad as the rest of 'em, for though I wasn't a member of the House of Deputies, yet when me and a lot more of us, who had votes, used to get talking together about municipal business and other things we didn't understand, we were always saying 'No' to everything. I remember I used to come straight slap out with the 'No' before I knew what the question was about; it was a habit I'd got into. But at present all that's changed. Our Emperor he says, 'I'm here to rule,' and he does what's good for us: builds new streets and the like without taking counsel of anybody. And quite right too; for you see, gentlemen, let each man keep to his own walk, say I: I'm a famous good hand at selling cloth, calico, and ribbons, but I understand next to nothing about governing a country, and I don't see what any of you 'ud have to gain by letting me try."

Emile gave a shrug, Horace laughed.

"Well, that's candid and modest enough, anyhow, M. Pochemolle," he said. "I can't say you've quite convinced me. In any case, I daresay we shan't be the less good friends from thinking differently."

"No, no, that we shan't, sir: we shan't, indeed," answered M. Pochemolle. "Only"—and here M. P., relapsing into a serious vein, cast another deprecating look towards the picture of the Revolutionists which he had abandoned on the table during his last harangue —"Only, trust me, gentlemen, and don't have anything to do with *them*. I've never known it lead to anything but fighting in the streets and imprisonment afterwards. If they were all cut out of the same cloth as your respected father, it might be another matter; but they're not. I knew a Republican who talked very handsome about the rights of man, and went away without paying my bill."

M. Pochemolle was very exhaustive when he got on the subject of his antipathy for revolutionists, and might have adduced numerous other instances of Republican shortcomings, had not a knock at the door interrupted him at this juncture, whilst a feminine voice from without cried—"Papa, you're wanted in the shop."

"Ah, that's my little girl, gentlemen," said M. Pochemolle; and opening the door, he revealed a bright young lady, who looked some seventeen springs old, and was as pretty as clear hazel eyes, thick chestnut curls (young ladies wore curls in '54), red lips, and neat dressing could make her. She reddened slightly at finding herself before two strange messieurs, but was not otherwise shy, for she repeated to her sire what she had already said, and added that it was "*maman*" who had sent her up to say that Monsieur

Macrobe and his daughter were downstairs. She begged the messieurs' pardon for disturbing them.

"Come here, Georgette, and let me introduce you to these gentlemen," said M. Pochemolle, with a not unpardonable look of fatherly pride. "Gentlemen, you only saw my wife and my son when you came to take your rooms the other day. Here is my daughter, who was away staying with her aunt then. Georgette, these are the MM. Gerold, sons of Monsieur Gerold, who faced the fire of revolutionary rifles to save your father's life.* Make your best curtsey to them. Gentlemen, this is my little Georgette—my pet child." And the worthy man led the young lady forward by the hand.

There was the most graceful of bows on the part of Horace Gerold, a not less civil but graver salutation on the part of Emile, and a demure curtsey with more blushing from Mdlle. Georgette. As Frenchmen are never at a loss for compliments, M. Horace, who was always collected in the face of the adverse sex, added a few pretty words, which seemed to please M. Pochemolle. Mdlle. Georgette herself cast her eyes on the ground with an almost imperceptible smile, as if the young man's compliments were not the first she had heard in her life.

"And now to business," exclaimed the draper. "Monsieur Macrobe and his young lady shan't be kept waiting long; my dear. Ah, gentlemen, you should see Mademoiselle Macrobe—a pearl, as we should have said in my young days, though I wouldn't ex-

---

* N. B.—This was not quite historically correct, for the firing had ceased when M. G. picked up M. P., and it is not so sure that the latter would have died even if he had not been picked up at all. But gratitude may be pardoned for exaggerating.

change her for my Georgette; but she'll marry a duke or a king before she's done, I'd stake twenty bales of cloth on it. Then there's her father, too. Lord bless my soul, what a long head! That's the kind of man to make a deputy of if you like. When he started in life he'd not two brass farthings to rub together, and no profession either, nor trade, nor teaching, so far as I could see; and yet now—why, he rolls his carriage, and I guess he won't live much longer in this quarter; he'll be emigrating towards the Champs Elysées or the Chaussée d'Antin: worse luck, for I shall lose a first-rate customer. A rising man, gentlemen, and thinks like me about politics; ay, it's not in his mouth you'd ever hear a word against the Emperor."

Mdlle. Georgette pulled her father's sleeve.

"M. Macrobe was in a hurry, father."

"Yes, my dear, coming; it won't do to offend M. Macrobe. Gentlemen, your servant; and if ever I can serve you, pray do me the honour to command me. Georgette, my pet, make another curtsey to the Messieurs Gerold."

And Mademoiselle Georgette did.

"Queer card!" laughed Horace, when the good M. Pochemolle had retreated.

"I hope we shall see as little as possible of him for the future," answered the younger brother, drily. "I don't like such cynicism."

"Oh! cynicism is a big word," observed Horace. "I don't see anything cynic in the matter. We can't all think alike, you know."

Emile, for all his gentleness, was much less tolerant of hostile opinions than his brother. His was the nature out of which enthusiasts are moulded. He answered bitterly, "It's those sort of men who've helped to bring France to her present humiliation, and to send our father into exile. What wonder that there should be despots to treat us Frenchmen like slaves, when they are encouraged to it by such people as this —fellows who are ready to stand up for anybody in power, and to truckle to any government that will fill their tills."

"Whew—w—w!" whistled Horace. "Why look at things so gloomily, brother? Let's have freedom all round in the community. Think what it would be if everybody professed the same opinions—half the fun of life would be gone. Besides, it seems to me that a man who goes out three or four times over, and risks his life for his opinions, however absurd these may be, has a right to be respected. It isn't the same as sticking to one's convictions only so long as they pay you."

Emile shook his head, unconvinced; but the discussion was not prolonged further, for Horace remembered the letter which the draper had brought, and which was lying unopened on the table. He had not looked at the address, but, on taking it, saw that it was in Manuel Gerold's handwriting. "It's from our father," he said, breaking the seal; and Emile having asked him to read aloud, he read as follows:—

"*Brussels, November,* 1854.

"MY DEAR BOYS—

"*I have just received your letters, informing me that you were almost installed; and by same post a copy of the* MONITEUR, *with your names amongst those of the new barristers admitted at the opening of the courts. It* is a great satisfaction to me to feel that you are now fairly launched, both of you, in a profession where merit and hard work are more surely and liberally rewarded than in any other calling you could have chosen. The Bar will lead you to anything, though your progress must be at first slow; but you can afford to wait, and you are too sensible not to be aware that the only stable reputations are those which are acquired laboriously, by dint of patience and energy. Had I stayed longer in Paris, I should have introduced you to such few of my friends as still remain there. The number of them is terribly dwindled down, for most of us men of '48 have been scattered to the four winds; but there is Claude Febvre, one of the leaders of your profession, who has always been my firm ally—you will do well to call upon him. He will be sure to receive you kindly, and may be able to help you forward. In the press, Nestor Roche, the Editor of La Sentinelle, is my old and valued friend. You might find him a little rough at first, but there is a heart of gold under his shagginess. He lives at the office of his paper, Rue Montmartre. I should think it not improbable that my bankers, MM. Lecoq and Roderheim, would wish to show you some civility, and ask you to their parties; in which case you would perhaps do well to go, for my relations with the firm have always been friendly. I hear that they have just taken a new partner, a man named Macrobe. If it is the same Macrobe I knew in 1848, he will be likely to invite you too. He was a curious fellow, whom I could never quite understand. I believe he was a very warm Republican, acted once or twice on my electoral committees, and during the Provisional Government asked me several times to assist him in getting army and navy contracts.

I mention this, because somehow he knew all about our family history, who I was, and the rest of it. I used to have some trouble in preventing him from trumping up my affairs in public, and paying me compliments. His object seemed to be to make friends with me; for though I never helped him in this contract-hunting, he always professed to be a great supporter of mine——"

"Macrobe!" muttered Horace, breaking off. "Why, that's the name of M. Pochemolle's customer downstairs. I wonder whether the two are the same."

"M. Pochemolle said his M. Macrobe was a Bonapartist."

"H'm, to-day—yes; but he said nothing about six years ago."

"If they *be* the same," remarked Emile, quietly, "M. Macrobe may spare himself the trouble of showing any civilities to *me*."

Horace said nothing, but took up the reading where he had left off, and finished the letter:—

"*. . . . Amongst my other quondam friends, I need not remind you of one whom you frequently saw come and visit me in old times: I mean M. Gribaud, who is now Minister of State. You remember the letter he wrote on the morrow of the coup-d'état, acquainting me with his sudden change of politics, and advising me to follow his example: you have not forgotten either the reply which I sent him. Under the circumstances, I scarcely think it probable that M. Gribaud will care to recollect he was once on such warm terms with us; and if he hears that you are in Paris, he will, doubtless, not trouble you with cards for any of those Ministerial* *soirées of his, which I hear are so much envied. Still, there is no knowing. My letter to him was not sharp: it was merely cold; and there is just a possibility that out of vanity or bravado, or from other motives difficult to analyze, he will invite you to go and witness his present splendour. Should this be the case, I confess it would please me to hear that you had held as completely aloof from this man as you would from any other individual who had shown himself openly dishonest. The world is indulgent towards men who have succeeded, and easily condones the villanies to which they may owe their triumphs; but for this reason it is the more important that strictly honourable men should build up a higher and sterner code of morality. You and I cannot harm M. Gribaud: neither would we if we could; but we can refuse him our homage, and so mark in our humble way that we draw no difference between the knavery that leads to the hulks and that which leads to the Cabinet.*

"*Let me hear from both of you as often as possible without intruding too much on your time, and believe me,*

"*My dear Boys,*

"*Your ever affectionate Father,*

"MANUEL GEROLD."

Whilst Horace Gerold was reading this letter to his brother, M. Pochemolle the draper, with his daughter Mdlle. Georgette, had returned to the shop on the ground floor, in order to attend on the important M. Macrobe. This gentleman — who at first sight looked like a weasel, upon closer inspection like a badger, and who, after mature examination, left one doubtful as to whether there were not a chimpanzee or two amongst his ancestors—was standing at one of the counters conversing volubly with the draper's wife, and holding up a piece of silk to the light to test the quality of the woof. The good Mdme. Pochemolle, stout, buxom, and blazing in scarlet capstrings, had been thrown into a sudden state of excitement and perspiration by the entry of this well-to-do but restless customer. M. Macrobe was one of those gentlemen who turn a shop upside down before they have been in it five minutes. At his bidding, M. Alcibiade Pochemolle, heir of M. Achille, had been made to haul down bales upon bales of silk, velvets, and satin, box after box of ribbons, until the counter was encumbered half a yard high with merchandise. The person for whose edification all this bustling and scurrying was supposed to take place was Mdlle. Angélique Macrobe, but it was her father who virtually did all the shopping. Mdlle. Angélique herself was a blue-eyed, blonde-haired, angel-faced child, who looked at people with a perpetual expression of soft wonder, and acquiesced in everything her sire proposed in a quiet, pleased sort of way, as if she quite appreciated the blessing of having somebody to take the trouble of thinking off her hands. In terming her "child," I must be understood to speak figuratively, for her pretty baby-face was eighteen years old, and she was decked out in all the finery which proclaims a candidate in that most moral of competitions called the marriage-market.

M. Macrobe nodded when the draper came in, and, continuing to look through the silk, "'Morning, M. Pochemolle," he said. "Brought my daughter here to lay in winter stores. Goodish bit of silk this, but I don't believe in the dye. What's the news?"

In Macrobian phraseology, "What's the news?" had no reference whatever to the state of anybody's health or to occurrences in the political world. M. Macrobe was better informed than any man in Paris as to things politic, and the condition of people's health was a matter of great indifference to him. "What's the news?" was a query intended to elicit information as to what M. M. called "possible bargains." If there was anything to be sold anywhere at a loss to the seller—anything from the stock of a bankrupt tradesman to the "Stradivarius" of a starving fiddler or the pug-dog of a ruined actress, M. Macrobe was the man to seize the occasion by the forelock. It was by constantly inquiring "What's the news?" during a course of thirty years that M. Macrobe had, bit by bit, picked up his fortune.

"I don't think there's much doing in the quarter, sir," answered the draper, hastening behind his counter, with a respectful salutation, first to the daughter, and then to the father. "Nothing in the way of news, I mean. Trade's brisk, and money's plentiful enough, though to be sure I heard somebody say that our neighbour the Armourer, three doors off, was in a bad way. Didn't you tell me something about it, my dear?" (this to his wife).

"Yes, indeed," answered Mdme. Pochemolle, looking up from the velvet she was spreading before Mdlle. Angélique. "An honest man, too, and was getting on well in his business; but they say his son's not turned out what he should have done; his father's had to pay his debts, and this coming on the top of foolish gambling in the stocks, has put him in a low way."

"What's the name and address?" asked M. Macrobe.

"Quirot, Armourer and Curiosity Shop, Number 9 in this street," said the draper; and down at once went the name of Quirot, 9 Rue Ste. Geneviève, in the note-book which M. Macrobe had whipped out from the breast-pocket of his coat.

"Generally, something to be picked up in a curiosity shop," he muttered. "Now then, my pet, have you seen anything you like? Fairish velvet, Mdme. Pochemolle; this year's make; can tell it by the touch. We shall want three ball-dresses—eh, pet? —what do you say to a white, a pink and white, and a light blue,—blue's what goes best with your hair."

Mdlle. Angélique smiled and said: "Yes, papa."

"Measure out the silk, please, M. Pochemolle; and now twenty *mètres* of that velvet for a dinner-dress; ten of that white satin for a petticoat; enough white cashmere to make an opera cloak."

"Four *mètres*, M. Macrobe?"

"No, no: a goodish cloak like a shawl; something like the burnouses those Arab fellows wear: a thing to wrap one up all over—it's warmer and it's more *chic*. You must tell Mdme. Pochemolle yourself, pet, how much trimming 'll be wanted."

Mdlle. Angélique said, "Yes, papa," as before, and turned with a helpless look towards the draper's wife, to wonder how much trimming would be required for four dresses. Whilst Mdme. Pochemolle was doing her best to enlighten her on the weighty point, M. Macrobe had inquired for a second time of the draper whether he had any more news to give.

M. Pochemolle was up to his neck in silk, which

was flooding the counter in waves a yard long as fast as he could measure it. He was full of merriment at the fine stroke of business he was doing that afternoon, so he answered with respectful joviality:
"Should you consider it news, sir, to hear that I've got two fresh lodgers?"
"Depends who they are," replied the financier, quite seriously.
"Their name's Gerold, sir." .
"Gerold!" echoed M. Macrobe, quickly; "any relations to Manuel Gerold?"
"They're his sons, sir; M. Horace and M. Emile Gerold."
Out came M. Macrobe's pocket-book in a trice.
"What floor, M. Pochemolle? what's the age of the two young gentlemen? and what are they doing in Paris? Manuel Gerold's a most intimate friend of mine, banks with us: a curious character, but—ahem! —very well off—very."
A little astonished, M. Pochemolle informed his customer that his lodgers were on the third floor, that they had not been with him long, that they were quiet young gentlemen, and that their profession was the law. "Wasn't aware that you knew them, M. Macrobe," he added; "I was just talking with them, when Georgette came up to fetch me; but they didn't say anything at the mention of your name."
"Nor do I know *them*," answered M. Macrobe, promptly jotting down, *Horace and Emile Gerold 3rd floor over Pochemolle's, Rue Sainte Geneviève.* "Manuel Gerold's the man I know; but his sons and I will soon scrape acquaintance. Angélique my child, remember the Messieurs Gerold, and tell your aunt,

when you get home, to have them down on her list for our next party. But stay; they live in this house: why shouldn't I go up and drop a card whilst you're making out your bill, M. Pochemolle?" and M. Macrobe fumbled in his pockets for a pair of black kid-gloves, which did duty with him on ceremonious occasions.

"I am sure they will be delighted to see you, sir," observed the draper. And the worthy man spoke as he thought; for, indeed, it seemed to him impossible that anybody should be otherwise than delighted at the sight of an individual so eminently prosperous as M. Macrobe. The latter drew on his gloves, gave his hat a brush with the sleeve of his coat, and walked out; but he was spared the trouble of climbing up three flights of stairs, for he had scarcely left the shop when the two sons of his most intimate friend emerged from the *porte-cochère* of the house in person. They had finished their decorating upstairs, and were on their way to make a few calls before dinner. M. Pochemolle noticed them through the window, went out and stopped them as they were passing his shop, and then ran after M. Macrobe crying: "Those were the MM. Gerold, sir, whom you met going in."

In another half minute M. Macrobe, with a most friendly smirk on his acute physiognomy, was holding out his hand to the younger of the two brothers. He had mistaken him for the elder, on account of his graver face and stronger build. "Monsieur le Marquis de Hautbourg, I'm truly glad that hazard should have thrown me in your way," he began; "hope I see you well? Only just heard you were in Paris."

"My name's not Marquis of Hautbourg," answered Emile very distantly. "Here is my elder brother."

"And I call myself Horace Gerold," continued the other, not less distantly, but with rather more curiosity in his tone.

"Ah! yes; I perfectly understand; aversion to titles; most respectable prejudice; am a Republican myself to the backbone. Your father and I are great friends, M. Horace: my name is Macrobe."

"Oh, you are M. Macrobe," said Horace, amused.

"At your service, M. Horace: Macrobe, of 'Lecoq, Roderheim and Macrobe,' your bankers. Dear me, what a likeness between father and sons. Do me the pleasure to step in a moment, M. Horace and M. Emile, and let me introduce my daughter to you."

From the moment when he heard the name Macrobe, Emile set his face rigidly and answered only in monosyllables. Horace suffered himself to be led into the shop by the arm and presented in due form to Mademoiselle Angélique. The draper's daughter, who remembered the pretty compliment with which the well-looking young gentleman had honoured her some twenty minutes before, raised her eyes slyly from the parcel she was tying, to see whether he was going to publish a second edition of this flattery for Mademoiselle Macrobe. But nothing save the usual courtesies took place. Perhaps Horace Gerold was too much struck by Mademoiselle Angélique's beauty to say anything; for in truth to those who saw her for the first time, the sweet candid-faced girl appeared the incarnation of all that was lovely and loveable in woman. Her curtsey to the two brothers was a model in its way, Mademoiselle Angélique being an adept pupil of M. Cellarius, her dancing-master.

M. Macrobe, not unmindful of the effect created by his daughter's beauty, followed up his advantages by at once inviting Horace and Emile—but especially Horace—to come and dine on an early day. "Quiet people we are," he said, with a bluffness not quite suited to the weas'ly mobility of his eyes and the fox-like acuity of his nose. "I live here in this quarter not far off from you—Rue de Seine, opposite the Luxembourg. Name a day, and we'll have as snug a dinner as you could get in Paris. Twelve at table, you know, just enough to be cosy, and I'll ask a solicitor or two: it's good for young barristers to be friends with solicitors."

Though the invitation was cordial, Horace politely regretted that the number of his pressing engagements would prevent him from naming a day; and there he was going to stop, but—after a second's hesitation and a glance in the direction of Mademoiselle Angélique—he promised he would do himself the pleasure of calling. Emile, more wary, promised nothing; but the assurance of the elder was enough for M. Macrobe, who appeared satisfied.

For the last five minutes the fingers of the entire Pochemolle family had been nimbly at work, folding, rolling, parcelling, and stringing. M. Alcibiade Pochemolle, the cashier of the firm, now went to his high desk and totted up the items of the various purchases into one grand-total, smearing the whole with sand by way of conclusion, under pretence of blotting it. "Shall we book to your account, M. Macrobe?" he asked.

"No, I closed my account last autumn," said the

financier; "for the future I pay ready money. Knock off the discount."

This was at once done, for the house of Pochemolle and Son transacted business on the fine old principle of deducting 6 per cent. for cash. The bill was a heavy one; but I daresay M. Macrobe was not altogether grieved. He read aloud the total—2,785 *francs* 75 *centimes*—with some ostentation, drew out three bank-notes of 1,000 francs each, and paid without a word. This feat, however, reminded him once more that Manuel Gerold banked with his firm: so, taking Horace by the button of his coat, he drew him a step aside, and said: "It's we, you know, who are to pay you your allowance, 3,000 francs a year; but I've been a young man myself and know what it is.—If ever you're hard up, don't forget where I live: my cash-box is not like the bank, it's open at all hours—to my friends."

"Thank you; I never contract debts which I have no prospects of paying," replied Horace curtly.

A few years before, whilst he was still a law-student, M. Macrobe's offer might have stirred him to emotion; at present, he felt inclined to resent it as an impertinence, the more so as he recalled the passage of his father's letter, in which the acquaintance of the financier with the Gerold family concerns was hinted at.

But M. Macrobe, who knew nothing about any passage in a letter, grinned at the young man's stiff answer, and, with a leer that was intended to be arch, said: "Oh, of course, of course, M. Horace, that's the proper reply to make—never accept a loan till you want it. Only, mind what I say, and if ever you do want, come to me. All in friendship, you know; no securities or anything of that kind—plain word of honour, and down goes the money."

And with this he turned on his heel, leaving no time for a second refusal.

Mademoiselle Angélique had risen at this juncture, and was preparing to leave the shop as soon as her father should be ready. Seeing the financier's brougham standing outside, Horace could scarcely do less than offer the young lady his arm to help her into the carriage. Even had he wished to evade performing this civility, he would have been unable to do so, for M. Macrobe, in going to the counter to get his bill receipted, cried, "I am sure, my dear, M. Horace will kindly give you his arm whilst Madame Pochemolle counts me my change."

And so the two young people walked out together, preceded by the Pochemolles male, both of them freighted with cardboard boxes and packets.

Mdlle. Angélique scarcely touched Horace's sleeve with her dainty gloved hand; and, in answer to a remark of his respecting the coldness of the weather, replied, "Yes, Monsieur, it is," with the same depth of earnestness with which she would have subscribed to an article of the Christian faith. Once she was safely stowed into the brougham, and had mildly thanked Horace, M. Macrobe came bustling out amidst the bows and murmured benedictions of the Pochemolles, and took farewell of the brothers. He did not attempt to shake hands with Emile, for he was a perspicacious man was M. Macrobe, and easily discerned where he was not welcome; but he shook hands warmly with Horace, and repeated: "Mind, M. Horace, Rue de Seine; always delighted to see you—Angélique too."

And with this, not forgetful of business, he directed his coachman to stop at the curiosity shop of the ill-starred M. Quirot, out of whom he hoped to be able to screw a bargain.

When the carriage had rolled off, the first remark of Horace to his brother was: "That's the most beautiful girl I've ever seen in my life; if she's as intelligent as she's lovely, she must be a paragon."

Precisely at the same moment M. Macrobe was discoursing to his offspring in this strain: "My pet, that M. Horace with the light moustaches is a marquis, and, at the death of his father, who is a little cracked—in fact, entirely cracked—he will be a duke, and have one of the finest fortunes in France. I'd no idea we should meet him in Paris in this way; but, since I've had the luck, why, I'll get him to come and see us, and—h'm—you'll try and be civil to him, won't you, pet?"

To which speech Mademoiselle Angélique replied with a smile of placid obedience, such as a seraph might have envied: "Yes, papa."

CHAPTER VI.

A First Brief.

HORACE GEROLD did not immediately redeem his promise of going to call on the financier. After thinking during a day or two of the sweet face and tiny hand of Mademoiselle Angélique, that young lady and her sire went out of his head, and it was fully three months before he renewed acquaintance with them. In the meanwhile, M. Macrobe spared neither letters nor invitation-cards, and when these were declined, he came himself to pay personal visits; but he never found the brothers at home. The fact is, they were hard workers. Ambitious to push their way quickly, they slaved at their trade as men must slave who wish to succeed. This is the life they led:—Up at seven, they fagged at law-books—but principally the Code—till eleven; at eleven they went out and breakfasted at their *table-d'hôte*, which took them till about a quarter to twelve; breakfast over, they walked down together to the Palace of Justice, put on their caps and gowns, and went from court to court, listening to cases until six; in the evenings, after dinner, they generally spent a couple of hours in the Café Procope, reading the papers and talking politics with fellow-barristers; and the remainder of their time was devoted to the same employment as the early morning: that is, either in studying law or in getting up history—one of the most indispensable branches of knowledge in a country where barristers have so often to defend political offenders. The time spent in the courts was that which seemed most arduous to them both, and here a marked difference in their characters became discernible. Unlike his brother, Emile seldom went into the criminal courts. He usually selected the most complicated case on the Civil Roll, and sat the trial out with stolid patience from first to last, often foregoing his breakfast to be earlier in his place, and taking notes with an unflagging attention which earned him the admiration of some of the judges, by whom he soon came to be noticed as "that young man who never goes to sleep." Frequently it happened that Emile was the only barrister—and, indeed, the only spectator—present, besides the counsel, and these last would marvel to see him follow all the mazes of some terrifically intricate argument concerning a disputed boundary wall, an unintelligible passage in a codicil, or a right of way over a footpath. They would have been much more astonished had they known that Emile Gerold generally studied these arguments a second time when he got home in the *Gazette des Tribunaux*, making it a principle, once he had taken up a case, to master it thoroughly. Horace could not have stood this uphill kind of labour. The cases he selected in preference were those which promised most excitement. The Court of Assize, the Sixth and Seventh Chambers of Correctional Police, during press trials, and the Third Civil Court, pending a suit *en séparation de corps et de biens*—these were his places of favourite resort, though his object was not to recreate himself by listening to scandal-mongering witnesses, for he commonly went out of court whilst evidence was being taken, and only came in during the speeches of counsel *pro* and *con*, and during the summing-up. Whilst his brother was laying down a solid stratum of law-experience, and learning to be a close, persevering reasoner, Horace was acquiring the gift of a ready tongue—not very strong in argument, but clever at that headforemost kind of rhetoric which capsizes a jury, and drags the public along with it. He was the disciple and admirer of the half-dozen leading barristers who held public prosecutors in check, kept a whole court fizzing with excitement whilst they spoke, and were known to the outside world through the medium of their daguerreotype portraits, purchaseable on the Boulevards for twenty francs.

One day Horace had been listening to a remarkable orator of this school, who, with much credit to himself and great advantage to society, had been rescuing an assassin from the scaffold, and he was walking along the gallery which leads from the Assize Court to the Salle des Pas Perdus (French Westminster Hall), musing what a fine thing it was to set twelve jurymen whimpering in concert, when, on reaching the hall, he was almost run into by a man with a preposterous-looking hat, who was wandering about in a purposeless sort of way, evidently seeking somebody, but not paying much attention to whither his steps led him. This man's hat at once stamped him as being out of the ruck of common humanity. It was a hat such as could only figure on the head of one who despised conventionalities, and was wont to pursue his own course in life, undeterred by sarcasm. It was a tall hat, made of silk, and towering into a peak, with an altogether obsolete brim, twice as wide as those ordinarily in vogue, and standing straight out from the crown of the hat without the least curve, like the balcony of a window. Underneath this head-dress gleamed the face of a man of sixty, round and smooth-shaven, all but the moustache, which hung grey and wild to below the chin. The eyes were bright and intelligent, though cold and searching. The nose, mouth, chin, and lips were all large and boldly-delineated, denoting a man who held pretty grimly by his opinions once he had formed them, and was no more to be bantered out of a crotchet than to be intimidated out of a resolution. There are faces like this on which one may read character as in an open book. The man was dressed, regardless of fashion, in wide loose clothes; he sported a broad collar, turned down over his coat, and leaving a good deal of his throat bare. His hands were in his trousers-pockets.

He made no apology to Horace for nearly running into him, but, seeing the latter was a barrister, he said: "Can you tell me where I'm likely to find Maître* Claude Febvre?"

Claude Febvre was the barrister upon whom Manuel Gerold had recommended his sons to call. The brothers had done so and were on very good terms with the great pleader, who had promised to take them in hand and help them forward as soon as he could. At that moment Claude Febvre happened to be in the provinces, standing counsel in a suit at Bordeaux, so that Horace was able to inform the stranger that it was no use looking for him at the Palace.

"At Bordeaux is he?" responded the man with the hat. "Well, it doesn't much matter; I should have

* Maître (Master) is the substitute for Monsieur in the case of French Barristers; the title is only used at the Law Courts.

retained him because he's a friend of mine; but my affair is as plain as a mill-board: anybody can plead it." He fixed his eyes on Horace Gerold, surveyed him half a minute as if taking measure of his quality, and then said: "Have you many briefs on hand, young man?"

Horace Gerold had not a single brief on hand. He was just then awaiting the return of this very Claude Febvre to make his début at the bar in the character of second junior in an action for damages against a railway company. He coloured, but, the sense of his professional dignity rising uppermost within him, he answered quietly: "If you want assistance, Monsieur, I daresay I shall be able to give it you."

"What's your name?" asked the stranger.

"My name's Horace Gerold."

"Ah! I thought I'd seen those eyes somewhere. Come you along with me, young man; we two are friends. Have you ever heard of Nestor Roche?"

"Yes, indeed," exclaimed Horace, stopping. "My brother and I called upon him twice by our father's special desire, but he was not at home either time—that is," added Horace smiling, "he was at home both times, but once when we called at twelve we were told he was in bed, and the other time, when we went at three, he was breakfasting, so we merely left cards."

"Yes, so would you be in bed at twelve if you were editing a paper till six in the morning," rejoined the man with the hat queerly. "But give me your hand. I was glad to see your honest cards on the table; next time you write to your father tell him from me that there's not a man I esteem more under heaven.

Come along now and I'll tell you about this case; you shall plead it for me."

It was a very hearty grip, something like a bear's, which he gave the young man. He then slipped his arm through his, and the two went together to a form in a corner of the Hall, where they could talk over matters in quiet. Horace, though a little chagrined that a man so worthy as Nestor Roche was known to be should wear so eccentric a hat, was pleased to have met his father's friend, and the prospect of now handling a first brief added very naturally to his elation.

"Look here," began Nestor Roche, drawing a copy of his paper, *La Sentinelle*, from his pocket. "My gazette's got into hot water. It would never get into hot water if I alone wrote in it; for though there's not a line I pen but what's against the Government, I'm an old hand, you see, and know how to steer clear. However, some of the others are not so wary, and the other day one of my young ones, Max Delormay, who does the 'Echoes,' wrote this note, which I didn't read carefully enough before it went into print; so that now we've got an action for libel on us in the Correctional Court. It's all my fault, for Delormay wouldn't be supposed to know; in fact, nobody does know what's libel, and what's not, until he's written twenty years. Of course we shall be convicted, so I don't ask you to try for an acquittal. The *Sentinelle*, an opposition journal edited by a Republican, and tried before three Imperialist judges without jury, for attacking an Imperialist stock-jobber, has no more chance of being let off than if I'd been caught in the act of firing at the Emperor's carriage. Delormay and I shall each get three months' imprisonment: that's what we shall get:

there'll be a fine into the bargain; and as the plaintiff has laid his damages at a hundred thousand francs, I expect the judges will award at least ten thousand. All that, however, is of no consequence: those are the risks of journalism, like the breakages in a china-shop; and I shall be able to edit my paper just as well in the prison of Sainte Pélagie as in the Rue Montmartre. But I'll tell you what I wish you to do. You must show in your speech that we've no personal rancour against this fellow whom Delormay has attacked; that we have merely hit at him as one of a disreputable class who are growing rank as weeds under this precious Second Empire of ours. Make of this affair one of commercial morality. Argue that it is the duty of the Press to expose people like this fellow, who rob the public just as truly as if they stood on a highway road and rifled the pockets of the passers-by. These are the facts:—A very loose fish named—but look, here is the note; you can read it for yourself."

Nestor Roche pointed with his finger to a passage of *La Sentinelle* in which figured the following lines:—

"We have noticed two very interesting items of news in yesterday's *Moniteur:* the first announcing that a certain Monsieur Isidore Macrobe has been appointed Knight of the Imperial Order of the Legion of Honour, and the second proclaiming through the advertisement columns that the same M. Isidore Macrobe has been elected one of the directors of the new *Société du Crédit Parisien*. We have no wish to say anything unpleasant either to the Members of the Legion of Honour or to the shareholders of the *Crédit;* but before congratulating the former on their new colleague, and the latter on their fresh director, we confess we should be glad to know whether this M. Isidore Macrobe is the same Isidore Macrobe who was declared a bankrupt in Paris in 1835, in London three years later, and in Brussels in 1842; whether he is the same M. Macrobe who, having returned to Paris in 1843, singularly well-off after his third bankruptcy, at once revealed himself to the world as Treasurer of a *Compagnie Générale du Pavage Départemental*, which Company never paved anything, but collapsed in 1845—that is, some months after M. Macrobe had with striking foresight resigned his post of Treasurer, and, as we understand, sold his shares at a most advantageous premium; whether it was this M. Macrobe again who, in 1846, bloomed out afresh as Treasurer of the *Société de l'Eclairage Rustique*, which did rather less in the way of lighting than the other had done in the way of paving, and from which M. Macrobe retired, as before, in time to avoid the catastrophe which soon after befell the share-holders; and finally, whether it is this M. Macrobe who, in 1848, being a zealous Republican, obtained of the Provisional Government a contract for supplying all the country mairies with plaster statues of the Republic, which statues have never been beheld to this day, although there is no mention of M. Macrobe having ever refunded the twenty thousand francs which he received on account. It is a correspondent who has suggested that we should ask these questions, and we do so in the hope that they will elicit an answer. If all the Isidore Macrobes just alluded to form but one individual, it will remain with us to speculate what can be the claims of this gentleman to be rewarded with an order of merit, and to act as director to a company which we had hitherto believed to be a *bonâ fide* enterprise."

Horace had not been able to suppress a slight exclamation at reading the name of Macrobe, and when he had finished he said to Nestor Roche: "I know this man a little; he's a partner in the firm of Lecoq and Roderheim, with which my father banks."

"Oh, you know him: will that prevent your giving him a dressing?" inquired the Editor.

"Not the least," rejoined Horace. "If all this is true, the man deserves to be shown up, and I think M. Delormay was quite right in exposing him?"

"Well, I don't quite know about that," grumbled Nestor Roche, removing his monumental covering and rubbing the grey, bristly head under it with a perplexed air. "You must stick to that line of arguing in your defence; but between us both, if newspapers set themselves to unmasking all the Macrobes in Paris, they'd have to issue a special edition every morning. I shouldn't have let in the paragraph at all if I'd been awake when I read it; but Delormay generally takes things so quietly that I didn't expect to see him fire out in this way, and so glanced at his note with only half an eye. The whole thing's true, though; for I remember all about those plaster statues of Liberty which were to replace the busts of Louis Philippe; but the fact of its being true doesn't matter, for French law, as you've learned, won't allow a defendant in libel to furnish proof. No, the job's a bad one for us; and it'll be useless to ask for any mitigation of penalty; but if you think you can manage it, I shouldn't be sorry to see M. Macrobe get a first-class lashing. Since he's rammed us into a corner, he may as well have the benefit of all the mauling we can give him."

Horace assented, told the Editor briefly all he

knew concerning M. Macrobe—which was very little—
and inquired for what day the trial was fixed. It was
down for hearing on the following Friday, that is, four
days off, it being then a Monday; but as postponements of a week or fortnight can generally be obtained
without difficulty as many as three or four times over,
there was no actual reason why the case should come
on for another six weeks.

"I wouldn't ask for too many postponements, though,
if I were you," remarked Nestor Roche. "The judges
are always as sulky as possible with our trade; and,
besides, it doesn't look well asking for adjournments
in a libel case: it gives the plaintiff the opportunity of
bellowing that we're afraid of him. Be ready to face
the fellow as soon as you can—without adjourning at
all if possible."

Horace, not sorry that his first client should be as
impatient of delay as he, readily promised that he
would have the case at his fingers' ends by Friday
morning. He was not likely to spare the midnight oil
over a maiden brief, and would have worked without
any sleep at all for the next three days if needful.
Nestor Roche gave him the address of his solicitor,
with a laconic recommendation, however, not to follow
the instructions of that luminary, solicitors being tem-
porizers by nature, addicted to adjournments and devoid
of taste for stand-up fighting. He added that he himself was always to be seen from three in the afternoon
to three in the morning inclusively; and matters being
thus pleasantly settled, he observed he must be off,
gave another grip to Horace, buried his hands in his
pockets and was gone, with as much unconcern as if

he had been ordering a new pair of shoes, instead of preparing to face three months' imprisonment.

That day was marked with a white stone by the two brothers, and assuredly they are the happiest days in our lives, those on which we first see our way to earning our own living. A first article or a first picture accepted, a maiden brief, a maiden fee—these are joys which may well console those whose lot it is to struggle, for not having been born with golden spoons in their mouths. Emile was as elated at his brother's piece of luck as Horace could be; he made no doubt that now his brother had got a foot in the stirrup he would quickly ride away to fame. But this was not all. Emile did not confine himself to mere congratulations; he was anxious, so far as in him lay, to help in assuring Horace's success. During the whole evening he pored over libel cases in records of French jurisprudence, and the following morning slipped out early, without saying where he was going, and remained absent till dinner-time. When he returned he handed his brother a paper, covered with precise notes as to M. Isidore Macrobe's career. He had spent his day in the public library of the Rue Richelieu, consulting the files of the French and Belgian *Moniteurs* and of the *London Gazette*, and had acquired proof indisputable as to the worthy financier's three bankruptcies. Further, he had been to call upon two members of the Provisional Government of 1848, and both had assured him that the details as to the statue contract were perfectly correct—though one of them added that the unlucky *Sentinelle* had placed itself altogether in the wrong box, for that suspicious bankruptcies, suspicious stock-jobbing, and suspicious practice with regard to

A FIRST BRIEF. 129

Government contracts, were only accounted stigmas when a man was ruined by them. This, too, was Manuel Gerold's rather sorrowful view. Horace had written to give him an account of the case, and on the very morning of the trial he received an answer, in which the old tribune said: "I am not sorry, my dear boy, that you should win your spurs in defending my old friend Nestor Roche, neither am I in any way concerned that you should be obliged to attack that curious M. Macrobe, well-wisher of mine though he profess to be. At the same time, let me warn you that, from the world's point of view, your clients have not a leg to stand on. Society—especially Second Empire society—will always be averse to having ugly truths raked up against a man who has made his way. Nothing that you can say against M. Macrobe will affect his reputation in the least. He will leave the court with a high head, and pocket poor Nestor Roche's damages with as much coolness as if the money were owing to him."

There was another person whose opinions in the matter of the libel leaned much rather towards law than equity, and that was the excellent M. Pochemolle. Coming home on the eve of the trial, after receiving one or two final instructions from the Editor, Horace was stopped by the honest draper, who dragged him by the sleeve into his shop, and said, in tones of dismay: "Dear me, M. Horace, what's this I hear—that you're going to speak against M. Macrobe? It can't be true, come now——"

And Madame Pochemolle, behind her counter, chimed in with the exclamation: "Such a civil young gentleman as you are, M. Horace; I'm sure you wouldn't say harm against anybody."

It took the good couple some time to understand that a man could actually reconcile it with his conscience to assail so extremely respectable a person as M. Macrobe. It was Mademoiselle Georgette who had first discovered in the paper the paragraph which said: "*The trial of* La Sentinelle, *in the person of its editor, printer, and of M. Max Delormay, a member of the staff, for libelling M. Macrobe, of the banking firm Lecoq, Roderheim, and Macrobe, will take place on Friday. Maître Giboulet is retained for the plaintiff, Maître Horace Gerold will appear for the defence.*"—For a while M. Pochemolle had clung to the saving hope that this might be a mistake, or that there were two Horace Gerolds, or that the names had been interverted; the correct reading being—Giboulet for the defence and Gerold for the plaintiff; but when Horace avowed without a blush that the announcement was perfectly correct, M. Pochemolle called to mind the words of solemn warning he had uttered to the young men at the sight of David's picture, and reflected that the present incident was a realization of his worst forebodings. Nothing but association with Republicans could ever have seduced a well-nurtured and generally quiet youth into taking part with a subversive print against a gentleman who paid ready-money, and had, as it was affirmed, at least two hundred thousand francs a year. He hoped that no harm would come of it, but it was his experience that bad beginnings generally led to evil ends. So spake M. Pochemolle, his wife assenting with a sigh, and had it not been for Mademoiselle Georgette, Horace would have been condemned *nem. con.* by the worthy household. But Georgette Pochemolle, who was accustomed to speak her mind, and who, besides, felt an interest in the two rising barristers (as what young woman will not feel an interest in a couple of young men who pass by the window several times a day, and on each occasion favour her with a bow?)— Georgette Pochemolle quietly confronted her scandalized father, in defence of the incriminated youth: "For," said she, "what if this M. Macrobe deserves to be spoken against, why shouldn't M. Horace do it as much as anybody else?" A mild query, which caused M. Pochemolle to stand bolt still and answer, with all the dignity he could command: "Mademoiselle, I am surprised that you should join in the cry against one of your father's most valued customers. When you grow to be older, you will learn that those who become rich are always pursued by the animosity of the envious. Let it be enough for you that M. Macrobe enjoys my personal esteem and that of his sovereign, who has just rewarded him with the Cross of Honour."

Georgette went on with her stitching, but scolding never yet convinced a woman.

It must be confessed, however, that neither his father's predictions nor the draper's lamentations much damped Horace Gerold. Of all the god-sends which could befall to a French barrister in the year 1854 that most to be prayed for was a brief in a political trial. At a time when public meetings were prohibited, when people held their tongues under double chain and padlock, when even the parliamentary debates were a secret, it was something for a man to have the opportunity of standing up in a full court and giving vent to whatever pent-up liberalism there might be in him. Not a few barristers would have cheerfully bartered one of their ears for such a chance; for, if taken good advantage of, it meant simply reputation, honour, and possibly fortune. No great talent, in fact no talent at all, was needed; all that was required was boldness. Talent is of use when a cause has to be won, but in 1854 the results of all press trials were known beforehand. Barristers accepted the defence of prosecuted journalists, not with any hope of obtaining an acquittal—*that* they were aware would have been an idle dream—but with the view to making sensation speeches, which should bring them into notice. Horace was in no way ignorant of this particular, and the more he thought over the matter the more clearly did he perceive that Nestor Roche had thrown an occasion in his way such as did not often fall to a pleader of but a few months' standing. It is true that the trial in which he was engaged was not strictly a political one, being virtually nothing more than an action for imprisonment and damages brought by a private person. But political is an elastic word: in France, where one of the parties to a suit is an Imperialist and the other a Radical, the judge would be a phœnix who kept politics out of the question.

Need it be said that Horace was up with the dawn on the morning of the famous Friday; and shall we blame him if he paid much more than ordinary attention to his toilet? Always neat—a dandy even for the Bar—he put himself this time into black, eschewing the grey trousers habitual to the younger members of his profession; and selected the stiffest of his shirt-collars, no doubt so as to be on a level with the luminaries of the judgment seat. He had not slept very soundly the night before, neither had Emile. The latter, quietly busy to the last, had remained working till long after midnight, and had compiled about twenty foolscap pages of notes, full of intelligent arguments and precedents drawn from past libel cases. "You would have managed this case better than I," said Horace affectionately, as he glanced through this labour of love. Emile had neglected nothing: the notes were plainly written in the darkest ink, and blank spaces were left between each, so that they might more easily catch the eye if consulted in a hurry; with patient thoughtfulness an appendix had been added to help in ready reference to the rest of the work.

Just as the two brothers were going to set out, soon after nine, Georgette Pochemolle came running up with a letter. By the way, it was not Mademoiselle Georgette's business to bring up letters, but the postman, when pressed for time, frequently made mistakes and left lodgers' letters in the shop along with the Pochemolle correspondence, instead of delivering them to the *concierge* at the private door. On such occasions Mademoiselle Georgette, with her father's sanction, would often run upstairs with the missive, and be rewarded with, "How good of you to take so much trouble," or "We're really ashamed to put you to so much inconvenience," which would make her sometimes say to herself that these Messieurs Gerold, especially the eldest —for it was commonly he who spoke—were certainly very well-bred young men.

The letter Mademoiselle Georgette brought was rather a curious one: it came from the imperturbable M. Macrobe:—

"My dear M. Horace—

"*I just hear that you are retained for the defence in my affair with the* Sentinelle. *Bad business for Roche—I am talking of the libel.—He'll be knocked down in heavy damages, and I reckon the costs will be biggish; but I'm glad we've got an honourable adversary like you against us. Of course the whole story of the* Sentinelle *is a lie; but I don't ask you to believe it from me. I only write to prove there's no rancour. We who've made money are accustomed to hitting from those who haven't—I don't say that for you, but for Roche.*

"*I shake your hand cordially,*
"Isidore Macrobe."

"*By-the-by, you've not yet kept your promise about calling. You know we've removed since I last saw you. Our present address is* 294 *Avenue des Champs Elysées. Easily find the house: two statues of naked boys with goats'-legs playing on the flute outside.*"

Horace crumpled up this calm epistle, laughing, and threw it into the fire.

"He's cool enough at all events," said Emile with a smile. And the two brothers set off together for the Palace.

CHAPTER VII.

A First Speech.

A ROOM forty feet long by twenty, wainscoted with light oak, and papered above the wainscot in green, studded with gold bees. Twelve rows of seats on either side of a passage running down the whole length of the room, and leading to a dais raised two feet from the floor. On the dais, a table covered with green baize, and three arm-chairs. To the left of the dais a low pulpit, to the right a dock. On the walls, in guise of ornament, a clock and a bust, in marble, of the sovereign—the bust faces the dock, the clock shows its face to the pulpit. Over the dais a life-sized picture of the Saviour on the cross, the arms stretched out in ghastly whiteness, and the forehead bloody from the crown of thorns. Add to this a fire-stove near the door, three glistening pewter inkstands with three black blotting-books on the dais table, a fourth inkstand and blotting-book in the pulpit, and you will have the Sixth Chamber of Correctional Police.

From ten o'clock till four, five days out of the week, thieves and swindlers are put to confusion there. On Fridays the thieves and swindlers only remain in possession till noon; at noon come the journalists, and the procession of them generally lasts till six. Sometimes the journalists are too numerous to be disposed of in an afternoon, and then the Wednesday is considerately set apart for them. Justice shows her respect for the Press by making the thieves and swindlers wait.

From 1852 to 1860 Press trials took place with closed doors: that is, none but the defendants, plaintiffs, witnesses, and members of the Bar were allowed to be present. Things were conducted snugly *en famille;* and when the trial was over, the papers were allowed to publish the indictment and the judgment, but not the speeches for the defence, or the despositions of the witnesses. This last precaution, intended to safeguard the public against the spirit of partiality that might accrue from hearing both sides of the question, is in force to this day; but the regulation which kept the public out of court has been kindly abrogated. There is nothing now to prevent people from going to admire how justice is meted out to the pen tribe.

Thus, in 1854, the trial of Macrobe *v.* Roche ought to have been pleaded with three judges, Monsieur the Public Prosecutor, and a few desultory barristers, for sole spectators. So said the law, and so said the besworded Municipal Guards, who kept watch at the door, inflexibly keeping back the curious, and disdaining blandishments, supplications, and bribes alike. But in France laws have from all time been much easier to make than to enforce, and there was one method by which one could elude both the vigilance of the "municipals" without the court and that of the ushers within. The way was simply this: to shave off one's beard and moustache, if one possessed such appendages, and to hire a barrister's cap, gown, and bands, of the robe-man at the Palace. It was impossible that the "municipals" could know the features of all the members of the Bar; the shaven or plain-whiskered face, with the cap and gown, were their only clues; they had no power to keep out barristers, and so in you walked. Press trials were such an attraction that a good many journalists kept themselves permanently shaved, so as to have the privilege of going to hear their compeers condemned of a Friday. The judges more than suspected the infringement, but were obliged to wink at it. One of them—a cantankerous judge— had tried to put a stop to the evil; but the "municipals" at the door are not a pre-eminently intelligent body, and when told to be extra careful, they kept out real barristers as well as spurious. This had led to complications. The Conseil de l'Ordre des Avocats had remonstrated, and demanded an apology. Judges don't like to apologize; and so the upshot of it was, that the shaven journalists remained masters of the situation.

On Friday afternoons the Sixth Chamber was always crowded. When Horace Gerold arrived there punctually at twelve with his brother, he found it so crammed that there would not have been standing room for a magpie.

You may be sure his heart throbbed as he threaded his way down the gloomy passage that led from the Salle des Pas Perdus to the grim sanctum of the Correctional Police, over the door of which might be read this significant couplet:—

Hic scelerum ultrices Pœnæ posuere tribunal;
Sontibus unde timor, civibus inde salus.*

He thought everybody was staring at him, and a good many of his legal brethren *were* doing so; for they deemed him a lucky dog, wondered rather scep-

---

* The Court labelled with this inscription has since become that of Correctional Appeal; the Sixth Chamber has been removed into the new buildings in the Cour de la Sainte Chapelle.

tically whether he would do justice to his luck, and, in any case, envied him cordially. The case had brought together not only a mob of journalists, but a powerful squad of moneyed men, many of whom had resorted early to the cap, gown, and bands expedient and had managed to squeeze into court. The remainder thronged outside with such journalists—and they were the majority—who were too well pleased with their moustaches to sacrifice them, and with those of the genuine barristers, who, less fortunate than their pseudo-colleagues, had been unable to find a place. Money-men, penmen, and law-men were making a fearful hubbub, and exchanging observations, interjections, and epigrams at the top of their voices, as the fashion is amongst Frenchmen. Everybody was perfectly good-humoured. The gentlemen of the Bourse laughed very pleasantly at the squibs of wit launched by the gentlemen of the Quill against the profession of stock and share jobbing; but they retaliated with genial irony, and the ejaculations "Oh! oh!" "Ah! ah!" succeeded each other apace, when a burly journalist, known throughout Paris as the editor of an extremely lively print conducted on the strictest catch-penny principles, put in a remark about the sacerdotal mission of the Press. It should be owned that the eyes of the corpulent editor twinkled somewhat as he ventured upon these tall words, which in his mouth were hailed as an amazingly good joke by the bystanders.

In the centre of one of the noisiest groups the two brothers descried the stupendous hat of Nestor Roche, his baggy clothes and naïvely grim face. The editor of *La Sentinelle* was talking about some recent Crimean battle and evincing the most supreme indifference as to what was going to happen to him personally that afternoon. Nevertheless, on catching sight of the Gerolds, he held out a hand to each, and introduced them without more ado to a good-looking companion of his, whom he announced as "the young one who has shoved us into the wasp's nest—Max Delormay." The brothers had both been several times to the office of the *Sentinelle* during the two or three past days, and had quite made the acquaintance of M. Roche; but they had never met M. Max Delormay, who seldom turned up for purposes of work until 10 o'clock P.M. He lifted his hat and thanked Horace with effusion for the trouble the latter was going to take in defending him; but it did not seem as though the prospect of losing his liberty for a certain length of time weighed very heavily on his mind. M. Max D. was the cynosure of a small circle of admiring *confrères*, in whose eyes he had become a sort of oracle ever since he had been fortunate enough to drag his paper into a legal conflict. *Non cuivis contingit adire Corinthum:* it is not every journalist whose editor will give a chance of figuring in the Sixth Chamber. Monsieur Max was not unaware of this, and there was an expression of modest contentment on his features, as on those of a man who feels conscious that fortune is dealing kindly with him.

Nestor Roche took Horace by the arm and drew him aside.

"Max didn't mean any harm against that fellow Macrobe," he whispered; "he published the questions of a correspondent without knowing that they would stir up this shindy. However, mind and stick to the commercial-morality line of defence—and give it our adversaries hard. We must make political capital out of the affair."

He said this simply, without excitement, and then turned to resume his talk about the Crimean battle. But in a few minutes an usher put his head out of the court and announced that the judges were coming in; which was a signal for witnesses to proceed to the waiting-room, and for the defendants with their counsel to go and take their seats. The crowd instantly made way to let Horace and his brother pass; the unmoved Nestor Roche and Max Delormay followed; and behind them came a lean and melancholy printer, who stood included in the indictment.

The solemn stillness of a court of justice, succeeding immediately to the noisy chattering of three or four dozen glib-tongued loungers, has something of the same effect as a bath of cold water in collecting the senses. Horace Gerold's head had been on the whirl all the morning—anxiety, impatience, and expectation all combining to make him restless and feverish. In the eyes of most frequenters of the Palace it was a very ordinary press suit that was going to be tried: to him the Sixth Chamber was a gambling-house, in which he was going to take his first throw with the dice. From ten till twelve he had been pacing up and down the Salle des Pas Perdus, rehearsing the main points of his speech with Emile, and stifling occasional qualms of nervousness by calling all his vanity and young ambition to his aid. A congratulatory shake of the hand or two from several of his friends, an encouraging nod and smile from one of the "great guns," who had said to him, "This is your maiden-speech day, isn't it, Gerold? I wish you success," and the flattering hums of "That's young Gerold." "That's the fellow who's going to defend the *Sentinelle*," which he had heard in the crowd outside the court, had been so many circumstances that had helped to buoy him up like corks in his small sea of glory. He did not regain complete and cool possession of his head until he found himself seated, with his brother to the right of him, Nestor Roche's solicitor to the left, and the three judges of the Correctional Court enthroned opposite him on their dais.

A deep silence, and business at once commenced. Not a moment was lost in vain formalities. The chief judge of the three—a florid magistrate, with a deal of starch, silk cassock, and red ribbon about him—lifted up a white hand, armed with a gold pencil-case, and said, in a voice agreeable as the abrupt closing of a steel-trap, "The first case is that of the *Journal de la Reforme*, for exciting to hatred and contempt of the Government. Are the parties here?"

Up jumped a slim barrister from close to where Horace was sitting, and mumbled a request for adjournment on grounds only audible to himself. The pencil of the chief judge traced a mark on the Cause List, and the trap-like voice rejoined, "Adjourned for a week. But this is your third adjournment, Maître Gribouille: we shall not grant you another. The second case is *La Gazette des Boulevards*, for false news."

The figure of the corpulent editor who talked about the sacerdotal mission of the Press, leaned forward suddenly and whispered something in the ear of a barrister with a red face. This man of law rose in an off-hand style, and with his tongue in his cheek, intimated that he was unprepared, having only been instructed last Monday week. At this a square-set form, hitherto imbedded in the folds of a black gown trimmed with ermine, started up in the pulpit facing Horace, and an indignant face, ornamented with a pair of blue spectacles, cried, "I oppose the adjournment."

"Monsieur le Procureur Impérial opposes," snapped the steel-trap; "the case shall proceed."

"Then we will let judgment go by default," replied he with the tongue in his cheek; "we can't plead if we're not ready."

There was a general grin, for he with the tongue in his cheek was a legal wag, and his client, the fat editor of the *Gazette des Boulevards*, was a favourite. But the Public Prosecutor hereupon leaped up again.

"Maître Carotte," said he, "I shall not allow judgment to go by default. Your client, M. de Tirecruchon, is in court at this moment; if he does not stand forward and plead immediately, I shall request the Bench to have him arrested and put into the dock."

"Usher, let no one leave the court," cried the chief judge significantly.

The grinning stopped. The fat editor, looking slightly blue, was seen leaning over and conversing again with the red-faced barrister. The latter, no longer with his tongue in his cheek, then stood up and expostulated meekly: He knew that the prosecution would be perfectly justified in taking the course proposed, but he relied upon the well-known courtesy of Monsieur le Procureur Impérial, upon his generous indulgence, upon his universally acknowledged sense of justice, to grant just one more week's respite; and he looked piteously towards the pulpit.

Monsieur the Public Prosecutor having vindicated his importance, which was probably all he wanted to do, was graciously pleased to unbend before Maître Carotte's humility. He announced that he withdrew his opposition for this once, but that such an act of condescension must not be taken as a precedent. Maître Carotte restored his tongue to its original position in his cheek. The chief judge made a second mark on the Cause List with his gold pencil-case, and, for the third time, the steel-trap snapped out: "The next case is Macrobe *versus* Roche, Delormay, and Dutison; action for libel; are the parties here?"

There was no immediate reply, for Maître Giboulet, the counsel for the plaintiff, being a great gun, had thought it incumbent upon his dignity to remain talking outside until he was being actually waited for. An usher had to go out and call him, and in a minute he came flustering in at the rate of eight miles an hour, mopping his brow with a cambric-handkerchief, and followed by a brace of juniors with bags. "I'm for the plaintiff, Mr. President," he shouted, lifting his square cap and planting it on his head again.

Horace Gerold stood up, and, as firmly as he could, said: "And I'm for the defendants."

"The case is opened," proclaimed the chief judge, and in another few seconds Maître Giboulet had started full gallop into his indictment.

As this is a record of the life and adventures of the two Gerolds, and not a chronicle destined to perpetuate the eloquence of the French Bar, it will be as well to make no more than a passing mention of all the fine things which Maître Giboulet said, and of all that part of the trial which included the examination of the plaintiff, defendants, and witnesses by the trap-voiced judge. To those who know how these things are managed in France it is quite needless to explain that Maître Giboulet, who was an Imperialist and an official member of the Legislature, animadverted with a great deal of warmth upon that base-born spirit of envy which attached itself to men who had rapidly attained wealth by dint of hard work and enterprise. Yet he did not rant, for he was a good orator—albeit the chief use to which he put his tongue in the Legislative Chamber was to cry "bravo! .bravo!" when the Ministers spoke. He referred in a few feeling words to the spotless and industrious career of his client, to the esteem in which he was held in all financial circles, "and also by his Majesty the Emperor himself, Mr. President, as you will see when he comes into court by the Ribbon of Honour on his breast." He then made a brief allusion to the newly founded *Société du Crédit Parisien*, which was to confer priceless boons upon humanity, and the shares of which were already at 300 francs' premium; and he concluded by a dignified protest against the licentiousness of the Press, and a prayer that justice would safeguard the sanctity of private life, and indemnify his client by heavy damages for a libel at once groundless, heartless, and malicious.

Maître Giboulet sat down, and a few of the moneymen, who had crept in with borrowed plumes, mumbled "Très bien!" the begowned journalists retorting by crying "Hush!" and "Silence!" with great zeal, though with good humour. The cross-questioning of the defendants was then commenced by the presiding judge, who, being an old hand, conducted matters roundly and with a rigid impartiality of which I will try and give an idea.

To Nestor Roche—"Stand up, sir: your name?"

Nestor Roche—"My profession is journalism; my address Rue Montmartre."

"Why do you libel honest men?"

"I never libelled an honest man."

"I beg, sir, you won't split straws with me. You have slandered an honest gentleman, a knight of the Legion of Honour, a director of one of the greatest financial companies in Paris; you can have had but one motive, that of sordid envy; and I advise you if you hope for the indulgence of the Court, to make an unreserved apology. On consulting the record of your antecedents, I find you have been imprisoned four times for Press offences: twice under the present reign, and twice under the last; you are evidently a danger to society. What have you to say for yourself?"

"That what you call a libel is a true statement. I..."

"Monsieur Roche, I cannot suffer you to bring into court the slanders which you have already endeavoured to propagate through your journal. Your misdemeanor is aggravated by this display of effrontery. Stand down!"

The next to come up was M. Max Delormay. Now, M. Max had made up his mind to be very downright and cutting. This is what his resolution came to:—

"Monsieur Delormay, I find you are twenty-five, and the only son of a mother who has tried to bring you up as a respectable member of society. On coming to Paris five years ago, the kindness of Monsieur le

Préfet de la Seine obtained for you an appointment as clerk at the Hôtel de Ville; but, last year, you left your place. Were you discharged for misconduct?"

M. Delormay (hotly).—"Certainly not. Who has dared to insinuate such a falsehood? I resigned because I earned only two thousand francs a year, and could gain more than double by my pen."

"Exactly. You preferred the disreputable gains to be had by libelling your betters to the modest salary obtainable by labour in an honourable career. Don't interrupt me, sir: I know what I'm saying. What business has a young man of your age to insult one superior to him in years, social position, and worth? It's a cowardly thing, do you hear, sir? But you may stand down. Your attitude sufficiently shows that I may appeal in vain to you for a spark of contrition and good feeling."

And so down went M. Max, looking very much as if he would like to say something, though too nonplussed to put that something into words.

Next came M. Dutison, the lean and melancholy printer, who observed, dolesomely, that seven daily newspapers and eight weekly ones were printed on his premises, and that, with the best intentions in the world, it was utterly beyond his powers to revise them all. He was disposed of in the following terms:—

"Monsieur Dutison, I informed you, when last you were here, that this excuse was shallow and frivolous. A printer should ponder over every line of manuscript before submitting it to his presses. He should be the paternal censor of all the writings put into his hands."

"Yes, and see all his customers go and get their

printing done elsewhere," ejaculated M. Dutison, with dismal irony.

"Sir, an honest printer would be consoled for the loss of custom by the possession of a blameless conscience."

M. Dutison seemed to consider this solace insufficient, and was sent back to his seat, with the gratifying assurance that, if he would only wait till by-and-by, he would see what would happen to him. The presiding judge then called the name of Prosper Macrobe, and the plaintiff was introduced, irreproachably dressed, be-gloved, smugly shaven, and looking the image incarnate of respectability. In the topmost button-hole of his frock-coat flashed a spick-span new piece of scarlet ribbon. He cast a quick glance round the room, leisurely drew off one of his black gloves, and, catching sight of Horace, nodded as amicably to him as if the two had been breakfasting together.

Wondrous was the transformation which the features, voice, and manner of the presiding judge now underwent.

"Monsieur Macrobe, will you be so kind as to answer the usual questions as to name and profession? They are a mere formality."

And, saying this, the steel-trap became softened as though it had been oiled, whilst a deferential smirk irradiated the thin lips of the speaker.

Monsieur Macrobe evinced no objection to furnish all the explanations that were required of him. He briefly stated who he was, hinted that he was uncommonly rich, and hesitated for some polite term by which he could intimate that he cared not two brass stivers what was said about him. The judge was evidently unwilling to keep a man of such parts long on his legs, and, after a couple of totally insignificant questions, would have dismissed him; but Emile, whose usually placid face had been settling into the rigidity of contempt under the influence of this burlesque of justice, nudged his brother and whispered, "Up at him, and cross-question him."

Horace Gerold had been undergoing during ten minutes a sort of wet-blanket infliction from the solicitor on his left, who, in despair at the youth of his client's advocate, repeated mistrustfully, yet with depressing persistency, "Mind and be prudent, Monsieur Gerold—mind and be prudent." At his brother's exhortation, Horace at once shook off this dotard, and, starting up, looked the plaintiff full in the face, and said, "Monsieur Macrobe, remember you are on your oath. Is it or is it not true that you have been thrice bankrupt? that you obtained a contract which——"

He could get no further. The blue-spectacled visage of Monsieur le Procureur Impérial leaped up in the pulpit like a jack-in-the-box, crying, "I protest!" The two minor judges, aghast with astonishment, exclaimed, "Order!" The presiding judge, quivering with the anger of outraged majesty, shouted, "Maître Gerold, I recall you to the respect you owe the court. You well know that it is against all rules for the Bar to interrogate a witness otherwise than through the Bench."

Poor Horace apologized. He had, indeed, forgotten this important rule. Reddening, and a little dashed, he resumed, "Will the Bench kindly ask the plaintiff whether——"

"I shall do no such thing, sir," broke in the chief

judge, indignantly; and the Public Prosecutor, without any such expression of his opinion being called for, rose anew, and cried, "I move that the question is altogether out of place. The *Code* lays down that, in cases of libel, it shall not be allowable for the defendants to adduce proofs of their asseverations.* Besides," added the Procureur, with triumphant logic, "even if the defendants possessed the privilege, it would be of no use to them, for we are entirely convinced that their assertions are false."

"Precisely so," assented the chief judge; "the libel is false and malicious, and it is against all law that the defendants should seek to establish the contrary."

Emile turned pale with disgust, and bit his lips savagely. As for Horace, the blood had flowed to his head; he made a couple of steps forward, and for half a moment it looked as if there was going to be a disturbance in court; but the cautious solicitor sprang up in terror, and pulled him back by the gown. "Oh! be prudent, M. Gerold—be prudent," said he. Horace turned with flashing eyes to Nestor Roche, who was seated behind him. "What am I to do?" he asked.

"Do nothing," answered the other, coolly. "Wait till it's your turn to speak, and then pitch in to everybody."

Horace sank into his place. The nonchalance of Nestor Roche discouraged him. Whilst his liberty was being weighed in the balances of Imperial justice, the Editor was unconcernedly writing a leading article in his note-book with an odd bit of pencil.

* This law was repealed by the National Assembly in 1871; but only so far as libels against Government functionaries are concerned. A writer libelling a private person is still denied the right of proving that his libel is a truth.

Neither of the parties desiring to call witnesses, the fluent Maître Giboulet at once set about delivering a second edition of his opening speech. He thanked the Bench for its impartiality; declared magnanimously that he bore no grudge against his young friend and adversary, Maître Gerold, for having made an abortive attempt to envenom the discussion; and renewed his impressive yet temperate appeal for substantial damages. Everybody admitted that it was a very gentlemanlike speech. Maître Giboulet was succeeded by the Public Prosecutor. As this functionary is supposed to intervene on behalf of whichever party he may, after honest consideration, deem aggrieved, it was only natural that he should inveigh with splendid energy against the defendants. "For, indeed," said he, with honest wrath, "who is there among us that would not revolt at the idea of having all his past life disclosed? What hope is there for any honourable man, if papers are suffered to reveal all he said or did ten or twenty years ago? The press, gentlemen, is becoming each day more and more a danger; the landmarks of society must soon be swept away if it be not kept in check. M. Prosper Macrobe will leave the court with the warmest sympathies of all upright minds, whilst his libellers will be branded for ever with the stigma of indelible shame."

M. le Procureur was always overpoweringly eloquent in anathematizing periodical literature. It is surprising what a number of prints and journalists he had branded with the stigma of indelible shame.

And now came the important moment when Horace Gerold was to speak. The Public Prosecutor had imbedded himself anew in his pulpit, well content with his own oration, and after the usual amount of buzzing, foot-scraping, and coughing that succeeds the delivery of half-an-hour's speech, a deep hush pervaded the court. The defence is the episode *par excellence* of a press trial. In this instance, too, those who knew the name of the counsel were a little curious to see how the son of the Tribune Gerold would demean himself.

The beginning was not very promising. For the first time in his life, Horace experienced that disagreeable and totally indescribable sensation of perceiving every eye in a crowded room fixed on him. Till he opened his mouth, he would never have believed that he could so falter and stammer and long that the floor might yawn and swallow him. He had counted on an easy triumph, for he was full of his subject; but on rising, and hearing the unearthly echo of his own single voice, and feeling beside him the leaden weight of his two arms, which he knew not how to lift or move, all his ideas seemed to go as clean out of his head as though they had been wiped away with a sponge. To add to his composure, the chief judge took the occasion of hinting that he hoped the speech would not be long, as there was really no defence possible.

It was Emile who saved his brother from premature collapse by whispering energetically, "Well said," "That's it," "Perfect," &c. By so doing he drew down on himself the sharp censure of the Bench; but his welcome excitations helped Horace to bridge over the first few moments of emotion, after which the horrible fear of breaking down and becoming ridiculous acted like a tonic and did the rest. The voice of the speaker, which had been running all wild, and scaling every note in the octave, from the husky to the shrill falsetto, gathered firmness, and became controllable. Horace spoke spasmodically, but one by one his ideas returned. He kept his eyes fixed on those of a friend opposite him, whose changes of expression served him as beacons. Gradually he warmed to his subject; the trumps were all in his hand; arguments began to crowd upon him. A low murmur of approbation soon told him that he had struck upon the right path, and was making straight for the sympathies of his audience. The last remnant of nervousness forsook him. He spoke out flatly, plainly, fearlessly. The judges, who at first had thrown themselves back in their chairs, leaned forward and stared uneasily; the Public Prosecutor, who had affected to prepare himself for a quiet nap, glared from behind his blue spectacles as if he was getting more than he had bargained for. Encouraged, emboldened, Horace Gerold branched out from the main argument of his plea into an appeal of that kind which always finds an echo in Frenchmen, and which, in times of oppression, sets fire to them like tinder. He spoke of lost liberties, and there was a thrill. The dullest can be eloquent on such a theme; and young Gerold, who was not a dullard, threw out the burning words with a fervour of earnestness that quickly stirred his hearers to the marrow. There are crowds whom it takes a great deal to move; next to nothing is required to animate a French crowd. It seemed to some of the spectators present as though in the excited young orator before them they saw the image of the rising generation standing forward to protest against the cowardice of its fathers, which had handed France over to slavery. A loud explosion of murmurs greeted an unwise attempt of the chief judge to check the speaker. The judge desisted, cowed; and from that moment the success of Horace Gerold was sealed. The arms no longer hung like lead now; they moved with the simple but magnificent gestures of scorn and defiance; the face was flushed, the hair thrown back; faster and faster fell the words, louder and braver grew the denunciations, until at last the speaker stopped amidst a tremendous uproar. Everybody in court had risen; enthusiastic cries of "Bravo" shook the rafters; the three judges, on their feet, and livid with rage, were shouting, "You shall apologize!" Nestor Roche had rushed from out of his place and embraced Horace, kissing him on both cheeks French fashion; Emile, with tears streaming from his eyes, was wringing his brother's hand, and crying, "Well done, Horace; admirably spoken."

"You shall apologize," vociferated the Bench. "You said 'corrupt judges;' we will have an instant apology."

"Did I say 'corrupt judges?'" asked Horace, and indeed it was in perfect good faith he put the question, for he could not have told for the life of him what he had been saying.

"An instant apology!" roared the judges.

"An humble apology," yelped the Public Prosecutor.

Apologize at such a moment! Apologize when a score of hands were being stretched out to him, and tongues were repeating clamorously, "Bravo, bravo!" In a clear, ringing voice, Horace replied, "I shall never retract. I said 'corrupt judges,' and I maintain the term."

The Public Prosecutor immediately cried, "Maître Gerold has been guilty of an outrageous contempt of court. I pray that the Bench will use its discretionary powers to punish him." There was no doubt about the contempt of court; the three judges caught up their caps, and swept out of the room by the door behind the dais to deliberate.

Impossible to describe the scene in court during their absence. Barristers, journalists, left their seats and scrambled over desks and forms, to cluster round Horace and shake hands with him. Half-an-hour before he had been a simple, struggling, and pretty nearly briefless advocate; now he was a hero. "Well said, indeed," "Your speech was inimitable," "You called the *coup-d'état* a crime; give me your hand; you're my friend." Such were a few amongst the hundred exclamations that rose like fusees from out of the transported throng. It was in vain that the ushers sought to impose silence; they were bidden hold their peace, and jostled with- ignominy—the noise was deafening. One must witness such a scene to realize it. In the midst of it all, as cool as a cucumber, M. Prosper Macrobe bustled forward, seized Horace's hand like the rest, and exclaimed, "My young friend, admiration knows no camp; splendid speech: always knew you'd make your way." At which the spectators around clapped their hands, thinking this was truly manly behaviour on the financier's part. M. Macrobe had quite relied upon this impression; that enterprising man never laid out anything save at interest.

At the end of twenty minutes the judges returned.

Horace was perfectly aware that he was going to get his share of whatever penalty was in store, but this did not affect him in the least—neither, I fancy, did the other thought, that his fine speech had perhaps not done overmuch for his client's interest. There was no need to proclaim silence anew: the lull in the court was instantaneous. When the judges reached their place, one could have heard a gnat fly. The chief judge held two written judgments in his hand. Still white with rage, and in a loud, rasping voice, he read out the first:

"*Whereas the newspaper* LA SENTINELLE *published in its number of the 15th April, 1855, a note beginning with the words,* '*We noticed in yesterday's* MONITEUR,' *and ending with the words 'a bonâ-fide enterprise;' and whereas the said note contains a wilful and malicious libel affecting the character and reputation of M. Prosper Macrobe;*

"*And whereas the said M. Prosper Macrobe never gave cause of just offence to the defendants, so that it is evident the libel can only proceed from a wanton spirit of mischief;*

"*And whereas the defendant, Max Delormay, wrote the note, knowing it to be libellous;*

"*And the defendant, Nestor Roche, editor, inserted it in the newspaper* LA SENTINELLE, *likewise knowing it to be libellous;*

"*And the defendant, Dutison, printer, rendered himself accessory to the misdemeanor by printing the said note:*

"*The Court,*

"*Conformably to the conclusions of the Public Proseculor,*

"*Condemns*

"*Nestor Roche to six months' imprisonment, and a fine of five thousand francs;*

"*Max Delormay to six months' imprisonment and a fine of five thousand francs;*

"*Dutison to two months' imprisonment, and a fine of two thousand francs;*

"*And the three defendants conjointly to pay five and twenty thousand francs damages to the plaintiff, together with all the costs of the trial.*"

Then came the second judgment:—

"*Whereas Maître Horace Gerold, advocate, practising at the Imperial Court of Paris, did on the —th day of April, 1855, speaking in the Court of Correctional Police, render himself guilty of a gross contempt of court, by uttering words reflecting on the honour of the Magistracy;*

"*And whereas the said Maître Gerold, on being summoned to retract his words and tender an apology, refused to do so;*

"*The Court,*

"*Conformably to the conclusions of the Public Prosecutor, and by virtue of its discretionary powers,*

"*Condemns*

"*Maître Horace Gerold to be disbarred from pleading in any Court of the French Empire during a period of six months.*"

That evening Horace Gerold was the most talked-of man in all Paris.

CHAPTER VIII.

Sweets and Bitters of Popularity.

POPULARITY does not come or go by halves in Paris; it encircles or forsakes one with all the suddenness of a change of wind. Previously to Horace's sensation speech, the brothers had led very retired lives, paying few visits and being themselves little visited, save by one or two young barristers of their own age, who had been their companions during their student-days. On the morrow of the speech there was not a café in Paris, not a club-house, not a drawing-room where Horace Gerold was not the leading subject of conversation. For the moment, he supplanted Sebastopol, which the Allies were doing their very best to take, without succeeding.

It may seem strange that the maiden speech of an unknown barrister should have been able to effect such a commotion; but stranger things than that used to happen in those days. Considered soberly, the speech was not a master-work. It failed a good deal in plain logic, and as a defence on behalf of accused men it was disastrous, for it had, without any doubt, caused the penalty of the defendants to be doubled. But Horace had had the striking merit of speaking out the truth flatly at a moment when scarcely anybody dared speak at all. Herein lay his success.

He was also helped a good deal into public favour by the fact that the judges had disbarred him for six months. To get one's clients sentenced to six months' imprisonment instead of three is well—it is like inserting the thin end of the wedge; but to get oneself disbarred into the bargain is splendid—it is like driving the wedge bodily in.

According to the courteous usage of a time when avowed Liberals were so few that they deemed themselves all friends, Horace Gerold received a congratulatory call from most of the men of mark in Paris. Nineteen-twentieths of the members of the bar, pretty nearly every one of the students in the School of Law, and some three or four score Opposition journalists, left their cards upon him.* It was a singular procession, which lasted three days, to the mingled consternation and pride of M. Pochemolle—consternation, because the honest draper could not but wince at the sight of so much factiousness incarnate walking up his staircases; pride, because the good man worshipped success, and felt all the importance of possessing a lodger who was getting on so famously.

After the cards came the anonymous letters and the albums; the former mostly eulogistic and feminine (there must be women who have an uncommon amount of time to lose), the latter feminine also, and accompanied by notes praying M. Horace Gerold kindly to write a few verses, a sentiment, or anything in the world, provided only he signed his name to it. After this arrived the artist of a comic paper, who requested leave to pourtray Horace with a head three times

* As an historical illustration of this graceful custom, it may be mentioned that, in 1867, after his very remarkable speech in the Senate in defence of free thought, the late Monsieur Sainte Beuve received no less than 12,300 cards. Liberalism was gathering strength then.

bigger than his body. This was the *nec plus ultra*. When a gentleman asks permission to draw you with a big head you have reached the acme of celebrity: Fame can do nothing more for you.

We must not forget the bank-note of 500 francs, which Horace Gerold received as his *honorarium*. There had been no previous agreement as to fee, no allusion even to the subject; but on the day following the trial Nestor Roche sent his counsel a simple and affectionate letter, in which he said, "The usual way, my dear Horace, is for the solicitors to settle these affairs; but there had better be no formalism between you and me. I am just off to pay nine-and-thirty thousand francs into court—twelve thousand for fines, five-and-twenty thousand for damages, and two thousand for costs. I would pay the whole cheerfully enough, if I might forward it to you along with enclosed; but I confess it rather goes against my heart to enrich the citizen Macrobe. However, I am not angling for sympathy; your speech has done a fine stroke of work for the *Sentinelle:* we sold twenty thousand copies more than usual this morning."

All this was the bright side of the picture, but there was also a dark side, or at least a side rather less agreeable. Horace was sitting in his study some two or three mornings after his triumph, when he was startled by a knock much more rapid and less ceremonious than visitors are accustomed to give. He was alone, Emile being absent at the law courts, and he had just finished a letter to his father, which was lying unfolded before him. On going to open the door it caused him some surprise to find Mdlle. Georgette.

"Oh, M. Horace," she said, blushing terribly, "I've run up to tell you that I think the police are coming to search your rooms."

"The police?" and Horace showed Mdlle. Georgette into his study, shutting the door behind her.

"Yes, yes," she continued, hurriedly; "ever since you made your speech there have been two such curious men loafing on the pavement outside the house; great ugly men with big sticks. I believe they took down the names of most of the gentlemen who have called on you these last few days; and yesterday evening when you were out, you and M. Emile, they came in with M. Louchard, the commissary of police, and wanted to search your rooms; but papa wouldn't let them."

"What could they want to search our rooms for?"

"I don't know, M. Horace," answered Mdlle. Georgette, contemplating him half-naïvely, half in terror. "M. Louchard said you and M. Emile were dangers to the Government, and that he'd got his orders about you from the prefect; and when papa refused to let him have the key of your rooms during your absence, he said he'd come back to-day when you were at home, and made papa promise not to say about his having been here; but *I* didn't promise: for M. Louchard didn't know I heard him."

"It's very good of you to give me this warning, Mdlle. Georgette," said Horace, with a look of gratitude; "but," added he, throwing a glance round the room, "I don't think the police can find anything dangerous here."

"Have you no letters from friends, no books against

the Government," asked Mdlle. Georgette, with ready woman's wit.

Horace hesitated a moment, and then struck his forehead: "Dear me, what am I thinking of?" he cried; "thanks a hundred times for reminding me;" and he went to a book-shelf half filled with volumes of that uncomplimentary kind which the presses of Belgium used to send forth, and send forth still, in such numbers against the Emperor of the French. There were Belgian papers, too, brought by the brothers when they came into France—papers interdicted by the police, and the importation of which was punishable with fines and imprisonment. Horace spread a towel on the floor, laid all this anti-dynastic literature upon it, emptied a drawer-full of his father's letters on to the heap, and tied up the whole into a bundle. But when he had done this:—"And now, where am I to put it all," he said, rather helplessly?—"We've no hiding-place that will be safe from M. Louchard."

"Give the bundle to me," replied Georgette looking at him. "I'll hide it in my room; they won't come and search there."

Horace fixed his eyes on the spirited girl, and said with a little wonder, "What have I done, Mdlle. Georgette, that you should act in so kindly a way towards me?"

"Why shouldn't I save you from getting into trouble if I can?" answered Georgette, in a would-be indifferent voice, with perhaps just the faintest tremor in it. She took up the bundle, and, without looking at him, added, "I must go now, M. Horace; good-by." And in another minute she was gone.

Horace Gerold did not at once move; he remained

standing a few moments where he was, gazing at the spot on which Georgette had stood. Then he returned to his seat and slowly folded the letter he had been writing.

This simple operation must have taken him a long while, for he was still engaged in it when a sharp rap at the outer door gave him to infer that the promised M. Louchard had arrived.

True enough. This time it was not a pair of bright hazel eyes and a pink, bashful face that met him; but three individuals buttoned up to the throat: the commissary and his two satellites, MM. Fouineux and Tournetrique of the Secret Police.

One must have lived in countries where the police is the despised, ever ready tool of a hated Government, to realize the ineffable look of disdain with which Horace Gerold received his visitors.

"I am a commissary of police——" began M. Louchard.

"That information is superfluous; your profession is written on your face," answered Horace, curtly. "I suppose you have come to ransack my rooms. Here are my keys: get your job done as soon as possible."

Even MM. Fouineux and Tournetrique, who were accustomed enough to be spat upon, looked a little sheepish at this greeting. Horace had not given the keys into M. Louchard's hands, but thrown them on the floor for him to pick up. The commissary, who was a man of education, reddened.

The three followed Horace into his study. They kept their hats on; seeing which, the young man said peremptorily, "Take your hats off in my room." It was not the custom of the three honest gentlemen to uncover themselves when paying domiciliary visits; but the expression of Horace Gerold's features was not pleasant in moments of anger. The police hate fighting about trifles. They took their hats off.

Without thinking of what he was doing, Horace went to his desk to resume the operation of closing and sealing his letter, in which he had been twice interrupted. In a trice, M. Louchard was down upon him with a swoop, made a grab at the letter, and snatched it out of his hand. "I beg pardon: that's a letter," he said. "I must have all letters."

"Ah, to be sure," rejoined Horace, unconcernedly, and, throwing himself into an arm-chair, he took up a newspaper, which he read, without paying any more attention to his guests.

It is the admirable privilege of all Frenchmen to be liable at any moment to a search visit, and to see all their papers fingered and confiscated. They have no right of appeal; no right, even, to know why their property is being violated. And the search is no mere formality. Messrs. Louchard, Fouineux, and Tournetrique remained above an hour ferreting in Horace Gerold's bed-room and study. They turned up the corners of the carpets, routed out the drawers and cupboards, probed the mattresses, pillows, and curtains, and made a parcel not only of such letters as they could find, but of every scrap of paper, however small, that bore a line of handwriting, tradesmen's bills not excepted. The object of a search is to obtain all the details possible as to the searchee's habits and acquaintances, and a tradesman's bill may be as instructive a document for this purpose as any other.

There was a sheet of blotting-paper on which Horace had scribbled a list of a few friends who had sent him civil letters which needed answering. Messrs. Louchard and Co. took that. There was a japanned bowl which served as receptacle for the thousand and odd visiting cards which Horace had received after his speech. The young barrister was, not unnaturally, proud of these friendly trophies, and had contemplated keeping them as mementoes. Monsieur Tournetrique shovelled them all into his pocket-handkerchief, tied the handkerchief into a knot, and dropped it into the tail-pocket of his coat.

Horace did not stir. Only, at the end of an hour, when the three representatives of justice and imperialism had inspected his own rooms, they were for going into Emile's. In order to do this they were obliged to pass Horace, whose chair was so situated that it blocked the door of communication between the two sets of apartments. On the first man presenting himself, Horace stood up and said: "Where are you going?"

"To search those other rooms," answered M. Louchard.

"Those rooms are my brother's," rejoined Horace quietly.

"Monsieur, we have orders to search your brother's rooms as well as yours."

"If my brother chooses to let you search his rooms I have nothing to say," was Horace's impassive reply, "but in his absence I am the defender of his property; no one goes in there whilst I am here."

"Do you mean to say you intend resisting by force?" asked M. Louchard, taken aback.

Horace caught up the fire-tongs that were lying close within his reach.

"Yes," he said calmly. To do M. Louchard and consorts justice, it was not the fear of a broken head that made them pause. If Horace Gerold had been an ordinary rebel—a mere journalist for instance—the three would have fallen upon him together, knocked him down, handcuffed him, and bundled him off to the station in a cab to be charged with threatening to do grievous bodily harm to Government functionaries. But a barrister is an awkward adversary. The barristers form a powerful corporation, and if one of them were knocked down, the Council of the Order, with the "Bâtonnier" at its head, would certainly insist upon reparation. M. Louchard was quite perspicuous enough to guess that this reparation would probably consist in his own dismissal. He thought it prudent to temporize.

"Monsieur, I am only doing my duty," he observed.

"And I mine," rejoined Horace; "but it is no use wasting further words. You have two courses open to you; either to wait until my brother returns, or to go and find him at the Palace of Justice and tell him that you want his help to turn his rooms upside down."

Monsieur Louchard did not smile at this joke; but he accepted the former of the two alternatives, after venturing upon one or two more remonstrances to which Horace did not even deign to give a reply. When Emile returned about a couple of hours afterwards, he found his brother composedly smoking a cigarette, with a pair of fire-tongs in his hand, and the three myrmidons of the law seated in a row opposite, looking at him.

On being told what was the matter, Emile threw down his keys as disdainfully as Horace had done. MM. Louchard, Fouineux, and Tournetrique thereupon resumed their search, repeating their conscientious investigation of beds, cup-boards, and carpets, and making an abundant harvest of paper scraps as before. In Emile's rooms, however, occurred an episode which Horace had not foreseen; for, in exploring the top drawer on the left-hand side of the bureau, the detective Fouineux lighted upon the tin box which contained the title-deed of the Clairefontaine estates. Emile interposed, observing it was only a family document; but this was reason the more why M. Louchard should keep firm hold of it. Delighted to have got possession of something that looked valuable, the commissary took the box from his subaltern and expressed his determination not to part with it on any account.

"But what can you do with it?" cried Horace, more amused than angry; "I tell you it's only a title-deed."

At the word title-deed M. Louchard redoubled his grip of the box, and resolved in his own deep mind that he had captured a prize. He set himself in the immediate vicinity of the door, ready to bolt if any attempt at snatching should be made; and in a quick voice directed his satellites to make haste and get done. This injunction had the effect of abridging the search by about half-an-hour. Less than ten minutes after the discovery of the box, the brothers were left alone, MM. Louchard, Fouineux, and Tournetrique having returned to the préfecture; where, amongst other things, they were mindful to state that Maître Horace Gerold was "a dangerous man of murderous propensity," an observation that was scrupulously recorded in that famous and mysterious ledger, in which are inscribed the names of all those who, at any time, and for any reason, have been brought under the notice of the French police.

This domiciliary visit was destined to have ulterior consequences that influenced in no slight degree the careers of the Gerolds; but the only immediate effect of it was to make the two brothers laugh, and to raise Horace a cubit higher on his newly erected pedestal. The explorations of M. Louchard furnished a capital paragraph for *La Sentinelle;* the Liberals of the Boulevard waxed indignant; and the general opinion of the public was that this young barrister must be a very remarkable man, since the Government evinced such spite towards him. So true is it that despotism sets a halo upon those whom it tries to persecute.

Emile profited by his brother's triumphs. At the very moment when MM. Louchard, Fouineux, and Tournetrique were making hay amongst Horace's papers, the younger brother was being retained in three or four press-trials, at the Palace of Justice. These briefs would have fallen to Horace had he not been disbarred; but the journalists who retained Emile thought that he would no doubt follow in his brother's footsteps and make a sensation speech, perhaps even more violent than the other. In this, however, they were disappointed. When the first of the trials came on the court was crammed to bursting, and the defendants, whose paper had not been selling very well of late, were building up soothing hopes on a rattling sentence of fine and imprisonment, which should quadruple their circulation and give them the *locus standi* of martyrs. But Emile's speech was so simple that it took everybody by surprise. There were no flights of oratory in it, no attempts at declamation, no allusions to the *coup-d'état*. It was a plain, lucid piece of argumentation, full of truth, admirably compact, and couched in language as unpretending as it was respectful. The judges did not acquit the prisoners— that, of course, was out of the question—but they were so much relieved that they only inflicted a month's imprisonment, without any fine at all; a result which transported the solicitors present, who at once marked down Emile Gerold for brief in the civil courts; but which not a little chagrined the journalists, who confided one to another their chagrined impression that Emile had not the same brilliant talent as his brother.

CHAPTER IX.

Horace starts in Journalism.

It would be fair to suppose that after the pretty rough handling he had got from Nestor Roche's counsel, M. Macrobe would have renounced all further acquaintance with the Gerolds. But M. Macrobe's was a soul devoid of vindictiveness. Perfectly conversant with the fact that Horace Gerold was heir to a dukedom, and that he would some day inherit at least 500,000 francs a year, the financier had allowed himself to indulge in certain private schemes with regard to the young man, and he was not to be baulked of them for a few ugly words, more or less. It was a maxim with M. Macrobe that where there's a will there's a way, and *his* will was to become Horace Gerold's friend. How he was to profit by the friendship when he had obtained it, and in what particular direction he was to work his schemes, were points upon which he had not altogether made up his mind, having never yet had the opportunity of becoming thoroughly acquainted with either of the brothers. But, like a skilful angler who knows of a fish in a certain pond, which he will proceed to hook when he has the time, so M. Macrobe bore Horace Gerold in his mind, resolving that he would "land" him some day, and determined meanwhile to lose no opportunity of throwing out clever baits. Within a week of the trial the two MM. Gerold received a card from Madame Roderheim, wife of the partner in the firm Lecoq, Roderheim and Macrobe, inviting them to a *thé dansant*.

Now, if this card had come by post, or been deposited with the concierge by one of Madame Roderheim's plushed footmen, Horace and Emile, out of deference to their father's request that they should keep on amicable terms with MM. L. and R., would, on the appointed evening, have put themselves into dress clothes and have gone through the civility, which consists in driving two miles to bow to a lady in a low-bodied dress, drink a cup of weak tea, and then drive home again. But, unfortunately, it was M. Isidore Macrobe who left the card (indeed, it was he who had especially asked it of Madame Roderheim), and this circumstance was not long in becoming known to Horace, to whom the missive was delivered by Mademoiselle Georgette, despatched by her father on this embassy.

Mademoiselle Georgette was very glad to be the bearer of the note. It was on the day following the visit of the commissary, and she was anxious to return the young barrister his parcel of contraband books and papers, which had lain hidden in one of her bonnet-boxes a day and a night. Perhaps she would not have been sorry even had she had no books to give back, but this thought was one that lurked too deep for human eyes, and one which she would have rejected with the utmost spirit, had any silent voice within ventured to whisper it to her.

With a slight flutter at the heart, due possibly to the number of steps she had been climbing, and to the fear lest anybody should see her on the staircase with the suspicious bundle, Mademoiselle Georgette

HORACE STARTS IN JOURNALISM. 171

knocked as she had done the preceding day. It being about four, Horace was alone as before, but he was just preparing to go out. The young man would have found it difficult to explain why he coloured at the sight of the draper's daughter; but colour he did, and so did Mademoiselle Georgette.

"Here are your books, M. Horace, and a letter," she said.

She was going to retire after this, but Horace stopped her, saying, thankfully, "Do you know, Mademoiselle Georgette, I have been reflecting all night that you have rendered me a great service. If those books had been found here they might very well have furnished a pretext for indicting me as a Revolutionist. You have probably saved me from imprisonment."

She took no pains to hide the gleam of pleasure in her eyes, but answered with candour: "You thanked me yesterday. I am glad I have been of use to you. But" (and here she looked up at him a little timidly) "why do you expose yourself to being imprisoned?"

"Oh, prison is not very dreadful," he answered smiling.

"Then the service I have rendered you is not so very great," rejoined she, biting her red lips and smiling in her turn.

"I mean," laughed Horace, embarrassed—"I mean that prison in our case doesn't mean iron chains and a straw bed. I was just going to see some prisoners when you came in; I daresay I shall find them comfortably enough lodged; but loss of liberty is always a hardship, Mademoiselle Georgette."

"I suppose you are going to see those gentlemen whom you defended," remarked Georgette, feeling some little curiosity on a subject so profoundly novel to her as the captivity of gentlemen connected with the Press. Mademoiselle Georgette was an occasional reader of the Official *Moniteur*, the only daily journal which M. Pochemolle deemed it consistent with his opinions to take in.

Horace nodded.

"I am going to Sainte Pélagie to see M. Roche and M. Delormay, who were to surrender to-day. Shall I tell them that you sympathize with their misfortune?"

"You may tell them so if you like," answered Mademoiselle Georgette, gravely; "though I think you would do better to tell them not to write any more against M. Macrobe. Why is it that all you gentlemen are so much against M. Macrobe?" she continued, yielding to the temptation of conversing for once with a person whose whole soul was not enwrapped in cloth and calico. "I thought he was a friend of yours, M. Horace."

"Not of mine, Mademoiselle Georgette; I know very little about him, and that little is not to his advantage."

"He has a very lovely daughter," observed Mademoiselle Georgette, gazing rather steadfastly at her interlocutor.

"So he has," replied Horace, recalling the fair hair and seraph-like expression of Mademoiselle Angélique; "but the daughter doesn't change the father. He would be a bold man who married Mademoiselle Angélique and accepted any dowry with her."

These words did not seem to displease Georgette, but she replied generously: "Are you quite sure, M.

Horace, as to all they say about M. Macrobe? Papa thinks so highly of him, for he is always very good to us. Though he lives right at the other end of the town now he comes to us whenever he wants to buy anything. He was here to-day and offered papa some shares in that new *Société du Crédit Parisien* which is making so much noise."

"Oh, M. Macrobe was here to-day, was he?" exclaimed Horace, interested.

"Why, yes; that letter comes from him; at least it was he who brought it."

Horace opened the letter with evident curiosity; but when he had inspected the contents he was amused, and said: "It appears to be your vocation to do me good turns, Mademoiselle Georgette; yesterday you saved me from prison, to-day you have kept me out of a trap."

"What trap?" asked Georgette innocently.

Horace was on the point of holding out his hand to Mademoiselle Georgette, but he checked himself and answered gently: "It would take too long to explain, and I don't think it would much interest you."

Georgette looked surprised, but she was beginning to reflect, that she had been talking long enough. She did not, however, return to the shop downstairs for another five minutes, and when she entered, her brother, M. Alcibiade Pochemolle (occupied in catching flies pending the receipt of custom) was the first to notice that she was a little pale, and held a parcel in her hands; which she at once went and showed her mother. This is how Mademoiselle Georgette came by the parcel.

Just as she was about to bring her interview with

Horace Gerold to an end, the latter had opened a drawer and taken out of some silver paper a handsome work-box which he had bought the evening before. It was one of those admirable and expensive knick-nacks such as are only to be found in Paris—a thing of rosewood with silvergilt corners and fittings, ivory silk-reels, satin lining, and golden thimble. To tell the truth the better part of Nestor Roche's 500-franc note had been bestowed on the purchase.

"I want you to accept this box, Mademoiselle Georgette, as a souvenir," said Horace, before the young girl had even divined his intention.

Georgette was so unprepared for the present that she turned first red, then white, and echoed in a pained tone: "A *souvenir?* Are you going away then?"

"No, I am not going away, but a hundred things may happen, and I should like you to accept this keepsake whilst the recollection of your thoughtful kindness of yesterday is still fresh with us both. Don't refuse," added he, seeing that Georgette looked hurt by his offer; "I shall tell Madame Pochemolle it is a gift in return for the number of letters you have had the trouble of bringing me, and if you refuse I will offer you the box in her presence." He said this gaily; but it was in a more serious tone he repeated: "Accept it in the same spirit as it is offered, Mademoiselle Georgette; if you refuse I shall think you consider me guilty of impertinence."

"You would be wrong to think that," she murmured quietly; yet she still looked pained, and it was only after Horace had taken the box and gently forced it into her hands that, not to wound him, she consented to keep it. There was an incident that helped to silence her objections: It has been said that Horace's parcel of books had been hidden by Mademoiselle Georgette in a bonnet-box. There were a few artificial flowers lying in this box and one of them—a moss-rosebud—had clung by its wire-stem to the folds of the towel in which the books were wrapped and been brought up, unnoticed by Georgette. Horace saw the rose, and, when he had placed the work-box in Georgette's hands, unfastened it and said: "May I, too, have my souvenir, Mademoiselle Georgette; will you let me keep this flower?" At this the look of pain vanished altogether from the young girl's face. She threw him a rapid look, loaded with gratitude and happiness and fled. But her emotion had not yet disappeared when she returned downstairs and—as already chronicled—encountered the gaze of M. Alcibiade Pochemolle.

M. Pochemolle senior was delighted with the gift. There are drapers who might prick up their ears at hearing that their daughter had been presented with a costly work-box by a gentleman on the third floor; but M. Pochemolle was of the old school: he believed in social distinctions: and just as he would have deemed it presumption to think of marrying his daughter to any one above her sphere, so he had a sort of honest and chivalrous confidence that no man in Monsieur Gerold's position would ever trifle with the affections of his child. Madame Pochemolle, though not quite so humble in her matrimonial views respecting Mademoiselle Georgette, was also pleased with the present; she might have looked grave at a brooch or a locket, but a work-box was such a brotherly offering that it proved the purest motives on the part of the young barrister. As for M. Alcibiade, he was all enthusiasm, wondered what was the price of the box, and would have been greatly astonished had he heard that his sister had ever refused such a gift. M. Alcibiade was of the new school of tradesmen.

"Georgette, my child," said M. Pochemolle, "we must make M. Horace some return for this. It is a pity that young gentleman is a republican, but he has the courtesy and gallantry of a Count. Let me see; what can we do for him? Ha, I have it: Alcibiade, measure your sister four yards of the finest lawn, Cambrai mark, and she shall inaugurate her box by hemming M. Horace a dozen pair of bands to wear in court. Meantime, give me my hat and gloves: I must go and offer my dutiful thanks to our lodger."

And the thanks of M. Pochemolle were all that could be desired. He met Horace Gerold on the staircase and made him a bow such as would not have disgraced that famous lace-purveyor of the Prince of Condé, who was said to bow better than the Prince himself. And the same hour Mademoiselle Georgette set to work upon the cambric bands, cutting and stitching with a diligence that somewhat surprised M. Alcibiade, who remembered that his sister never worked so fast when she had to hem any of his pocket-handkerchiefs.

Now, are we to conclude from this gift of a work-box that Horace Gerold, the heir of the Hautbourgs, or, what is more to the purpose, the rising pleader already renowned in Paris for his good looks, his good luck, and his eloquence, entertained any deeper feeling towards the draper's daughter than the parents of that young lady suspected? Maidens of Mademoiselle Georgette's age are apt to imagine that every soft word, playful smile, and kind glance are so many indications of attachment, and poor Georgette, as she hemmed the cambric bands, doubtless built many a fancy mansion that would have crumbled into dust could she have witnessed the extremely leisurely gait and placid air of M. Horace as he went on his way to visit his friends at Ste. Pélagie. Lovers do not wear the expression that Horace Gerold wore. He trod the pavement like a man who is exempt from cares of every sort, whose blood flows cheerily in his veins and who would not change his present lot for a kingdom. Well-a-day, how far he was from thinking of Clairefontaine now, and what a good joke he would have considered it, had any long-headed soothsayer lifted the veil of the future and shown him .... but why anticipate? let us follow the young man on his visit to the prison.

Sainte Pélagie is a fine grey building, devoted, like the Sixth Chamber of Correctional Police, half-and-half to the accommodation of thieves and of journalists; the thieves occupy the back part, the journalists the front. Let us be just, however, towards the Imperial Government:—When a journalist was sentenced in the courts of the Empire, he was not laid hold of there and then in the dock, and carted off to bondage in a van, as is done in certain freer countries. He was left to surrender pretty much when he pleased (save in very exceptional cases). He might take a fortnight, or a month; sometimes he took three months; and when he at last made up his mind to go and be locked up, he drove to his destination in a cab, bearing his boxes, portmanteaus, and writing materials with him, and leaving word with his friends to come and call upon him, just as if he was off for a hydropathic establishment, and was merely about to undergo a few months' cure.

Of course the Government was not bound to make things thus pleasant, and occasionally, when sulkily disposed, it would order that such and such a captive journalist be rendered as miserable as possible by being debarred from all intercourse with the outer world. But such instances of waspishness were not common. It was always borne in mind that the imprisoned writer of to-day may be the cabinet minister of to-morrow: journalism being a career that leads to anything—provided you abandon it.

Horace Gerold's purpose in visiting Sainte Pélagie was two-fold: in the first place he had a duty of common courtesy to perform, and in the next, being thrown out of work by his six months' interdiction, he wished to ask for employment on the staff of the *Sentinelle*. He found Nestor Roche installed in a room that looked much more like an apartment in a middle-class boarding-house than a cell in a prison. It was tolerably large, the walls were papered, there was a carpet on the floor, and two workmen were engaged in nailing up a book-case, which Roche had obtained permission to bring with him, as well as a bureau, a couple of easy-chairs, an enormous ottoman, and a shower-bath. On a peg above a small camp bedstead hung the monumental hat of the captive, which at once arrested the eye like the helmet of a cloistered knight; and the captive himself was seated at a table smoking a meerschaum pipe and correcting a proof, whilst a printer's devil, his legs tucked up on the bar of a chair, was waiting to carry the said proof to the printing-office.

"*Salve, puer,*" exclaimed Roche, holding out his hand, "I shall have done in a minute. Meanwhile, you'll find Delormay at home; he's next door."

M. Max Delormay had not arrived above an hour and was standing in his shirt-sleeves amidst a litter of portmanteaus and carpet-bags, from which he was extracting bottles of eau-de-cologne, hair-brushes, pots of pomatum, razor-strops, and the adjuncts of a well-furnished toilet-table. M. Max felt deeply grateful to Horace Gerold for having secured him six months' imprisonment. Ever since his sentence, the value of his signature as a writer had risen considerably in the literary market. A whole collection of articles, tales, and sketches, of which he had been utterly unable to dispose in the days of his freedom, had passed triumphantly into the columns of various broad-sheets the moment he had become a martyr. Moreover, he had obtained promotion on the staff of the *Sentinelle*, having been raised from the note and paragraph department to that of leader-writing. Encouraged by these results, M. Max felt equal to facing any amount of persecution for the truth's sake. He shook Horace warmly by the hand, planted him in a chair, and offered him a cigar.

"You'll stay and dine with us, I hope? We make up a capital mess: Roche and I, two writers of the *Siècle*, Jules Tartine of the *Gazette des Boulevards*, and three members of a Secret Society who are in here for two months more; the famous Albi's one of them. We're to mess in Roche's room, dinner from the restaurant over the way, one franc fifty centimes a head. Here, you, my friend, just cut downstairs to the canteen and get us a pint of cognac, two lemons, some sugar, and a jug of hot water; catch hold of the money."

This order was addressed to what appeared a workman, who was putting M. Max's clothes into a chest of drawers. Like the two workmen in Nestor Roche's room, he was attired in grey garments, and wore his hair cropped close to his head.

"Most intelligent man," remarked Max Delormay, when his attendant had vanished. "The Government, you know, gives us some of our fellow-prisoners from the other part of the building to wait upon us. We have one between three. They are chosen for their good behaviour. I daresay you saw those in Roche's room. One's in, I believe, for spoiling the good looks of a policeman; the other for putting stones through the window of a publican who refused him credit. This one of mine used to make mistakes in computing the change to which his fares were entitled, and then molest them when they objected. He was a cab-driver, and means to reform when he gets out."

The cabman who made mistakes returned with the cognac, lemons, &c., and declared himself competent to brew "*un grog*," if need were. Soon after, the voice of Nestor Roche was heard shouting, "I've finished now," and M. Max accompanied Horace into the other room, each bearing their share of the refreshments. The printer's devil, a boy with one eye (but what a perspicuous one was that single orbit!), had slid off his chair, and was receiving directions not to loiter with the proof by the wayside. He snivelled as he listened, and, I regret to state, more than once made use of his sleeve in guise of pocket-handkerchief.

"Have you any copy, M'sieu Delormay?" inquired he, upon the entrance of this gentleman.

M. Max had no copy; but he laid a hand on the shaggy poll of the small Cyclops, and bade him tell his name to Horace Gerold. The boy fixed his one eye on Horace, and answered sturdily, "My name's Tripou, but they calls me Trigger."

"And now tell M. Gerold why they call you Trigger."

"They calls me Trigger," answered the young Tripou, with pride, "because in '51, when there was the fighting, and I was seven years old, I prigged the gun of a sentry at the Louvre when he wasn't looking, and shot him through the head with it."

"Good lad!" exclaimed M. Max, dismissing him. "You'll grow up to be a valuable citizen,"—an assurance which encouraged Trigger to add, for the enlightenment of the stranger, "The gun kicked, and that's how I lost my eye."

The presence of two gentlemen in grey proving an impediment to confidential intercourse, nothing was done but grog-sipping and cloud-blowing for a quarter of an hour or so; but when the book-case had been nailed up, the shower-bath established in its corner, and the ottoman wheeled near the fireplace, the gentlemen in grey vanished, and then Horace plunged at once *in medias res* by saying, "I've come to ask you to take me on your staff, M. Roche."

"H'm," grunted the editor, from out of a curling wreath of shag-smoke. "Does our condition seem so delightful as to tempt you to become one of us?"

"If you think me good enough," was Horace's modest reply.

"You'd be good enough in any case," answered the editor, shaking the ashes off his pipe. "You've made yourself a name, and the public'll read anything you write. Only, I'll tell you what, journalism's not the easy thing you may think."

Max Delormay confirmed this statement by ejaculating with feeling that he had often sat up a whole night elaborating notes which wouldn't be coaxed out of his head—a reminiscence which evidently gave him a very sublime estimate of the difficulties of literature.

"Yes, but I didn't mean that," rejoined Nestor Roche mildly; "what I mean is, that there are two kinds of journalism—one for which any man who can spell is fit enough; and the other, the real journalism, which sucks in its man like a whirlpool. Those among us who take a liking to our craft don't leave it; our pens stick to our fingers, and there we sit scribbling until brain-fever grabs us, which it generally does, in the long run. I don't want to deter you from following your own bent, but I warn you of this, that if you once take to printer's-ink you'll soon be throwing off your gown. It's easier to write articles than to read up briefs and make speeches; it's pleasanter work too, but after a time it squeezes your brain as flat as a sucked orange. Yes, I know what you were going to say," proceeded the editor, observing that Horace was preparing to reply. "You were going to cite half-a-dozen journalists who have been at work close upon fifty years, and who write leaders as much as ever. Yes, but just read those leaders: they are washed-out copies of others written long before you were born: the authors of them take it easy; they have given up fabricating new thoughts, they say the same things over and over again, they are like those looms that throw off mechanically a piece of cotton of the same length, breadth, colour, and texture every day. And mind, it needs a certain merit in its way to be able to do that. It requires a good, thick, solid head that goes 'thud' when you rap it, and doesn't contain two straws' worth of enthusiasm or conviction. Those men have no passion for their work; their blood flows coolly and evenly through their veins like the waters of the St. Martin's Canal; journalism with them is not a calling, it is a trade; they take to it in the same spirit as they would have taken to boot-making had they been born a few steps lower down the ladder. But you, Horace Gerold, will never make one of this band. If I am any judge of your character, you will throw yourself into your work with all your might — ambition, vanity, conviction, and talent all pushing you together; and so sure as ever you throw yourself into journalism it will use you up—unless indeed," added the editor, rather gloomily—"unless it leads you to a prefecture or a seat in the Cabinet—but I don't see much chance of that, for you are not of the stuff of which nature makes renegades, and I am not very sanguine as to our having a Republic whilst you and I are on earth to enjoy it."

"Why not?" asked Max Delormay, astonished at this dispiriting prediction.

"Because we are a nation of parrots, Max," rejoined Nestor Roche, laying down his pipe.

It was not often that the editor indulged in such long speeches; he was habitually curt in his dialogues, and seldom went the length of developing his views. But his esteem for his old friend Manuel Gerold was so great that he treated Horace and Emile to a share of it, and spoke more at length with them than he did with anybody, save his wife and his niece, who kept his house for him.

Horace answered, without much hesitation, "I never thought of taking to journalism as a profession. All I want is employment to keep me from rusting until I can go into court again."

"Dangerous," muttered the editor. "I took to journalism five-and-thirty years ago, waiting until I could pick up a practice as a doctor, and I have been at it ever since. But you shall have your way; the *Sentinelle* is open to you; write me leaders, or articles, or anything else you like; only, in six months from this, I shall remind you of what you've just said, and expect you to drop the pen: for you can't drive two trades together."

A few minutes later Nestor Roche drew a pencil from his pocket, and said, "Listen: this is just the position of the *Sentinelle* at the present moment: We are selling 40,000 a day ever since the trial; at three sous a copy, that makes 5,600 francs a day; deduct 6 centimes per copy for the stamp-duty, and there remains 3,200 francs. Expenses of printing are 1,300 francs; publishing and remittances to agents, 800 francs; carriage, 400 francs. This leaves us 700 francs, to which we may add another 800 from advertisements. Out of this 1,500 you must subtract again 750 as payments to the staff, and the remaining 750 may be said to constitute the profits, which are supposed to be divided equally between my partner and me. To my partner, however, who is a money man, I pay over and above his share in the profits the sum of 5,000 francs a year, being the interest on the 50,000 francs he was obliged to deposit in the Treasury as caution-money when we started the paper; moreover, it is I who must meet such liabilities as may spring up in the way of fines and damages; for instance, the nine-and-thirty thousand francs of the other day. This statement will show you that the *Sentinelle* is at present a paying concern; but you must remember, on the other hand, that the normal circulation is not 40,000, but 20,000, and that, as the *Sentinelle* has already received two '*admonitions*' from Government, it may, on its next offence, be suspended for two months, and after that be suppressed altogether, in which last event I am bound by treaty to pay my partner 100,000 francs. Do you follow?"

"Yes," answered Horace, a little surprised.

"Well, then," said the editor, shutting up his pencil-case and relapsing into briefness, "you won't make any mistakes as to my reasons if I sometimes cut down your articles until there's nothing left of them but the paring. Supposing the *Sentinelle* were suppressed I should be as good as ruined; but, what is infinitely more serious, there would be a liberal organ the less in Paris: for, as you are aware, it needs a special licence from Government to start a new paper, and that licence the Government would refuse."

"Cut down my articles as much as you please," answered Horace, smiling. "You may be sure I shall respect your reasons."

Upon this understanding the young barrister temporarily joined the staff of the *Sentinelle*, and wrote his first leader the same evening.

CHAPTER X.

New Friends, new Habits.

A BARRISTER may go into society or not as he pleases, and perhaps the less he goes the better for his professional work; but with a political journalist the case is just the opposite. Before long, Horace Gerold found himself thrown into daily intercourse with a number of personages whom, hitherto, he had only considered from afar: eminent liberals for the most part, and leaders of the party, whose organ the *Sentinelle* was. These gentlemen represented a considerable variety of shades in opinion and, under a freer form of government, would have been pretty certain to detest one another cordially. But one of the beauties of despotism is that, like fox-hunting, "it brings parties together as wouldn't otherwise meet," and Legitimists, Orleanists, and Republicans formed in those days one happy family, coalesced in common hatred of the reigning dynasty.

As, owing to the law which prohibited the founding of political newspapers without special licence from Government, the number of opposition prints was extremely limited, some honour attached to being on the staff of an independent journal. It was something like belonging to a crack club. All the members of the independent press hung very much together, maintaining a sort of freemasonry, and holding carefully aloof from the writers of the semi-official or Government press, whom they despised as little better than hired menials. Naturally, the Bonapartist writers resented this contempt, and affected to reciprocate it, and this kept up a feud which evinced itself in little things, such as frequenting different cafés, walking on opposite sides of the Boulevards, and adopting dissimilar slangs. In 1855, the favourite café of the opposition press was the Café des Variétés, that of Government journalists the Café des Princes on the other side of the way. It should be added that the face-to-face situation of these rival establishments not unfrequently led to unpleasantnesses, such as meetings in the middle of the road between foes crossing from one pavement to the other; and so sure as ever this happened, there was either a treading on toes, or a jostling of elbows or something to necessitate an exchange of cards, perhaps an exchange of slaps on the face, and on the morrow an encounter at daybreak. Those were times when MM. Grisier and Pons, the fencing-masters, had a rare number of pupils in the literary profession. Horace was cordially received at the Café des Variétés the first time he appeared there at the "hour of absinthe," *i. e.* 5 P. M., on the arm of a M. Hector Tampon, sub-editor of the *Sentinelle*. Preceded by his quickly-won reputation, he was hailed as a valuable recruit. Nobody asked whether he wrote well—that, in the opinion of journalists, was a secondary consideration—but he thought well: he seemed to hate the Government well, and that was enough.

M. de Tirecruchon, the stout editor of the *Gazette des Boulevards*, whom he had already seen once in the Correctional Court on the occasion of the Macrobe trial, held out his hand and shouted with a bluffness which at first surprised him: "Welcome, M. Gerold. You're quite right to try the press. I predict you'll make your way in it."

"Oh, I'm only a visitor," answered Horace modestly: "the *Sentinelle* has taken me in like a passenger on a cruise."

"Tut, tut! When passengers like you come on board they don't go off again in a hurry. It's ten times pleasanter writing leading articles than cramming briefs, and so you'll find when you've had time to compare. If you leave the *Sentinelle* give me the preference; my columns are open to you." M. de Tirecruchon here drew an immense flat cigar from a Russian-leather case, and wreathed his solid face in smoke. "I'm a Legitimist," he continued, "but it doesn't matter, for it's Liberty Hall in my paper; all my contributors are free to write as they please. Do you see that small man yonder, sucking iced-punch through a straw? he's my sub-editor, a Red Republican like yourself, opposed to luxuries, and all that sort of thing. Take a seat. I'm going to prison next week, at least, as soon as Number 9 at Ste. Pélagie is vacant. I was sentenced yesterday, but I like being always in my old quarters, so that when I heard Number 9 was tenanted —(I look upon Number 9 as almost mine, for I've been there five times, and always leave a carpet-bag and a few shirts there,)—I asked the Public Prosecutor not to make out the commitment until it was vacant again. Very civil fellow, the Public Prosecutor. He'll do anything for you if you treat him properly; I called on him in dress clothes and a white tie, and that touched him.—I see you smoke cigarettes; they're too weak for me; try one of these *panatellas*. I suppose you've made it up by this time with Macrobe. Uncommonly clever fellow, and gives capital dinners at that new place of his in the Champs Elysées. His daughter's one of the prettiest girls I've ever seen. You let fly pretty hard at the Crédit Parisien the other day, but it's a splendid concern upon my word; and if you've any spare cash I advise you to invest in it. I've done so. Nominal value of shares 500 francs, issued at 360; they're selling now at 800, and rising steadily. That man Macrobe is a genius."

Thus M. de Tirecruchon. Horace had expected a little more austerity from men who gave themselves out as the defenders of public morals, the champions of might against right, the victims of oppression, &c.; but he soon discovered that liberal opinions and a good-natured tolerance of successful capitalists go very well hand in hand. Even the Red Republican who was sucking iced-punch through a straw, admitted that there were few things like the shares of the Crédit Parisien, and that though he despised riches he had bought two dozen of them. Excessive strait-lacing was out of fashion at the Café des Variétés, and it was only in his own editor, Nestor Roche, whose rugged soul was all of a piece, that Horace found that uncompromising sternness of principle which he had been disposed to think was inseparable from republicanism.

It was his habit to go and call upon Nestor Roche every day with either a leader or some occasional notes; and these visits afforded him the opportunity of learning what a real talent there lies in careful editing. Nestor Roche was not a man of many words, and the few he uttered were apt to mislead those who would have taken them as an earnest of the man's secret thoughts. In conversation he seemed indifferent and sceptical; in reality he was imbued to the marrow with theories of his own, and cherished, with a child-like veneration, the political creed in which he had been educated. This became, to a certain extent, apparent when he corrected the articles of his younger contributors; for, without appearing to do it designedly, he would, by a word inserted or expunged here and there, alter the whole tone of passages which jarred on any of his favourite chords. Men seldom make very good journalists until thirty, and Horace's writings profited considerably by the searching discipline to which they were subjected. They left the editor's hands strengthened and furbished, and yet the corrections were so few, that the most susceptible of literary vanities would not have found a pretext for taking umbrage. Horace was often astonished at the fine figure his own articles cut in print, and even wondered slightly at his own talent. Amongst his brother journalists too, it soon came to be remarked that young Horace Gerold was an elegant and thoughtful writer. The truth was, he wrote neither better nor worse than most intelligent young men of four-and-twenty, and so the public would have judged had his compositions passed straight out of his own hands into those of the printer.

Invitations and civilities began to flow in apace. Society does not run after those who shun it, but it soon adopts those who make any advances. From mixing with journalists at the café and elsewhere, it was not long before Horace was solicited to dine with them at their homes and meet their wives or connections. Then came introductions to eminent statesmen who had held high office under former governments and deemed it politic to surround themselves with the rising men of the press and the bar, with a view to a possible return to power in the future. There were also nobles of the Faubourg St. Germain, who, to cement the coalition of all parties against the Usurper, filled their drawing-rooms once or twice a month with human salads concocted of all the prominent elements then in Opposition.

Horace was everywhere received pretty much as a budding hero. His good looks, his literary and oratorical merits—(recommendations always powerful in France)—would alone have sufficed to open many doors to him; but the interest he inspired was heightened by the mystery in which he enshrouded his real name and distinguished birth. At the Café des Variétés few knew or cared whether he was a nobleman or not; but it was very different in society where there were ladies. A little to his vexation, although that vexation was not unmingled with a small dose of incipient complacency, Horace Gerold discovered that his titles were a secret for nobody, and that the fact of his repudiating them as he did was accounted to him for stoicism and abnegation beyond the common. In fact he would never have suspected how hard it was not to wear one's coronet had not people marvelled more than once, when they thought him out of earshot, that any young man should prefer such a name as Gerold to that of Clairefontaine.

One evening after he had heard himself addressed as M. le Marquis five or six times by different persons in the course of an hour, he turned rather impatiently to the lady with whom he was conversing, and said,

"Why do people insist upon labelling one with these absurd titles?"

This was at a rout given in the hospitable mansion of a very famous man—none other than the small and eloquent M. Tiré, who had been Prime Minister under Louis Philippe, and had helped not a little, by the way, in bringing the dynasty he loved to grief. The lady in conversation with Horace was an extremely pretty Baroness de Margauld, wife of an Orleanist banker.

"Why do you call titles absurd?" she replied. "I wear mine bravely enough, and should be sorry not to possess it."

"I don't mean that they are absurd for everybody," he answered, blushing; "though even in your case, Madame, I might well say, of what use is a title to you? But it is absurd to inflict upon me a distinction which I do not choose to bear."

"You must blame your own friends for that," said the Baroness, with a little tinge of slyness. "If they *will* sound your trumpet so loudly, you must expect people to do you honour."

"What friends, what trumpet?" inquired Horace, with innocence.

"Oh, you have so many friends, M. Gerold; but to cite only one instance, there is M. Macrobe, who misses no occasion of praising your good qualities; he was talking to my husband, only this morning, of your high principles and your generosity."

"M. Macrobe my friend!" exclaimed Horace, sceptically; "why, he is the man against whom I pleaded the other day."

"I am certain he bears you no ill-will then," rejoined the Baroness, "but why *did* you plead against him? Surely you do not believe all the wicked stories that have been circulated against him?"

"I neither believe, nor disbelieve," answered Horace, "but it seems to me that people judge M. Macrobe much more leniently than they would if he had failed in his curious speculations instead of enriching himself as he had done."

The Baroness gave a pretty little shrug.

"Is not success the best touchstone of merit; I believe, for my part, it is the touchstone of honesty too."

"Of honesty!" echoed Horace with surprise.

"Yes, my confessor says so. He asserts that Heaven would not allow bad men to prosper, and that consequently when we see a man very wealthy and successful, we may be sure he has deserved his good fortune, however much his enemies may say to the contrary."

"Truly a convenient moralist," observed Horace, smiling; "a sort of man to consult when one's conscience is in trouble."

"Yes, he is indeed," answered the Baroness, naïvely; "you should know him. His name is Father Glabre, of the Society of Jesus."

"I guessed the Society of Jesus," responded Horace, "and I suppose Father Glabre exemplifies his principles by being a Bonapartist. He must regard the success of the *coup-d'état* as the divine consecration of Napoleon."

"Father Glabre never talks politics," answered Mdme. de Margauld. "He says that one of the Apostles enjoined us to submit ourselves to the powers that be.

And, after all, what does it matter who is King or Emperor?" added she, fixing her bright eyes on the young man; "life was not given us to spend in wrangling as to who should sit in a velvet arm-chair. Why cannot we put up with the government we have, and try and make the best of it, it would be so much pleasanter."

Horace had too much tact to wage a war of opinions with a lady, cut he said gaily, "All I wonder at, Madame, is that, holding these views, you should risk facing such a sturdy anti-imperialist as our host."

"Oh, I come here because of the nice people one meets," answered the Baroness, playing with her fan. "If one desires to see men of any real worth in art, or literature, or politics, one must look for them in Opposition drawing-rooms. It has been the great mistake of the Emperor that instead of calling to him all the men who had rendered themselves illustrious under past reigns, he has made himself a court with a crowd of persons whom nobody knows. It's a pity, for I adore talent, and think that a sovereign cannot have too many distinguished men about him."

"I daresay he had no choice," muttered Horace, a little dryly. "Doubtless he would have been glad enough to fill his court with distinguished men, if distinguished men had consented to be employed for that purpose."

"Then you believe it is the men of talent who are holding aloof from *him*."

"Why, assuredly, Madame; have we not the proof in M. Tiré himself?"

"How good it is to be young and to have all one's illusions," murmured she, with arch but not unsympathizing raillery at the young man. "Do you not see, M. Gerold, that what has so angered all our great friends is, that they have been played? Their vanity is stung. They deemed it impossible that a stable government could ever be established without their help, and the way in which the Emperor has dispensed with their assistance, has been like telling them of what small account they were in the land. Our host, M. Tiré, is a charming man, but as vain as they say we women are. He thought himself necessary, and the Emperor has obliged him to drink gall. Depend upon it, if he were offered place to-morrow, he would accept, and with alacrity. He would consider such an offer an avowal of weakness; it would soothe his ruffled self-love; and self-love always goes before principle."

"You take a dark view of human nature," said Horace, rather moodily.

"I take the same view of it as you will when you have been ten years in society like me," replied Madame de Margauld, with half a sigh. "You are a rising man, M. Gerold. If you aspire to lead your contemporaries you must not estimate them above their worth."

The same night, going home, Horace revolved these last words in his mind with a dawning and discomforting conviction, that a society which condoned the shortcomings of such people as M. Macrobe, for the sake of the gold they possessed, did not deserve to be esteemed very highly. Somehow, though, he felt that his own contempt for the capitalist was lessening. Suspect and dislike a man as we will, we can seldom be totally indifferent to his repaying our ill-feelings by going about and speaking well of us.

It was long past midnight when Horace reached his lodging, and he walked quietly in on tiptoe for fear of awaking his brother. Something like a pang went through his heart on thinking of Emile. The two brothers were seeing less and less of each other every day. Since Horace had taken to journalism their ways lay apart. They no longer breakfasted and dined together at the modest *table-d'hôte*. Horace frequented the restaurants of the Boulevards Montmartre and Des Italiens; he rarely got up before ten in the morning; spent his evenings either out at parties or at the theatre, and when he returned home towards the small hours, usually found Emile in bed. On this occasion, however, the younger brother was still up, at his desk, writing.

Horace crept in softly behind him and put an arm round his neck: "Working so late, old fellow?" he said kindly.

"Yes, Horace," answered Emile, squeezing his hand. He pointed to two or three parcels of papers tied with pink tape, and added, "I have been entrusted with a brief that requires some study."

This was putting the case very mildly, for ever since that *début*, in which he had disappointed the hopes of the unprofessional public, but won golden opinions from the solicitors, Emile had been entrusted with several briefs, all most arid, voluminous, and tough. Solicitors were delighted to find a young man who was devoid of vanity, and had no ambition to make himself a name at the expense of his clients. Briefs were offered him which were not important enough for the stars of the profession, but which demanded an immense amount of reading, and required to be handled by a man of talent, content to work hard with small prospect of glory, and, often, for not very high remuneration. Barristers of this kidney are scarce in all lands, but in France, perhaps, more so than elsewhere. Whence it happened that Emile was getting as much employment as he could manage.

He was looking pale, however, so that, after they had talked a little while together, Horace prevailed upon him to go to bed. They wished each other affectionately good-night; but before retiring to his own room, Horace passed into his study to see if there were any letters. There were several, chiefly invitations, and in the midst of the heap a little packet fastened with blue ribbons.

"From whom does this come?" said he, returning to his brother's room with the parcel opened, and displaying a dozen cambric bands and as many pocket-handkerchiefs, exquisitely embroidered with his initials.

"Oh! I forgot to tell you," exclaimed Emile, already in bed, and raising himself on his elbow; "they were brought up to-day by our landlord's daughter, in return for a work-box which she says you gave her."

"Kind little Georgette!" ejaculated Horace.

"She seems an amiable girl," continued Emile; "but I met her father to-day in the street, and he tells me that she is growing serious and silent, and doesn't look well."

CHAPTER XI.

Love and War.

No, Georgette had not been well lately, and the excellent M. Pochemolle, his wife, and even M. Alcibiade Pochemolle, had been growing a little uneasy at seeing that the blooming young girl, once so gladsome, had become by degrees unaccountably subdued and pensive. They questioned her as to whether she felt unwell, but she replied that she had no consciousness of being otherwise than usual—that there was nothing the matter.

And yet matter there was, though probably Georgette was sincere enough in asserting that she was not conscious of it. Several weeks had elapsed since the present of the work-box by Horace Gerold. She had hemmed him the cambric bands; then, fearing that the gift would not be complete, she had wished to add a dozen handkerchiefs, and this had taken time—it takes time to work twelve times over the letters H. G., when there are so many pauses for reverie between the stitches. And during the weeks that she had slowly plied her needle in marking the cambric with the two initials, she had seen Horace pass the window every morning and lift his hat and smile to her as he went on his way to the newspaper-office; and she had heard of his having entered journalism and of his new triumphs in that profession. Out of compliment to his lodger, and although he indignantly repudiated the doctrines advocated in that print, M. Pochemolle had made it a point to subscribe to the *Sentinelle*, and in the evening, when she retired to her room, Georgette took the paper with her and would sit up in her bed reading the articles by Horace. She did not always understand them at first, but she would read them over and over until she did; and if she was not successful after many readings, then she would read the signature a multitude of times, and that pleased her: she fancied, somehow, the letters were in his own handwriting. When she had read the papers she put them all carefully by in a drawer. M. Alcibiade Pochemolle sometimes wondered what became of them.

She no longer carried up their letters to the brothers when they were brought to the wrong door. There is an instinct in these things. But she would gaze with curious scrutiny at the envelopes directed in feminine hands. When there were none such she was happier.

She had noticed, with the quick eye of a woman for such trifles, that Horace Gerold was turning fashionable. He had an eyeglass, wore light-coloured gloves and lacquered boots, smoked cigars instead of the cigarettes which he used to twirl himself, and always came home at night in cabs. She could hear the vehicles stop in the street outside, and then his step as he mounted the staircase. She never went to sleep until she heard that step—not if it were delayed till four o'clock in the morning. One day, Horace had come into the shop and brought them a private box for the opera—she had once remarked in his presence that she loved music. The performance was *Robert le Diable*. Nothing could have been more hospitable or more full of tact than the arrangements made by him for their comfort. He had chartered a private brougham to convey and bring them back; and in the second entr'acte had paid them a visit in their box, bringing two bouquets, one for herself and one for her mother, and a fine *cornet* of bonbons, without which the happiness of a Parisian *bourgeoise* at the "playhouse" is never complete. Upon the drawing up of the curtain he had discreetly taken his leave. It had been a great evening for everybody. M. Alcibiade Pochemolle had never put on so much bear's-grease in the course of his existence, and the sight of the *corps-de-ballet* made his fingers tingle; M. Pochemolle had reckoned that there were at least a hundred square yards of canvas in the drop-scene; Madame Pochemolle had been much impressed by the resurrection of the ghost-nuns in the churchyard scene. As for Georgette, she had remarked but one thing, and that was, that Horace on returning to his stall had bowed to several stately and beautiful ladies in the boxes, and that at the close of the third act he had appeared in the box of one covered with diamonds, whom M. Pochemolle had recognized for a Marchioness of the Noble Faubourg. Alone in her room after the opera, and with her bouquet in her hand, the poor child shivered mournfully. Who was she that she could hope to vie with ladies who wore diamonds and were Marchionesses? It was evident M. Gerold had never given her a thought.

Nevertheless, she had moments of flitting compensation; and her cheeks mantled on the morrow of the day when Horace had found her present on his table and came down to thank her with his bright voice, which seemed to her more refined and gentle each time she heard it. He drew out one of the handkerchiefs, which was lightly scented with mignonette, admired the embroidery of the initials—indeed no common piece of workmanship—and playfully observed he intended keeping this fine linen for great occasions: "My wedding-day, for instance," said he, "providing I ever do marry." And at these words she turned pale anew; it was like a cloud passing rapidly over a furtive sunbeam.

The probabilities are that Horace did not remark this pallor, though he could not help noticing in a general way that she was changed since he had spoken with her last. He told her how sorry he was to hear she had been unwell, and drew forth the rather faltering answer that, indeed, she felt in perfect health.

This time he was struck with the tone of the reply, and it recurred to him at intervals in the course of the day, and again once or twice during the week when passing by the shop he remarked that Georgette's eyes lowered under his with a new expression which he did not understand. Then this circumstance faded out of his mind under the pressure of graver preoccupations which soon beset him.

He underwent the common lot of Parisian journalists, and got engaged in a quarrel with a brother pen-man in the opposite camp. The fault was not his, nor altogether his adversary's, but that of the admirable political system under which they both lived. The conditions of the French Press were then such that journalists could not well help coming to loggerheads try as they might. The unlucky law Tinguy-Laboulie (named after the two old gentlemen who promoted it), which rendered it binding upon the writer of an article to sign his name to it, had completely disorganized the old anonymous Press by substituting individualism for combined action and conflict of personalities for polemic of opinions. The staff of a newspaper was no longer a disciplined company, but a band of sharpshooters, each of the members of which, being personally responsible for the opinions he emitted, naturally did his utmost to assert himself. Had the Press been free, the discussions between man and man need not necessarily have degenerated into violence, for it is not the tendency of educated men to abuse one another when they have fair arguments at their command. But, hemmed in as journalists were on every side by penal clauses, which made it impossible to write on any subject with latitude, the temptation to glide from trammelled controversy into exchange of personal invectives was often irresistible. Opposition writers would break out into vituperation, as a train will jump off the line because obstacles are set in the way of its straight course; but more frequently the aggressors were the members of the semi-official Press. These gentlemen, being obliged to defend the acts of their Government, by hook or by crook, might have found the task an up-hill one had the only weapons allowed them been those of logic; but matters were much simplified when they could champion Imperial policy with a pen in one hand and a foil in the other. If the pen found nothing to say, the foil came to the rescue, and it was not an unusual thing to attempt silencing troublesome writers in the liberal ranks by picking a series of bones with them, until they either held their peace, overawed, or retaliated by spitting a few of their antagonists one after the other. This was what was tried with Horace.

There was an Imperialist paper named *Le Pavois* and on the staff of it one M. Paul de Cosaque, a Creole, with a frizzly head of hair, large round eyes, and hands like small shoulders of mutton. This promising youth, though not above five-and-twenty, was the Quixote of his party, serving the dynasty in a devoted Creole way, and hating oppositionists as a tough young bull-dog might vermin. He was not long in taking offence at the successes of Horace. Hearing his name so constantly mentioned, he ended by growing tired of it, and did not conceal his longing for an opportunity of coming into collision with one whose popularity he was pleased to regard as in some sort a personal affront to himself. So he proceeded to do what is called in journalistic phrase "laying a man on the gridiron," which means that he collared Horace Gerold and served him up every day to the readers of the *Pavois*, skewered through and through with an epigram. They were somewhat blunt, these epigrams of M. Paul de Cosaque, but the intention of them was plain enough, and, at the outset, Horace was for despatching a couple of seconds to request that satisfaction might be afforded him. But, with a shrug, Nestor Roche pooh-poohed this notion, saying it were best to take no heed of the barking of a cur; so that M. Paul, perceiving a reluctance to quarrel, set down his adversary for a chicken-heart, and began unwisely to crow cock-a-whoop before the time.

Now one day, after this fleabiting had been going on for some weeks, Horace wrote a leader in the *Sentinelle* on the subject of the privacy of the parliamentary debates. It was a very temperate article though, not without a dash of acid, and it had been ably revised by Nestor Roche, who had given it the backbone it at first wanted. Several foreign papers, and most of the liberal provincial organs, quoted it; and as the law which debarred the public from knowing what went on in their own Parliament was an ever-chafing sore, the author received a good many congratulations from Boulevard politicians. This was just the sort of occasion M. Paul de Cosaque had been looking for. He was down on the article in a trice, dipping his pen in his smartest verjuice, and howling out abuse much as a faithful negro might do who had seen his master's shins scraped. Horace was on a visit to his editor at the prison of Ste. Pélagie when the number of the *Pavois* containing M. Paul's attack fell into his hands. Nestor Roche, Max Delormay, and another captive journalist named Jean Kerjou of the *Gazette des Boulevards*, were sitting at the table writing. The printer's devil, Trigger, who had just brought all the morning papers in a vast bundle under his arm, was planted on a chair, whence his legs dangled, and his one eye squinted, waiting for "copy." Horace himself was lounging on the ottoman and smoking as he read.

He started up with the colour rising to his face and an indignant glare in his eyes.

"Look at this, M. Roche," he said, and began to stride about the room, biting his lips. "It is time this should end now. I shall send the fellow my seconds this afternoon."

"No; wait till to-morrow," put in Jean Kerjou. "I shall be out of prison then, and I'll act for you. Who is the man?"

Nestor Roche ran his quick glance through the column and presently answered: "Well, my boy, it's one of the necessities of our trade to fight as well as scribble. This whelp's trying to draw you; you must break his teeth. But, first, we'll just give him a rap with his own weapons and make his copper-coloured knuckles ring."

The four journalists were soon in consultation round the board with the open number of the *Pavois* before them. What they wanted was to draw up a retort which should strike at the weak place in M. Paul's armour, and make that sword-clinker yell. This weak place was not difficult to find. M. Paul, like many other worthy people, was not above the foible of vanity, and had tacked on to his patronymic a name which did not lawfully belong to him. His real style and title was Paul Panier; but Panier being an ugly name, signifying "basket," he, or rather he and his father between them, had discarded it in favour of the more sounding designation De Cosaque, which was derived from the country residence of the elder Panier. But these usurpations are formally prohibited by law under pain of imprisonment; and it was, therefore, very much like throwing projectiles out of a glass-house when M. Paul delivered himself as follows in his attack upon Horace:—

".... As for these so-called Republicans, who go about under false names, being ashamed to wear the titles which their fathers bore lest they should compromise their popularity with the rabble; as for these self-styled Democrats, who refuse homage to a king, but fawn sycophantly upon the mob, and see no better way of currying favour with their masters than by making litter of all the distinctions their own ancestors won, just like those low birds who befoul their own nests;—as for these men, we know what is their object in asking that the debates of the Chamber may again be thrown open to public audiences. They have not forgotten 1793, when the galleries were filled with drunken trollops, whose bloodthirsty howls gave our precious Republicans the courage they needed to send old men, women, and fallen kings to the scaffold; nor 1848, when the scum of our galleys infested the Strangers' tribunes to cheer the dismal buffooneries of such men as the citizen Manuel Gerold. We should not wonder if those who ask that the tribunes may be thrown open again, had an eye to some day becoming deputies themselves; but, being aware of the contempt with which their utterances would be received by men of sense, they wish to make sure of having an audience of kindred spirits—like those tenth-rate actors who, unable to excite applause in the stalls and boxes, pick some poor devils out of the gutter and hire them for five sous a night to go and clap their hands in the pit."

There was nothing uncommon in the form of this effusion; it was the true semi-official style of the period.

Nestor Roche prepared the following reply, which Horace signed:—

"*The* MARQUIS OF CLAIREFONTAINE *to* M. PAUL
"PANIER.

"THE gentleman on the staff of the *Pavois* who calls himself M. 'de Cosaque,' is respectfully informed that the undersigned writer will resume the title he inherited from his ancestors on the day his courteous antagonist does likewise. M. Paul 'de Cosaque' will doubtless see fit to perform this resumption without delay, lest the Public Prosecutor, forgetting that M.

'de Cosaque' is a Bonapartist, and remembering only that he is a transgressor of the law, which forbids persons to adopt nobiliary particles to which they have no right, should order his transfer to Mazas, and so afford him the opportunity of making a closer acquaintance with those 'scum of the galleys,' with whose language, as well as with whose habits, M. 'de Cosaque' appears so conversant.   "HORACE GEROLD."

This again was a very fair specimen of an Opposition retort.

"This will save you the trouble of sending a challenge," remarked the editor. "The whelp will probably begin operations himself;" and he handed the slip to Trigger, who, after receiving his usual instruction not to loiter with fellow *gamins*, shambled off with it to the printing-office.

The effect, however, was not quite what Nestor Roche and his acolytes expected. On reading the stinging paragraph M. Paul de Cosaque blanched, but he did not set out in quest of seconds. He caught up his hat and went off prowling in the direction of the Boulevards, grinding his white creole teeth and clenching his fists so tight that the nails left four dents in each of the brown palms. He wanted to find Horace and knock him down; then fight him with steel afterwards. There is no profession like literature for making a man mild and brotherly.

Horace was breakfasting at one of the great restaurants, and with him, as it chanced, was Jean Kerjou, the man of the *Gazette des Boulevards*, who had been released from confinement in the morning. He was a Breton, this journalist, short, but thick and powerful, and amazingly prompt with his hands, like all Bretons. He had taken a fancy to Horace, who knew but little of him, and the pair were, so to say, watering their new-sprung friendship in this breakfast.

Suddenly Jean Kerjou, who sat opposite the door, dissecting a woodcock, abandoned his bird, crying, "Haro, Gerold, look out!" and sprang to his legs. The mulatto face of M. Paul was darkening the doorway, and in less than two seconds was within blow-reach of them.

M. Paul held a newspaper crunched up in his right hand. He strode up to the table, jabbered something unintelligible, and, before any one in the crowded restaurant could stop him, delivered a tremendous cuff, which missed Horace's head by an ace, alighted, with a loud thwack, on the countenance of a waiter, and sent him sprawling on to a table where lunched a peaceful English family, who set up piercing cries.

There was an inconceivable uproar, amidst which a huge slap resounded, and simultaneously an unholy crash of broken glass, as some one not distinguishable was hurled, all of a lump, into a corner. The slap was administered by Horace; the crash was caused by Jean Kerjou, who had caught up M. Paul like a bundle of linen, and shot him to the other end of the room.

Twenty arms at once pinned down the creole, gnashing and struggling to rise; twenty others pulled back Horace Gerold and Jean Kerjou, to prevent further mischief. Then uprose a deafening contestation as to who was the aggressor—the English family shrieking all together that it was the negro, and the waiter thundering that it was Horace, seeing that, had the blow fallen on his cheek as it was meant to do, half

the disturbance would have been avoided. In the midst
of the hubbub entered two policemen, who took down
the names of everybody all round, apprehended the
waiter on the ground that, being splashed all over with
lobster-sauce, he was presumably the culprit; and, on
being eventually induced to release him, retired bewildered, leaving the field clear to a gentleman with a
countenance like a weasel's, who, having been witness
of the whole scene, stepped forward, with his mouth
full, and spluttered, "I maintain, it's an act of the most
brutal aggression. M. Paul de Cosaque, you've conducted yourself like a villain. Do you hear that?"

There was no mistaking this twanging voice. It
was M. Macrobe's. He had been lunching with a stock-
broking friend, and this friend, fearful that he would
get himself into trouble, now sought to restrain him by
the coat-tails; but M. Macrobe would not be restrained.
He rushed up to the infuriated creole, who was with
difficulty kept from flying at his throat, and shouted,
"Men like yourself are a disgrace to the Press, M. Panier.
You convert what should be the noblest of professions
into a bravo's trade. You deserve to be stamped out like a
pestilent toad, and if M. Gerold doesn't kill you, I will."

M. Paul de Cosaque was forcibly dragged out of
the restaurant. M. Macrobe turned, apparently trem-
bling with the holiest indignation and sympathy, and
walked to where Horace and his friend were standing.
The least Horace Gerold could do for a man who had
taken his part so warmly was to thank him, which he
did at once and with gratitude, though coldly. M.
Macrobe, not minding the coldness, continued to strike
whilst the iron was hot.

"My dear young friend," said he, "that man is a

very cut-throat. He has had half-a-dozen men out already, and will nip your brilliant career short if we let him; but trust to me: I will be your second. It was he who first raised his hand on you. This makes you the offended party, and gives you choice of weapons."

Horace did not much relish the proposal of M. Macrobe to be his second; but to refuse would, under the circumstances, have been both discourteous and ungracious. Besides, Jean Kerjou did not leave him time to do so, for, delighted with the pluck of "the small man with the ferret face," he held out his hand, and said, "Sir, my name is Jean Kerjou, and I am M. Gerold's other second. Between us we will see our friend well through this scrape."

Further breakfast being impossible, Horace threw down five napoleons to the landlord to pay for the breakages, and two more to the waiter to soothe his throbbing jaw. Then he, Jean Kerjou, and the banker, slipped out by a back door to escape the mob, which had already congregated outside, wide-mouthed, and so home to Horace's lodgings. The two policemen, before retiring, had suggested that everybody should call upon the Commissary of Police during the afternoon to explain matters; but this formality was omitted, for the police official could neither have undone that which was accomplished nor prevented that which was to come. In the course of a couple of hours Jean Kerjou and M. Macrobe had routed out Emile from a musty court, in which he was acting as junior in a fearfully musty case, and hastily apprised him of what had happened: after which they had called upon M. de Cosaque, and arranged a rendezvous with the latter's two friends at five. By dinner-time the duel was all settled. It was to come off at seven the next morning, in the Bois de Vincennes, with foils.

Of course the news spread quickly along the Boulevards, and was received with no inconsiderable glee by the do-nothing portion of the public. These tiffs between journalists were the one thing that saved the press of the period from monotony, and a duel was always a welcome little episode. All the evening papers gave accounts of the fracas at the restaurant; but, in order not to spoil sport, *i.e.* bring the police on the ground, they fraternally abstained from divulging the spot where the fight was to take place. Nevertheless, they printed the names of the contending parties in full, with those of their seconds, and hinted significantly that M. Paul de Cosaque was one of the best swordsmen in Paris.

By the advice of his two friends, who took bodily charge of him during the evening, Horace dined lightly, and gave an hour to fencing, in which he was already tolerably proficient. At half-past nine he was escorted to his door, with injunctions to go to bed as soon as possible, and be up by six the next day.

The day might be called an eventful one, but he mounted his staircase with a very quiet pulse for a man who was going to risk his life at sunrise.

Just as he reached the *entresol*, however, a door was timidly held ajar, and he was confronted by Georgette.

She had read of the impending duel in the newspaper, and ever since her mind had been distracted by visions of blood and death. She was pale and terrified, and held the newspaper in her hands. When she saw Horace she said nothing, but shed a few tears.

He was touched by this unexpected meeting, and

by the simple display of grief, of which he could not but guess the cause.

"Why are you crying, Mademoiselle Georgette?" he said, gently.

She made no answer, but pointed to the paragraph in the newspaper.

He took one of her unresisting hands in his, and said with gaiety, "But there is nothing to be afraid of in that. Duels happen every day."

"You may be killed," she sobbed.

"And if I were, would you grieve for me?" he asked, half in jest, half gravely.

She threw him a sad, reproachful look.

"Don't speak like that, Monsieur Horace; you know how unhappy I—how unhappy we should all be," added she, correcting herself.

He took her other hand, looked into her eyes, and said, "I shall run no danger, Georgette."

This was the first time he called her Georgette. She strove gently to free herself: but the effort was short-lived.

"Promise me you won't fight to-morrow," she faltered.

"I promise you he shall not hurt me, Georgette," he answered, encircling her waist with his arm.

"Oh, but if he should——" she said, making another feeble attempt to disengage herself.

"But he won't, Georgette."

And, stooping, he pressed a kiss on her lips.

But theirs was the bliss of a few instants only, for at that moment the house-door opened, then closed, and the steps of a lodger in the vestibule below warned them to separate.

"Good-night, Georgette," he whispered. "I shall

be safe to-morrow if you return me my kiss. It will be my talisman."

He was still holding her waist. She blushed; looked over the balusters to see if the lodger was coming, and then returned him his kiss.

* * * * *

The next morning betimes, one of the keepers of the Bois de Vincennes, returning to his cottage from night-duty, beheld two broughams, following each other at an interval of a few minutes, sweep along the road to the race-course and stop near a secluded knoll, distant some couple of hundred yards from the Grand Stand; and, being a man of experience, he knew what that meant. Chancing to be further a shrewd man, he resolved upon retracing his steps, and, instead of going home, to take up his position at a distance, though within eye-view, so as to be ready to come forward when everything was over and earn an honest twenty-franc piece, by undertaking to preserve secrecy. To these ends he ensconced himself behind the trunks of some felled trees.

M. Macrobe, who had managed matters for Horace, had done everything very well. He had brought his brougham, with store of lint, bandages, restoratives, &c. concealed in the pockets; the most eminent surgeon in Paris on one of the front seats; and a pair of the finest duelling-foils in a chamois bag. He had quite won the graces of Jean Kerjou, both by his energy, his practical hints, and the loud-spoken sympathy he evinced for Horace. In sooth, M. Macrobe had been somewhat gloomy the preceding afternoon, on his principal insisting upon fighting with foils; and his gloom had not cleared up until he had seen how Horace bore himself in the fencing school. Horace, though he never boasted of it, and never sought to air his talent, was a good fencer; having been originally taught by his father, who, first as a nobleman, then as an officer, and finally as a journalist, had served a treble apprenticeship in sword-craft. M. Macrobe was elated to see the manner in which he could parry and lunge, and though he would still have preferred pistols, on the ground that a man with steady nerves can blow his adversary out of life with this weapon, and not allow time to be shot at in return, yet he felt considerably reassured as to his principal's prospects even against such an antagonist as M. de Cosaque.

Horace Gerold's party were the first on the ground. Upon the others appearing, the eight gentlemen all bowed together, but there were no negotiations attempted—the insults exchanged being such as could only be washed out by blood-shed. The two seconds of M. de Cosaque—one a colonel of the Imperial Guard and a man of the *coup-d'état*, the other, M. de Gargousse, an official deputy—selected the ground along with MM. Macrobe and Kerjou, and then examined the different pairs of foils that had been brought. By common consent those of M. Macrobe were chosen; they were very ribbons of steel that could be bent so that the point touched the handle without snapping. Whilst these preliminaries were being adjusted, the two principals took off their coats, waistcoats, hats, cravats, and boots—so as not to slip on the wet morning grass;—and opened their shirts a little, as etiquette required, to show that they wore no mail-coat next the skin. Meantime, the two surgeons, standing aside and conversing in a low voice, fumbled in their pockets to open their surgical cases, in order that no time might be lost when their cheerful services were needed. The morning was deliciously balmy; and in the wood could be heard the tinkling of a cart-bell, and the lively voice of the carter speaking to his horse as they jogged together to their work. It is only human beings who could think of fighting on such a morning as that.

There was a silence. The combatants were face to face, two yards apart. The Colonel having measured the foils, gave one to each, then joined the two weapons by the points, and, stepping back with head uncovered, said, "Allez, Messieurs."—Then the guard ensconced behind the fallen trees saw this:—

The strongest of the two duellists, he with the dark face and large hands, bore down upon his adversary with a terrific onslaught, forcing him to "break" and parry wildly; then, when it seemed as though the quickness of the retreat must cause the slighter combatant to lose his balance, the other made a rapid, furious lunge. The attack was so formidable that any but a first-rate fencer would have been carried off his legs by it. The guard—an old soldier—winced. But the slighter man rallied with desperate strength, struck up the sword that was within a hair's-breadth of his heart, plunged forward, and with the suddenness of lightning thrust his foil through his adversary's chest up to the hilt. The whole thing did not last fifty seconds. M. Paul de Cosaque rolled over on the grass, with the foil still in him, quite dead.

Four out of the seven spectators turned pale. The Colonel glanced at Horace and saluted him with respect. M. Macrobe pressed up and wrung his hand. The guard loomed from behind his trees and came up slowly, in pursuit of his twenty francs.

CHAPTER XII.

M. Macrobe offers Money.

The lucky hazard that had thrown M. Macrobe in the way of Horace at the restaurant, had gratified one of that sagacious financier's most deep-rooted wishes. A few days before, talking with M. Louchard the Commissary of Police, with whom, as with a good many strange persons, he was on affable terms, the latter had said to him: "By the way, M. Macrobe, do you know that the young radical who spoke against you in the libel-suit is by birth a marquis, and owns vast wealth?"

"Yes, I know it," responded M. Macrobe curiously; "but how did *you* know it?"

"Why, after the trial, seeing that the popularity of this young man threatened to become a danger to public order, the Prefect sent me to search his apartments." Here M. Louchard lowered his voice, for they were in a public place, and gave an account of his domiciliary visit to the brothers' lodgings, omitting that episode, however, which related to the threat of Horace to break his head. "And, odd to say," he concluded, "we found a deed by which the old Republican, Manuel Gerold, makes over to his two sons the whole of the estates of Hautbourg during his own lifetime."

M. Macrobe pricked up his ears.

"Have you that deed still in your possession, M. Louchard?"

"Why, yes," answered the commissary, glad to interest the powerful financier. "I took it to the Prefect, who read it, but ordered me to return it, the document being a family paper of no use to us. I should have done so ere now, but forgot. However, this deed has not been so useless as M. le Préfet pretends: for it has proved to us that these two young Gerolds are an extremely suspicious pair. Having wealth, they yet live as if they had nothing, which is evidence enough that they must lay out their money to unlawful ends. We suspect they are subsidizing secret societies, and we have got them under close supervision."

"Oh, they are under police surveillance?"

"The very closest. We have men watching them day and night. There is not a thing they do but we know of it."

"Yet, I'll be bound you don't know who they bank with, though this piece of knowledge might have stood you in better stead than many others which I daresay you've picked up." And M. Macrobe looked rather sarcastically at the man of Police.

"No, we've not found who they bank with," answered M. Louchard reflectively. "And I suppose *you* can't tell us."

"They bank with us," replied M. Macrobe carelessly; "but I can't tell you anything as to where their money goes. The revenue of the estates is paid into our hands every quarter-day by the agent; but it is drawn out again almost as soon by this same agent with cheques signed by old M. Gerold. That's all we know about it." Then turning pensive, he added, "You will show me that deed, M. Louchard."

"Willingly," rejoined the other, who counted that his civility would be repaid by financial hints; since none knew better than M. Macrobe how to give hints as to securities worth dabbling in, and shares which, though prosperous in aspect, had best be avoided. Everybody gambled on the Bourse in those days of jobbing, and M. Louchard did like the rest. But it was not every one who had such a master tipster as M. Macrobe to guide him.

The two went together to M. Louchard's office, and the banker had a sight of the deed of gift, which he scrutinized long and narrowly. In return for the favour he thus advised M. Louchard:—"The shares of the Crédit Parisien are quoted to-day at 850. I'll let you have twenty of them at 800. You shall pay me in a month. Hold fast to them till they're quoted at 1,500, which they will be in less than a couple of years, and then sell out." M. Louchard almost went down on all fours, thanking him with transports as a benefactor.

The deed of gift set M. Macrobe thinking. He was an astute man, and soon put his thoughts into plain figures. So long as he had imagined that Horace Gerold would have to await his father's death before stepping into the Hautbourg estate, he had treated the angling of him as a thing that could be undertaken leisurely; but now that Horace was actually master of his property, he was a fish to bait and hook with the least delay possible. M. Macrobe had reached that pitch of wealth where gold comes flowing in like a Pactolus, on the immutable principle by which rivers always roll their waters towards the sea, which has enough without them. But his were paper riches. They were the riches that give a man consideration on 'Change, make his name familiar among brokers, and cause the outside public to speak of him as a warm man. M. Macrobe, however, desired something more than this. With opulence had come the ambition which opulence begets. The enriched stock-jobber longed to be somebody, and the surest way to become somebody is to be at the head of an ancient name and a substantial landed estate—neither of which essentials M. Macrobe possessed. Under the circumstances, it was not very surprising that a man, accustomed like him to put things in black and white, should think of his daughter and propose making her minister to his honest ambition. If she should marry a nobleman with influence at his command, that influence would naturally be at the service of her father, and give him a lift into that political world, where M. Macrobe now longed to try his powers. He turned over this thought maturely and in an infinite variety of lights, but always with the same result, to wit, that Horace Gerold and his daughter Angélique were evidently made for one another.

With M. Macrobe to plan was to resolve. Obstacles did not daunt him. He had surmounted so many already to make himself what he was, that the aversion which the two Gerolds testified towards him struck him as a mere vexatious circumstance—nothing more. That he should finally overcome the ill-feeling, he did not for a moment doubt; and he set himself to the concoction of sundry diplomatic schemes, by which he and Horace were to be brought together. But the merit of these schemes he never had the need to test, for as we have seen, hazard suddenly played his cards for him, and did more in a day than he, by his wits unaided, could have done in a twelvemonth.

After the duel Horace was bound to him by one of those ties which men of honour regard as strong. He had espoused the young man's quarrel openly and fearlessly in public, thus risking his life for him—there being no question that, had M. Paul de Cosaque triumphed, he would have visited M. Macrobe's interference in such a way as to lay that gentleman and his schemes of glory six good feet under ground. Horace might regret not having acted with more caution in accepting M. Macrobe's friendly offices; but it was too late for repentance now. He was under an obligation to the financier, and the latter determined, by a skilful stroke, to put all that remained of his antipathy to flight.

It had been somewhat of a shock to Nestor Roche, when he heard that his young ally had gone out to fight, with the slippery stock-jobber for his second; and though, upon Horace rushing into the prison-room a couple of hours after the duel, the joy at beholding him safe was such as, for the moment, to dispel all other pre-occupations, yet by-and-by, when the old editor had had time to grow calm and gruff again, he said, with a shade of pain, "I could have wished to see you with a worthier henchman on the field, my boy."

"I could have wished to have had you," replied Horace, gravely; "but I owe a debt to M. Macrobe."

And he proceeded to relate what had occurred, being backed in his narrative by Jean Kerjou, who spoke of the financier as having behaved throughout "like a trump." This did not convert Nestor Roche, but it appeased him, though soon his brow grew dark again when Horace said, a little timidly, "And, do you know, I have a message from this very M. Macrobe to you, M. Roche?"

"To me!" exclaimed the editor, impassively.

"Well, yes. This morning, after the duel, M. Kerjou, here present, and I breakfasted with him, and he fell to talking about the libel-trial. He was very frank, but full of tact about it. He said we must not bear him a grudge for having defended his good name, but that he sought to make no profit out of the action, and that he hoped you would take back the five-and-twenty thousand francs damages the court had made you pay."

Here Horace drew out a pocket-book.

Nestor Roche frowned.

"You needn't offer me that man's money. If he is lucky enough to persuade you that he is an injured man, I have nothing to say; but you know my opinion of him. I've 'not changed it."

"Yet it seems to me this should induce us to mitigate our judgment," observed Horace, sticking up for the man who had stood by him. "After all, I daresay he's no worse than thousands of others we call honest men; and here he has sent you back your twenty-five thousand francs, which is a great deal more than many others would have done."

Nestor Roche eyed him rather compassionately, and answered with dryness:—

"My boy, men will always get the weather-side of you with smooth tongues. Think well of this stock-jobber if you like, but take him back his money."

And he would hear not a word more on the subject.

Horace felt hurt at this shortness, and so did Jean Kerjou a little, for it did not suit this straightforward

Breton to suppose that he had been shaking hands with a man who had any taint on him. He said so frankly, and was putting it with some earnestness to Nestor Roche whether the latter had anything definite to allege against the banker Macrobe, when Max Delormay, the editor Tirecruchon, and a number of other political captives, tumbled in, attracted by the report of Horace Gerold's presence.

Much hand-shaking ensued, as well as congratulations on the issue of the duel; but of pity for the fallen man not a word. To be sure, M. de Cosaque was not a personage in whose favour one could get up much sympathy. He had been as a Goliath in the midst of his party, overshadowing his foes with his shoulder-of-mutton fist, slapping their faces on slender pretexts, and transfixing them afterwards without remorse. To have wished him alive would have been to wish an ever-threatening foil over one's head.

"A more bloodthirsty dog I never set eyes on," ejaculated the fat M. de Tirecruchon, with a sigh of relief. "Egad! he had *me* out once. Happily, it was with pistols, but he blew half the rim of my hat away."

"*De mortuis*—" began honest Jean Kerjou. He had not yet got over the tragic episode of the morning.

Soon the room was hazy with tobacco-smoke, and a dozen prisoners lay or sat recumbent on sofa, armchairs, and ottoman; Horace forming the centre of the group, seated on a low stool, and being made much of by the rest. Still a little sore at Nestor Roche's strictures upon M. Macrobe, he was rather moody and silent, and hoped the financier and his offer would be allowed to drop for a while, until he could be alone with Nestor Roche, and talk the point over with him. But Jean Kerjou, who was uneasy, and wanted to get his mind clear, made haste to resume his interrupted appeal to the editor, and so drew on a general discussion concerning M. Macrobe's proposal to refund the damages. The case was quite a novel one, and tolerably difficult to pronounce upon impartially. Opinions were pretty equally divided.

M. de Tirecruchon, who was nothing if not indulgent of everybody's foibles, his own included, held stoutly with the Macrobians.

"Corbleu!" he exclaimed, rolling one of his flat *panatellas* between two thick fingers, and glancing at his editorial brother with surprise—"Corbleu! Roche, you're not going to refuse such an offer as that? Of course Macrobe is more or less of a rogue, but aren't we all rogues, present company excepted? I wouldn't give a fig for a man who wasn't something of a rogue. Besides, don't you see that the more you've got to say against the man, so much the greater is the reason for taking his money. If what you said against him was true, *ergo* it was no slander: consequently, the damages were unjustly assessed, and, therefore, obviously, you have a right to repocket them."

Horace bridled up.

"I didn't wish to see the matter viewed in that light; I would rather the offer were accepted generously, as it was made, and that we should acknowledge, some of us, that we may have been a little hasty in judging M. Macrobe."

"Yes, so should I," assented Jean Kerjou, candidly; —"or, at least," added he, "I should like to hear something plain and proveable against this man."

M. Max Delormay here felt it due to himself to

protest energetically. The famous paragraph he had written against M. Macrobe, and for which he, as well as others, were suffering fines and imprisonment, had gradually come to assume in his eyes the proportion of an historical event. He was not very remote from the idea that since this paragraph the financier had become somehow his own peculiar private property, and that to speak of him in any way, either *pro* or *con*, without his, Max Delormay's, sanction, was to defraud him, Max Delormay, of his just privileges. Accordingly, he claimed his right to protest, and, in that sober tone which Frenchmen have when they don't know what they are saying, made a speech which nobody understood, he least of all; but which concluded with a panegyric of the Spartan Republic as being a place where commercial morality flourished.

M. de Tirecruchon puffed his jovial face with an air of bewilderment, and cried: "Tut, Max, you're running off with the wrong bone. The question is, whether Roche shall accept back 25,000 francs paid by him as damages for an article you wrote. I say yes; and I've given you my reasons. As for morality nowadays, I'll tell you what it just amounts to—not being found out. Go you into the streets and take at haphazard out of our church-folk, politicians, tradesmen, or out of us journalists, any hundred men, and I will be bound there are not two out of the lot whose lives will bear looking into with a microscope. Hang it all! let us not get to prying too closely behind each other's curtains. I don't know who this Macrobe is. In times past he may have been a coiner, for all I can tell; but at present the Government accepts him, the Law accepts him, and Society accepts him, so why shouldn't

I? For come! what would it profit me, if, after making the acquaintance of the man, finding him pleasant, sensible, ready to do one a good turn, &c., I were to go and rake up the diary of his life, to see if I could discover one soiled page in it? To-morrow the fellow might die; and what should I have gained by my trouble then?—not even the pleasure of cutting him. Much better seek to know nothing about the soiled page, and take the fellow's hand so long as I find it agreeable. Of course if I receive proof positive that the fellow is a cur, that's another question; but I haven't.'

A small, dark man, squatting near the fire and smoking a clay pipe, whom Horace knew as the Citizen Albi, a political conspirator, who unaffectedly admired Robespierre, and was of opinion that the Reign of Terror had failed in its effects from not being quite stringent enough, here broke in vehemently:

"Your views are as immoral as they well can be. If adopted they would be the charter of successful rogues. When you are hiring a servant you rake up all you can about him, and if you find a speck you draw back. I see no difference between rich rogues and poor. I have never yet given my hand to a man whose life was not as clear to me as the noon-day, and, so help me my own contempt for scoundrels, I never will."

"And what is the result, my poor Albi?" rejoined the stout editor, unruffled. "Why, ever since you could hold a musket you have been in open war with Society. Out of your short life of thirty years you have spent eight in transportations or imprisonments: and I daresay if I could read in your heart I should find smouldering there the scheme of some new communistical era of guillotining, by which you hope to regenerate us. Those are gloomy principles, my poor friend, which make you thirst for our blood so ardently, and oblige Society in its own defence to make you pine away the best years of your young life behind prison bars."

"I do not see that I am to be pitied," answered Albi, in the same energetic tone as before. "Every man has his ambition. That of some men is to fill a pocket with gold pieces, that of others to tie a piece of red silk round their necks; yours is, I believe, to sell more copies of your newspaper than your neighbour over the way. I have mine too, which is to establish a Republic of honest men. I care not the price I pay."

"And what is your idea of an honest man?" inquired Horace, eyeing him with curiosity.

Albi took the pipe out of his mouth and looked at him hard.

"You Gerolds are honest men," he said slowly: "your father is an honest man and a credit to human nature. Your brother promises to be like him; and I trust you will too. You have been so hitherto." And he laid a marked stress on that word *hitherto*.

CHAPTER XIII.

M. Pochemolle's Request.

THERE was no more talk about the five-and-twenty thousand francs. The conspirator Albi's utterances had fallen upon the free and easy conversation like a blast of hot air, withering it up by the roots. M. de Tirecruchon lapsed silent; and, presently, two of the crop-haired inmates of the penal wing coming in to lay the luncheon-cloth, Horace Gerold and Jean Kerjou took their leave.

"Lucky dogs!" sighed the fat editor, accompanying them to the end of the passage. "Yet two months before I may taste fresh air with you." He shook Horace's hand warmly, but holding it an instant, said: "Listen, M. Gerold. You pull too strong an oar for the *Sentinelle*. You're a man of independent views, and don't like running in grooves: as well harness a race-horse to a stone-cart, as keep you on a Radical paper. Your six months will be over soon. Come to me, you will find no dogmatism, and I don't set up for lecturing my contributors as to the acquaintances they choose."

Horace coloured at this inuendo. Truth to say, he felt humiliated by the rebuke of Nestor Roche, and by the covert warning implied in the last words of Albi. Time was when he might have submitted to be sermonized by the old Republican, whom he esteemed; but success had raised his spirit, and he resented the stiffness with which the overtures of M. Macrobe, as conveyed through him, had been repulsed. There was something quite unreasonable in this frame of mind:

for Nestor Roche might surely be excused for not feeling gushingly towards the man who had put him into prison; but reason is not the forte of youth; and in his pique, Horace bethought him seriously that he had a grievance against his editor.

He said as much to Jean Kerjou as they left Sainte Pélagie; and emitted one or two bitter reflections as to the obstinacy of old Republicans.

Jean Kerjou, being a Breton, was a Legitimist and a Catholic, and one who did not understand Republicans, nor quite realize what it was they wanted. His attachment to Horace had been formed on entirely personal grounds; but as he himself wore amulets next his shirt, signed himself when he swore, and never mentioned the name of Henri V. without doffing his hat, it was a subject of wonder to him how any one of birth and talent could profess the opinions which Horace Gerold did. In a simple tone, and rather puzzled, he answered: "I can't quite make out your party; you don't seem to agree among you as we do."

"Are there no men in your party who set up for oracles?" asked Horace; the puritan sternness of Nestor Roche, and the caustic fervour of Albi, recurring to him and nettling him.

"Perhaps there may be, but I don't know them," replied the Breton, naïvely. "I am sure, though, we have none who lecture about morality as I've heard them do every time I have been in the company of Republicans. Why don't you join our paper?" he added. "Tirecruchon is a loose fish on the surface, but a good fellow underneath; and he sets us no tether, you know: our staff is like a winter soup, full of herbs of all colours; we have two or three of your hue, but we all get on together swimmingly as beans in a pot."

Similes were one of the strong points of Jean Kerjou; they garnished his eloquence as the small dice of garlic do the roast legs of mutton in the province which was his birth-place. Horace, however, made no answer; and soon they reached the Rue Ste. Geneviève, where the first person they met was the courtly M. Pochemolle, who fingered a long piece of stamped paper which he had just received from an individual with a blue bag.

"This is for you, M. Horace. Something about this morning's business, I'm afraid," he added, in a tone of condolence.

True enough. It was a summons to appear before the Public Prosecutor, on the charge of having wilfully killed and slain one Paul Panier, commonly called de Cosaque. M. Macrobe and Jean Kerjou were both included in the summons, for having unlawfully, and of malice prepense, aided and abetted the perpetration of that crime.

Horace had already seen the Pochemolles once that morning, for on his way to Ste. Pélagie, after breakfasting with M. Macrobe, he had stopped to shake hands with Emile and show Georgette, who had been in sickly suspense since daybreak, that he was safe. He now walked into the shop with Jean Kerjou, under pretence of reading his summons, and found Georgette still pale, but with a ray of happiness in her eyes. She had just come in from out of doors, and was drawing off some tiny grey kid gloves, much smaller and finer than the daughters of drapers usually wear. So at least thought Jean Kerjou, who was observing her.

Madame Pochemolle was as gracious and smiling as it was her wont to be whenever M. Horace paid her a visit. M. Alcibiade Pochemolle, from sheer admiration at the sight of a man who had sent a fellow-being to his last account, allowed his ell-measure to drop. According to M. Alcibiade, the next best thing to having courage enough to kill a man oneself, was to behold some one who had performed such a deed. M. Alcibiade much regretted that he himself knew not how to fence. He was not ferocious; indeed, he was rather mild than otherwise; but he thought he should like to kill some other draper's son in fair combat.

Jean Kerjou, casting his eyes about the shop, which was fitted and wainscoted with the fine old oak of a century ago, lit upon the two famous prints showing the Rue Ste. Geneviève such as it existed in the reigns of Louis XIV. and XV., and having ventured to admire these heirlooms, was soon led to discover the monarchical, aristocratical, and clerical proclivities of the Pochemolle household. The draper, his wife, and the journalist then fell into harmonious talk and regrets over those good times when kings had no legislatures to plague them, when there was a gibbet stationed permanently in front of Notre Dame, and when a tradesman of the Rue Ste. Geneviève would not so much as have eaten an egg on a Friday without leave from the Bishop of Paris. Horace followed Georgette into the little back parlour, where she went to take off her bonnet. The door remained open, but there was no reason why any words spoken there should be heard in the shop. Horace spoke low.

"You have been for a walk, Georgette?"

"No," she murmured; "it was not a walk."

"Where then?"

She looked at him with more tenderness than she was aware of in her glistening eyes:

"To church," she whispered.

"To church, Georgette! But this isn't Sunday."

"It's more than that to me," she replied, with a touching accent.

"And to what saint did you pray?"

A tear or two welled up into her eyes as she blushed and said, almost inaudibly: "Could I keep away from thanking the Virgin on the day when your life has run such dangers and been spared?"

There was so much delicate modesty in her manner of murmuring these words, and when she had uttered them the emotion that suffused her face, and the grace which love lent to her demeanour, as she wavered between the fear of having said too much and the consciousness that all she might say would ill describe the tenth of what she felt—gave her such a charm that she looked to Horace more lovely and attractive than she had ever seemed before. He gazed on her with a sort of spell-bound and astonished admiration as one contemplates a picture whose full beauties one had not at first suspected. But even as he was gazing the current of his thoughts was turned by a sudden reflection. A voice rose up within him and put the question, like a note of reproof:—Whither was all this tending, and what did he hope would be the result of the love which he was encouraging in this poor girl?

He was not flippant or profligate, and the question unsettled him. The finer feelings in his nature revolted at the thought of trifling with the affections of a woman—a child almost—who seemed to have given him her heart; and yet, except an illicit passion—seduction and its attendant ties—there was but one possible course open to him, and that was to let Georgette think that he intended marrying her; and to do so. He was not prepared for this last step; and as the conviction forced itself upon him that he was drifting into straits where no man ever yet steered right who did not arm himself with inflexible resolution, a cloud passed over his brow, and he bit his lips.

Their eyes met—hers candid and trustful, his restless and uncertain. Then he said to himself: "I must remove from this house, else there will be misfortune on us all."

He rose abruptly, shook hands with Georgette without looking at her, muttered a few words about hoping soon to see her again, and passed through the shop, telling Jean Kerjou they would meet by-and-by, but that for the present he had letters to write. He hurried upstairs to his rooms, repeating to himself in a troubled frame of mind that he must go, and would explain why to Emile when the latter came home. But before he had reached his door he heard steps behind him, and the voice of M. Pochemolle hailed him with a petition for a minute's interview: "M. Horace, sir, if you could be so kind as to give me a moment of your time. I want to ask your advice."

"Walk in," answered Horace, absently.

When they were alone together—M. Pochemolle planted on a chair, and rubbing his ear to find a suitable exordium; Horace seated at his desk, expecting it was a legal opinion that was going to be asked of him—the draper began: "It's about Georgette, sir."

Horace started, and felt moisture bedewing his forehead.

"Yes, it's about my Georgette, sir," continued M. Pochemolle, not noticing anything. "If I might make so bold as to say so, M. Horace, I look upon you almost as an old friend now. You're a wiser man too than I am, notwithstanding your years, which comes of learning; and I want you to give me advice. To tell you the truth, sir, our Georgette has not been well of late; I told your honoured brother, M. Emile, so the other day. She's grown thin and pale, and doesn't talk as she used to do, nor laugh, nor seem to care much for things: all of which signs have been alarming her mother and me. But you know how women are, sir, and I don't think my wife and I would be likely to agree about our child's ailment, nor about the remedy for it. I ascribe a good deal of it to study and book-reading" (Horace gave a sigh of relief), "which is very well for men,—at least, for gentlemen —but isn't worth a rush for women. My respected mother—God bless her!—never read in any book save her ledger and her breviary, and this didn't prevent her making a true wife and a fine woman of business. But in these times old customs are dying out, and nothing would serve my wife but to have our Georgette brought up at a convent, where they taught her to strum on the piano, and paint flowers, and tell straight off on her fingers' ends who was Pope of Rome five hundred years ago, which seems to me about as useless knowledge for a tradesman's daughter as well can be. However, it was no good my attempting to say anything, for when I wanted our Georgette to be taught cooking, and book-keeping, and all that makes a useful housewife, her mother wouldn't hear of it. My wife, you see, is of the modern sort. She wants me to make haste and get rich, and outshine our neighbours, and be a finer man than my father was; and as for Georgette, she dresses her up in silk, and counts upon marrying her to some gentleman who'll be several cuts above us, and shut his door in our faces when we go and call upon our child. Now, that's all very well in its way, but in Georgette's own interest, M. Horace, I want to prevent it. Not that I should grudge my daughter a husband after her own fancy, if I thought she had set her heart upon any one, and I found the man was respectable and paid his bills punctually; but I don't think she has; and there's a youth I've in my mind who's in love with her, and a very thrifty, intelligent lad into the bargain, who'd be sure to make her happy, and I should like to bring the two together."

Horace took up a quill, and hacked it with a pen-knife.

"Who is this youth, M. Pochemolle?"

"Well, sir, he's a commercial traveller. He's not often in Paris, but when he does come he lodges up on the sixth floor above our heads, renting a room there all the year round. He's a cheerful young man, always ready—too ready some say—to crack his joke, and has known our Georgette ever since they were both no higher than this chair."

"Indeed!" broke in Horace, rather drily; "is it the gentleman I have met once or twice on the staircase, who wears a Scotch tartan waistcoat, with a brass chain over it, rattles pence in his pockets, and whistles the *Marseillaise* every time he comes upstairs?"

"That's he I daresay," assented M. Pochemolle thoughtfully; "though I've never heard him whistle the

Marseillaise; but his chain's gold, M. Horace, I assure you, and probably eighteen-carat, for he's very well off. His name's Filoselle; he's been travelling since he was twenty, getting five per cent. profit on all his commissions, and he's now twenty-eight, which makes a good deal of money. If he marries our Georgette, as he hopes to do, he means to set up in business for himself with the savings he has laid by."

Horace closed his pen-knife with a snap.

"And in what way can I assist you, M. Pochemolle?" he inquired.

"Well, sir," responded the draper, too intent upon his own thoughts to remark aught unusual in the tone of his lodger,—"Well, sir, M. Filoselle is a great favourite with us all, on account of his amusing ways. I sometimes think he'd make a stuffed bird laugh would that young man. Of a winter evening, when he's in Paris, he often comes in, and makes himself sociable, telling stories, and playing tricks with cards, and the like; and turning the things upside down; and my wife thinks well of him, I'm sure; but between that and accepting him as a husband for Georgette, is a long way; and, as for Georgette herself, why, I fancy she looks upon him as an old playfellow, but nothing else: so that Filoselle feels in a fix, and last time he was here, he told me that he shouldn't like to touch upon the question with the women downstairs until I had put in a good word for him."

Here M. Pochemolle shrugged his shoulders, and continued, dolefully, "But my putting in a good word would be just about as much use as arguing with a deaf post. My wife is a good woman, and I don't say but that she and I have got on smoothly together; but there's no tackling her about her daughter. On that point she's hoighty-toity, and as foolish as women are when they get any fixed idea into their heads. I think, though, M. Horace" (and here the honest draper became appealing),—"I think you might help us. My wife has a high opinion of you, which is only natural and properly respectful on her part, and supposing, for instance, one day you had dropped into the shop by hazard like, I was to set the talk rolling on commercial travellers, and you were to join in and say there wasn't a more honourable profession going, and that they earned a deal of money, and were quite on a level with gentlemen, I think, sir, that might settle it."

M. Pochemolle fixed his eyes interrogatively on Horace.

"And have you yourself this high opinion of commercial travellers?" asked the latter.

"Well, I've a good opinion of those who get on in the business," answered the draper. "My wife she's all for scented gentlemen—even when they've got nothing in their pockets, which is less seldom than one supposes. If she could, she'd make a gentleman of me. As it is, she talked me into doing what I'd never done in my life before—invest money in one of those giant new companies that are all full like a balloon to-day and all squash like nothing to-morrow. Happily, it's the Crédit Parisien, which, M. Macrobe tells me, is as safe as the Bank of France—and there's no denying it pays up well, and the shares are rising like quicksilver; but, to speak my mind, M. Horace, I don't fancy those kind of things. It's always been a motto in our family to sell fairly, to be content with few customers but good, and to look to small profits but safe; and the man I want for my son-in-law is a man who thinks like me as nearly as possible—as I believe Filoselle does. He's not a genius, maybe, though geniuses behind the counter seem to me as much out of place as whales in a fish-tank; but he's a shrewd fellow, who'll give his wife a good home, never let himself be caught with chaff, and keep clear of the Tribunal de Commerce."

The two purple ears, which ornamented the sides of M. Pochemolle's head like the handles of a jug, deepened in hue as he concluded the panegyric of his prospective son-in-law, and looked at the young barrister for an answer.

Had Horace prayed for it he could not have lighted upon a better opportunity of bringing his as yet innocent but dangerous *liaison* with Georgette to an end. Nevertheless (O consistency of human nature!) the idea of Georgette being married now caused him, of a sudden, unaccountable vexation bordering on jealousy. He dismissed M. Pochemolle with a vague assurance that he would see about the matter, and do his best; and, when the good man had departed, happy with having obtained his powerful co-operation, he paced about his room, pondering how he might best thwart this intended marriage. Such is man where women are concerned—a being more capricious than woman herself.

Of course he did not acknowledge to himself of what nature were the feelings that prompted him to think as he was doing, for the human mind, in its queerest fits of selfishness, is ever ingenious at putting a colour of honesty on its schemes. He argued with himself that Georgette was too good for this commercial traveller, who wore a tartan waistcoat, and looked like a snob; that he would be doing her a service in preventing her being tied for life to this man; that she was a refined, well-educated girl, who deserved a better fate, &c. &c. The Devil, who was close at hand, found him logic as much as he needed.

Whilst he was thus brooding peevishly, not very well-pleased with himself, he strayed into his brother's room, and stopped, with his eyes fixed on the portrait of his and Emile's mother hanging over the mantelpiece.

Their mother was as a dim vision to both the brothers, for she had died when they were too young to miss the guiding spirit they were losing. Horace, however, being by three years the eldest, could remember more than Emile, and he would often gaze abstractedly at the portrait, trying to recall a living image from out of the faint pencilled features. He did so now; and the effect upon him was soothing and beneficial as all thoughts of a loved and lost mother must be. Whilst he looked, the unworthy impulses within him seemed slowly to subside, then to melt. His better nature regained the mastery. He felt ashamed of having wavered even for a moment, and took the resolution there and then to do his duty. "I must not see Georgette again," he murmured; "and I had better do what her father wishes—put in a word for this tradesman."

"Ah! they told me you were at home," cried a voice behind him. "I've come to fetch you off to dinner. You know we've got things to talk about. We're going to be tried for manslaughter together."

And M. Macrobe, who had intruded himself noiselessly into the room, held out his hand.

Horace gave a start, but he shook the hand, though it seemed to him that in doing so he was swearing friendship to a sort of black-coated Mephistopheles.

CHAPTER XIV.

M. Macrobe inserts the thin End of the Wedge.

M. MACROBE'S face was against him, but if you gave him half-an-hour to talk it away, and another half-hour to make you forget the suspicious stories you had heard concerning him, he was a pleasant companion. He took Horace to dine at his own house in the Avenue des Champs Elysées: not a formal repast with guests eyeing one another ceremoniously over white neck-ties, but what he called a quiet dinner *sans façon*, to which he had invited a few nice fellows, and at which there were no ladies present. Our young friend was a little surprised at the luxury of the banker's residence, to which he had as yet seen nothing comparable, not even in the one or two lordly mansions of the Faubourg St. Germain where it had been his fate to visit. Everything, from the glossy livery of the porter, who swung open the gilt bronze gates as they drove up, down to the cypher and crest engraved on the massive plate of the dinner-table, bore the impress of solid, although new-made wealth. It was not foolish wealth however, such as does not know where to bestow itself, and heaps around it vulgar and cumbersome splendour which dazzles without exciting admiration. M. Macrobe had seen too much of life not to have learned good taste. As he ushered his guest through a series of spacious and elegantly appointed saloons into a dining-room teeming with brilliancy and light, he flattered himself that if there were houses in

Paris equal to his own, there were few superior, and he was not wrong.

The emotions of the day had been so numerous and varied that they had slightly unnerved Horace, and disposed him to accept any diversion as welcome. He was in that state of mind when friendliness comes as a balm, and slight attentions are received with a gratitude deeper sometimes than the occasion warrants. His duel of the morning—the gloomy horror of which was beginning to strike him with dull force now that he was cool and could reason;—his unsatisfactory interview with Nestor Roche; the doubts that he could not altogether allay as to the conduct he ought to have adopted and should adopt in the future towards Georgette; all these were harassing topics, which he was glad to dismiss for a while from his agitated brain. So the dinner was a relief to him, and, therefore, from M. Macrobe's point of view, a success. That gentleman had indeed spared nothing to make it so. The viands were choice, the conversation agreeable, and the guests all men famous in their respective walks, who treated Horace with a courteous deference that flattered him. Jean Kerjou was there, endowed with the excellent appetite that befitted his mediæval tastes, and, like his friend, not sorry to place the fumes of champagne between himself and the bloody scene of the morning. The Breton journalist had a constitutional horror of bloodshed—which was the more remarkable as he himself had been out twice, and each time killed his man. But, perhaps, in his opinion this did not count, for he was a fiery Papist, and the two brother-journalists he had slain were only Voltairians.

The other guests were: Baron Margauld the banker,

husband to the Madame de Margauld Horace had already met in society—a grave, emphatic man, suspected of Orleanism, but respected by the Government on account of his solid credit and his unaffected detestation of Radicals; M. Arsène Gousset, a sparkling novelist, in great favour at court, and mightily popular with women, though he passed his time in railing bitterly at the former and inditing cutting satires upon the latter; and the Prince of Arcola, descended from one of the first Napoleon's Field-Marshals—a young gentleman of eight-and-twenty, with a very grand air and high tone, tempered, however, with a good-humoured listlessness, which generally rose to the surface once the ice of formalism was broken. This, with the eminent surgeon who had attended the combat in the morning, made seven who sat down to table. But presently, when the soup had been removed, and two giants were handing round turbot and salmon-trout, entered, like a rush of wind, Mr. Drydust the celebrated correspondent of a London penny paper, who, with florid grace, excused himself for being late, on the ground that he had just been having an interview with the Minister of State. It was the peculiarity and good fortune of Mr. Drydust that he was always having interviews with Cabinet Ministers.

As the duel had created a considerable sensation and was for the nonce the one subject of gossip about town, it was unavoidable that some allusion should be made to it, and that Horace should receive the congratulations which are customary under such circumstances. Mr. Drydust, especially, seemed to know more about the occurrence than the parties themselves. He had written a full-length and erroneous account of it to his paper that afternoon, and on learning that he actually had opposite to him the man who had rid Paris of the dreaded M. de Cosaque, he proceeded, somewhat to the dismay of M. Macrobe, to rattle off with immense volubility, and in first-rate French, the names of all the illustrious persons of his acquaintance who had fought duels—winding up with the case of two distinguished British nobles who had wished to exterminate one another on Calais sands, but had been happily prevented by his timely interference. Horace listened with a rather embarrassed air; and Jean Kerjou furtively made the sign of the cross, in obedience to the superstition which holds it unlucky to speak of slaughter at table. But Mr. Drydust soon turned his attention to other themes. He apostrophized the Prince of Arcola:

"Prince, I was at Chantilly the day before yesterday, and saw your filly, *Mogador*, do her canter. Take my advice and back her in preference to her stable-companion, *Namouna*, for the *Prix de Diane*. I was talking about it to Lagrange; he thinks she'll win."

"Ah!" said the Prince, languidly, "I thought Count de Lagrange had got a filly of his own in the race."

"So he has; but I told him it wasn't worth a stiver. Lord Martingale was of the same opinion."

"Why, what has come over the filly then? Last week Lord Martingale backed her against my stable at five to one."

The Prince of Arcola had two passions: horse-racing and nobility. On the first he spent two-thirds of his income, which was large; on the second he lavished what spare time he had, reading books of heraldry and chivalrous chronicles. It was a most sore point with him that his title dated no further back than half a century, and had been conferred, in a batch, by a Napoleon. He would have bartered it with all his heart, high-sounding as it was, for a simple barony of mediæval creation; and when M. Macrobe whispered to him, in introducing Horace Gerold, that this was the young barrister who might call himself Marquis of Clairefontaine if he chose, he eyed Horace much as one contemplates a phenomenon, and soon set the conversation going on the Castle of Hautbourg, which he appeared to know from roof to basement, furniture included, as if he had been residing there for the last twelvemonth. He had a way of talking, when launched on his favourite topics, which lacked neither fire nor grace; and Horace followed him with a secret and altogether new interest as he dilated with enthusiasm on the broad acres, grey towers, old pictures, arms and sculptured halls of Hautbourg. "One of the finest domains I know," said he, "in this or any other country. Do you often go down there for shooting?" he added: and this question breaking the spell, Horace answered, a little drily, that he never went there at all. Whereat the Prince stared, and by-and-by observed with a sigh: "Political conviction must be very strong, M. Gerold, to make one renounce such treasures. *I* couldn't do it."

Mr. Drydust, who was patronizing the banker Margauld, giving him information as to scrip and share, current quotations, and the prospects of the new Irrawaddi loan, here cut in. He had caught the word "shooting," and immediately started upon a description of the great estates with which he was familiar— Windsor Castle, Knowsley, Chatsworth, Stowe, Eaton

Court, &c.: all places where, by his own account, he was wont to go and divert himself with a few weeks' sport when he had nothing better to do. His rapid sketches were so vivid and well-coloured that M. Arsène Gousset, deferring modestly to him as a superior genius, remarked how much democratic France was behind aristocratic England from the artist's point of view.

"With our code of equality and our parcelling of land," said he, "we have suppressed great wealth and pomp, and, consequently, picturesqueness. Wishing to be all of a size, we have dragged the nobles off their high towers and forced them to stand shoulder to shoulder with us in a flat plain, where no man's head may rise above those of his fellows under pain of making the rest cry out. French society has become a landscape without hills, a sea without waves, a house without gables;—anything you please that is dull and commonplace. It may be correct, but it is very ugly."

"Yet equality is one of the first conditions of progress," remarked the eminent surgeon; who, like most eminent surgeons, professed extreme liberalism, the more so at this moment, as he had expected to be made surgeon to the court, but been disappointed.

"Ah! progress," exclaimed the novelist, with a shrug, as he put down a glass of Tokay,—"progress, doctor, is a word coined by journalists and barristers, to signify that now-a-days it is they who rule the roast. We have superseded the nobles, and given ourselves for a prey to the men who talk and the men who write, and we call that abolishing caste rule. They say merit has better chances than it used to have; but, pray, when was merit more respected than when low-born Froissart consorted on terms of equality with the proudest noblemen of France? when Rabelais, a witty curate, was the friend of Francis the First? when Charles the Ninth did homage in verse to Ronsard? and when Louis the Fourteenth himself, who would not have bared his head to an emperor, waited at table upon Molière? If we look past history through, we shall scarce find a man of any worth in art, politics, or science, who was not petted, honoured, and enriched by the great of his time. With all our boast of progress and equality, there is not a court in Europe that would receive a goldsmith as Benvenuto Cellini was received at the Court of France; there is not a potter of our day who could hope to win the distinctions that Bernard de Palissy earned. Charles the Fifth of France ennobled the man who set up the first clock; did we do as much for the man who invented photography? Gutemberg, it is true, led a struggling life, but was George Stephenson's path strewn with roses? and of the two, which, think you, were most to blame, the mediævals who were tardy to acknowledge the advantages of writing by machinery instead of by hand, or the moderns who, after recognizing what they term the benefits of railways, suffered the inventor to be laid in the earth without a single token of gratitude from the state? In politics, again, because we stock our cabinets with superannuated lawyers and jaded leader-writers, carefully excluding the rest of the world, we cry out that we have thrown open a broad career to talent, just as if our ancestors had not done so before us, and more liberally. What were Richelieu and Colbert but friendless men of middle-class estate, who, by mere dint of adroitness, acquired the patronage of powerful noblemen, by whom they were introduced and pushed forward at court? The fact is, any man with brains and pleasant manners could make his way in former times, and was not obliged to wait until his teeth were loose and his hair fell off, as seems to be indispensable in our day. A fellow of parts attached himself to the suite of a noble, became his patron's adviser, then his friend, was presented to the king, flattered him—and why not? I would as lief flatter a king to obtain a bunch of seals as a ragamuffin to catch a vote—and with a little patience and wit rose to be Prime Minister, like the two I have named; or High Chancellor, like L'Hôpital and Harlay; or Marshal of France, like Turenne and Catinat (who were the sons of small country gentlemen); or Bishop, like Bossuet and Fléchier,—the latter of whom was bred a tallow-chandler. The best of it was, too, that we took these men young, when their intellects were in their vigour: for progress had not yet made it a law that our statesmen should be old men stricken with the gout, and our generals aged cripples, with all the genius frozen out of them by rheumatism. Had they lived in our day, Richelieu would have been, at thirty, a curate with fifty napoleons a year; Turenne a lieutenant, wondering whether he should ever be a major; and Colbert a government clerk in the office of Mr. Drydust's friend, Monsieur Gribaud."

Mr. Drydust nodded assent. He thought the atmosphere of modern civilization stifling. Nevertheless, he was in favour of penny papers. All things considered, he should like to be living under Louis XI., with the cheap press flourishing as an institution.

THE THIN END OF THE WEDGE. 247

But the novelist was averse to such a combination. He was not fond of the Press, and took no pains to conceal it. Cracking filberts composedly, and smiling within his well-trimmed yellow beard, he amused himself and the rest of the table by passing in review the Paris Press, and grimly bespattering the whole journalistic profession, without bitterness, but without mercy. He made an exception in favour of the *Sentinelle* and the *Gazette des Boulevards*, out of respect for the two writers present; but he could not refrain from giving a side cuff to the editors of those journals, MM. de Tirecruchon and Roche: the former of whom he described as the most agreeable humbug he knew, and the latter as a vinegar-cruet—cold without and sour within. It was pleasure to watch the starched features of the Baron Margauld relax whilst this performance was going on. He, too, was no friend of the Press: "a dangerous, meddlesome institution," as he termed it.

His satisfaction bordered upon mirth when the novelist continued: "You are right to call the Press a power, for it is a power for destruction, like gunpowder or corrosive acid: but it has never built up anything, and never will. Since daily newspapers have come among us, the word 'stability' has ceased to have any sense, and should disappear from the dictionary. Nothing is stable now-a-days: neither thrones, nor constitutions, nor religions. A journalist is a man who devotes his time to finding out the weak points in human institutions, political or social, and hammering upon them continually until the whole structure falls to pieces. There is very little discrimination in his work: for with him it is not a question of being right or wrong, but of filling up three or six columns a week. If the times be fertile in large abuses, so much the wider his choice of subjects; but if the Government be an honest one, and there be only small abuses, he will assail these small abuses at just the same length, and with precisely the same vigour of invective, as the larger ones. Louis Philippe was attacked more severely than Charles X., and the Republic of '48 more pitilessly than Louis Philippe. There is not a government on earth can bear up against the three-column system; heaven itself couldn't stand it. If ever the millennium arrives, it will have to begin by gagging the Press, else in twenty years it will go the way of all other governments."

The banker Margauld bent his head and coughed, in token of enthusiastic concurrence. But the Prince of Arcola whispered, with a smile, to his neighbour: "I fancy M. Gousset is himself a victim of the three-column system. His last novel met with some rather rough handling, did it not?"

It was now time for coffee; and M. Macrobe rose to lead the way to his smoking-room—an apartment of sybaritish comfort and luxury, fitted up like an Arab tent, with Turkey carpets a foot thick, and low divans, into which the human form sank, stretched enjoyably at full length.

In the passage to this *buen-retiro* Mr. Drydust naturally contrived to push to the front once more as leader of the conversation,—the only post his coruscating genius brooked. Cigars, with curiously outlandish names, but of exquisite smell and savour, were produced from cedar-wood cases; the powdered gentlemen poured fragrant coffee, steaming hot, into cups

small and transparent as egg-shells; and whilst the
fumes of Mocha, blending with those of Havannah,
were rising spirally towards the ceiling, the British
journalist resumed his observations upon men and
things, and the company were soon wrapped in the
pyrotechnic blaze of that gentleman's utterances, which
were always entertaining, sometimes even dazzling to
his audience. The performance was not so engrossing,
however, but that the Prince of Arcola, who was seated
on the same ottoman as Horace, found occasion to
strike up with the latter what the French call an exchange of good proceedings. He admired the modest
young barrister. He paid him compliments with that
insinuating and polished grace of which the French
are such masters, asked him to breakfast at his house
in the Rue Lafitte—one of the largest and most hospitable in the Chaussée d'Antin—and ended by offering
to propose him for election at the club of the Rue
Royale.

"You should belong to a club," said he: "clubs
are social ménageries; one meets all the lions there.
They are one of the many good things we have borrowed from the English, to whom we are indebted
for pretty nearly everything that makes existence toler-
able."

"I shall be happy to second you," added Baron
Margauld, whom Horace struck as a quiet, earnest
young man, and worth weaning from Radicalism.

Horace thanked them, but declined: for a Paris
club and a London one are not quite the same things.
In four cases out of five the former is little more than
a sumptuous gambling-house in disguise; and of all
the gambling-houses of the capital, the Cercle de la

Rue Royale was the most celebrated as well as the most splendid. The Prince did not press his offer, but wondered a little that Horace should allege want of means as one of the reasons for declining it.

The court novelist volunteered on his side to introduce Gerold to some of the leading authors, and this proposal was accepted gratefully.

"I know most of the journalists," said Horace, "and I have seen Monsieur Hugo at Brussels; but I should feel it an honour to be acquainted with our other national glories—M. de Musset, M. Ponsard, M. Gautier, and Mdme. Sand." He added something gracious as a hint that he had perused all M. Arsène Gousset's works, and ranked him, too, amongst the national glories. The novelist was sensible to the homage, and, towards midnight, when Horace had retired with his friend, Jean Kerjou, after accepting the Prince of Arcola's invitation to breakfast, and making a luncheon appointment with M. Macrobe for the next day, that they might appear before the Public Prosecutor together, he exclaimed with some admiration: "Good blood will out. That young Gerold has the manners of a duke: he is serious, dignified, and absolutely unaffected. It is incomprehensible to me that he should elect to be a *sansculotte*."

"He has fallen into bad hands," sighed M. Macrobe unctuously.

"Yes, but what makes him talk about the mediocrity of his means?" interposed the Prince of Arcola, with curiosity. "The Hautbourg estates are worth a million francs a year, if they are worth a centime. What do the Gerolds do with all their money?"

"Ah, there you put a question I should like to

solve myself," replied M. Macrobe. "The Gerolds are millionaires, I know, but they live as if they were poor. The father has a small lodging on a fifth floor at Brussels; I had inquiries made there by our correspondent. The police think they spend their fortune on secret societies; but this is probably a guess."

"There would be no derogation in it," said the Prince. "If a man of birth goes in for people's rights he is quite right to do it grandly; and there would be something not unbecoming in young Gerold putting himself at the head of an occult social movement destined to revolutionize the country. After all, he would only be re-enacting the part the Montmorencys and the Colignys played when they took the lead of the Huguenots, who were the Radicals of their time."

"For myself," chimed in the court novelist, composedly, "I should not be sorry if there were a good sanguinary break-out, like the Reign of Terror, only worse. I am convinced that if the Radicals were allowed their head for a few years, they would lead France such a gallop that she would leap madly back into royalty, feudalism, and rabid popery to get rid of them. Then we should have a century or so of peace."

"God bless my soul! you are surely not speaking in earnest," cried out the banker Margauld in disgust. He had seen revolutions face to face, and thought them no themes for jocularity. Happily Mr. Drydust was by to reassure him. According to this eminent person the Second Empire was unshakable, having the sympathies of democratic England with it. These sympathies found expression in the penny sheet, to which Mr. Drydust contributed, and were enough to keep any throne stable to all eternity. "Besides," added he, "you may make your mind perfectly easy, Baron, and you too, M. Macrobe, for M. Gerold does not spend his money on secret societies. I will tell the Prefect of Police so next time I talk to him. I know the man who is the soul of all the French secret societies: it's that arch-revolutionist Albi: he's in prison now—an intimate friend of mine—but a dark-minded character, who would no more agree with young Gerold, nor roost in the same nest with him, than a crow would with a starling." Then Mr. Drydust proceeded to explain how secret societies were organized; after which he speculated as to how the Gerolds spent their money; but eventually finding the problem insoluble, branched off into a disquisition upon "odd people," whose lives were a mystery to the community. M. Macrobe reiterated his regrets that Gerold had fallen into bad hands, and Mr. Drydust assented. He further engaged to bring him back by degrees to the right way, by giving him as much of his society as was compatible with his—Mr. Drydust's—other and multifarious occupations.

Meanwhile, the subject of these remarks, rolling homewards in a cab, was reflecting with satisfaction on the delicate, and even generous, behaviour of M. Macrobe: for just as Horace was leaving, the financier had drawn him aside and said: "My dear young friend, I am not surprised at M. Roche having refused the twenty-five thousand francs: for, though honest, I fancy he is a little opiniated—isn't he?—and not quite exempt from narrow-mindedness. Such at least is the character he has always borne in the Press, and, if you will allow me to say so, I have heard it deplored that a man of your wonderful and shining abilities should be tied to the same wheel as a person so cramped in intellect. The money must now go to the poor, and here I should really esteem it a favour if you could recommend me any worthy persons on whom to bestow it. As a liberal writer, you are, probably, often besieged with applications from needy people, whose political opinions make it difficult for them to obtain relief through the usual channels. There must be numerous families of poor Republicans who took part in the affair of '48, and who would stand no chance of obtaining anything from the Municipal Bureaux de Bienfaisance: these are the very people I should like to assist. And now, as to this trial of ours, I suppose you are aware that, from a certain point of view, it is a less serious matter to kill one's adversary in a duel than to wound him. If you wound him, you are tried in the Correctional Court by three judges, without jury, and you are safe to be imprisoned; in the other case, you are arraigned at the Assizes before a jury, and are invariably acquitted. However, we shall have to prepare a defence of some sort, and so I have been thinking we could not do better than have one counsel for the three of us, and that counsel your own brother, whose abilities I hear so warmly eulogized. The trial will be sure to draw a great crowd, and will help him forward in his profession. I shall instruct my solicitor to offer him my brief, and I trust you will prevail upon him to accept it."

"It was thoughtful," mused Horace; "and it was gracious. The man is a gentleman, and it is a pity I ever joined in calumniating him."

CHAPTER XV.

How Empires are governed.

ON the morrow, at about the time when Horace Gerold, Jean Kerjou, and M. Macrobe were being minutely cross-questioned by the Public Prosecutor as to their motives for maliciously slaying an official journalist, his Excellency M. Gribaud, Minister of State, was holding audiences at his residence in the Louvre, and it was noticed by all whom applications for patronage, favours, or redress brought into contact with that great man, that his Excellency was not at all in a good humour that morning.

Towards mid-day M. Camille de Beaufeuillet, one of the Minister's secretaries, a grave diplomatic young gentleman of irreproachable attire, issued from his chief's presence, and remarked to a brother secretary in an ante-room: "The governor has turned out of bed the wrong side this morning."

"Ah!" exclaimed the other, with an intonation that betokened neither amazement nor great concern; and looking up from the *Moniteur* with which he was beguiling the tedium of business hours, he added: "Summer heat doesn't agree with the old fellow; he's been bitter as a weed this some time past."

"He has sent me out to take stock of the unfortunates who are kicking their heels about in the waiting-rooms," resumed M. de Beaufeuillet; and saying this, he touched a bell on the table.

An usher with a silver chain round his neck, appeared.

"Is the slate very full, Bernard?"

"Very, sir; I much fear his Excellency will have a heavy morning; there are above twenty people waiting." And at the bidding of the young man, the venerable Bernard recapitulated the names of all the persons in attendance—a goodly list, on which figured many ladies of beauty come to solicit distinctions for their husbands; many gentlemen devoid of beauty, but replete with ambition, come to beg honours for themselves; and a remnant of individuals whose errands were purely disinterested and undertaken only from a desire to serve the State. Amongst these last was our friend Mr. Drydust, who stated that his business was important.

"I think you had better show in the English journalist first," hazarded M. Camille. "I believe the Government considers him useful."

But at that moment, entered a second usher, who said: "M. Louchard, the Commissary of Police, has just arrived." An intimation which caused the secretary to vanish for a minute, and, on returning, to say: "M. Louchard takes precedence of everybody. His Excellency will see him at once."

In another couple of minutes M. Louchard, the commissary, had been conducted deferentially through the ante-room, and was closeted in private with the Minister. The two secretaries pulled faces behind him when he had passed; but this M. Louchard did not notice.

His Excellency M. Gribaud was one of the bulwarks of the Second Empire. Formerly, he had been one of the bulwarks of the Republic, and indeed it was his mission, in a general way, to be the bulwark of every party that happened to be in the ascendant. In appearance, he somewhat belied his Christian name of Augustus, for he was not august at all; but he had a curious penetrating eye, that partook of the vulture's and the money-lender's, and a tongue as pointed and insinuating as a gimlet. It was this tongue that had helped to make the fortune of M. Gribaud. Most people when speaking in public are apt to hesitate now and then to find the correct term: but not so M. Gribaud. Nobody had ever known him pause for a word. Correct or no, he spoke straight on with imperturbable assurance, and the policy he pursued in elocution he followed, also, in all the aims of his life —never allowing himself to be impeded by a scruple, nor baulked by a regard for others. Such a man was sure to succeed. He was just the Minister to ride rough-shod over opposition, for there was no silencing him, and he was not in the least particular as to his choice of argumentative weapons. If pressed close by the logic of an adversary, he quietly called him a liar. One of his greatest oratorical triumphs had been obtained by accusing an honourable political opponent of being sold to a foreign government. He had no proofs to support the charge, but neither had his antagonist any to refute it; and, in such cases, it is always the more worthy of the contending parties— *i.e.* the man in office—who is believed. The charge almost broke the heart of the political opponent, but it greatly added to the credit of M. Gribaud, who came to be looked upon in Imperialist circles as a debater of no ordinary value.

When the Commissary of Police entered, M. Gribaud was seated at his desk, dressed in black clothes too large for him, and a stiff white cravat, that gave him the appearance of an unusually ferocious Dissenting minister. With a thick, knotty hand he was holding up a pair of double eyeglasses, through which he scrutinized, narrowly and frowningly, a despatch from a prefect. At sight of M. Louchard he wasted no time in vain courtesies, but cried out, "I can't make out what your agents are about, M. Louchard. They never tell one anything. All the information I get as to passing events comes from private sources. Two Roman republicans spent the day before yesterday in Paris, and you were quite ignorant of the fact; yet your orders are to keep the closest watch upon every Italian who sets foot in the city."

"I am sure they did not put up at any hotel, your Excellency," pleaded M. Louchard, humbly but firmly, "else I should have known it, and sent you a report."

"They came by the mail-train from England, and returned the same night. Your detectives at the railway-terminus should have recognized them for Italians, and followed them. Had they been bent upon assassinating any of us, they might have done it with complete security. But that is not all. Why have I had no report about the three medical students, who hissed a loyal song at a music-hall last Monday night? nor about M. Giroux-Ette, my predecessor in office, and a senator, who, on Tuesday, conversed amicably for a whole hour in a public place with the Radical barrister, Claude Febvre? nor about Madame de Masseline, the wife of an official deputy, who spoke slightingly of me at one of her dinner-parties?—Why have I been apprised of none of these circumstances? The police are growing either blind or careless, M. Louchard."

"Not blind or careless, your Excellency," protested M. Louchard, with meekness; "but the police have a great deal to do, and it is difficult for them to be everywhere at once."

"What is the use of them, then?" retorted the Minister, roughly. "It is the business of the police to have their eyes everywhere. We don't stint you with money. You should see into every house as if its walls were of glass."

"We do our best," muttered M. Louchard. "There are few houses of consequence where we have not one or two emissaries on the visiting list. Madame de Masseline herself is most zealous in conveying information as to all she hears, and I am certain that if she allowed herself to speak disparagingly of your Excellency, it was rather for the purpose of sounding her guests than to emit any opinion of her own."

"Humph!" murmured his Excellency, who appeared less certain than the police official. "I did not know Madame de Masseline was on your books, M. Louchard. If I were you I would rely as little as possible on women; their information is seldom accurate, and there is generally some woman's quarrel or jealous pique at the bottom of their denunciations. I have noticed they never tell tales of a man who has a good figure and curly hair, unless they have been jilted by him. But enough of this. What have you got to tell me this morning?"

"I have come about this Gerold affair—this duel," began M. Louchard. "I thought your Excellency might have some orders to give me."

"A pretty piece of work that duel," grumbled the Minister, his brow darkening. "You suffered this pestilent young Radical to kill one of our most serviceable writers; yet you had several hours' notice of the duel, and might easily have stopped it."

"I counted that matters would turn out differently. I imagined M. de Cosaque would kill M. Gerold," observed the commissary, naïvely.

"You don't seem very lucky in your calculations," was the Minister's dry answer; but he passed lightly over the subject, for he too had known of the duel beforehand, and if he had not thought expedient to stop it, there is a presumption that some such motive lay uppermost in his mind as had actuated M. Louchard. He remained silent a moment, stroking his short pointed chin with his hard hand, and peering with a brooding expression at the commissary. Perhaps during that moment he recalled the time when the two young Gerolds were bright boys, whom he used to go and see at school, and when their father was a friend whom he honoured and by whom he was esteemed. Those were far-off days, and probably the remembrance of them was not over-pleasant: for M. Gribaud broke out morosely: "Look here, M. Louchard: I've had enough of this M. Horace Gerold. Things were going on very well before he turned up; the Opposition were almost silent: but now it looks as if the old nonsense were coming back. This young Gerold is becoming a power. People talk about him in society, he has all the women on his side; in a word, he is dangerous. It is time you saw to him. That was a very suspicious document you showed me some time ago—I mean that deed of gift. If those two youths are already possessors of the Hautbourg estate, they are millionaires, and their leading the bread-and-water life they do is a queer circumstance that has a strong smell of conspiracy about it. You must have a close surveillance set upon both the brothers;

they must not be lost sight of a minute; you must ascertain what they do, where they go, whom they see: their letters must be opened at the post-office, and if you discover that they habitually frequent or correspond with men of extreme opinions, there will be enough in that to furnish a handle to the Public Prosecutor. At all events—and I hope you understand me, M. Louchard—M. Horace Gerold must be got rid of; we must frighten him into running back to Belgium, and if he won't go, why" (M. Gribaud threw a significant glance at the commissary)—"why I daresay it won't be very difficult to send him where tougher men than he have gone—on a forced voyage to Cayenne."

Accustomed as M. Louchard was to the mention of Cayenne and Lambessa as fitting places of resort for Liberals, and animated as he moreover was, against Horace Gerold by the recollection of how the latter had treated him on the occasion of the domiciliary visit, he felt a creeping sensation in the back at the grim coolness of the Minister's tone. M. Gribaud, indeed, made no more bones about removing an enemy from his path than about filliping a speck of dust off his coat. The commissary answered with his usual abject deference: "It shall be done as your Excellency wishes." Then he twirled his hat for a few moments between his fingers, as if doubtful whether to proceed with certain other communications he had intended making, until, finally, a thought seemed to strike him, and he said:—"If your Excellency will allow me to express an opinion, I think M. Horace Gerold, though dangerous, may turn out to be less so than his brother. My men have had their eyes on both for some time, and M. Emile is the one who appears to me the most vicious. He never goes into society nor to the theatre; he works very hard; he has few friends, and those all of the worst sort—hardened Republicans; he distributes a great deal of money amongst the poor, and visits them at their own houses; he also lends them books, which I take to be a mischievous symptom: for the poor who read become unmanageable. M. Horace, I am bound to say, is just the contrary. He mixes a good deal with everybody, and just now he has got into good hands—those of M. Macrobe, the banker, your Excellency. If your Excellency would have very precise information as to M. Horace Gerold's sayings and doings, there is not a better man to apply to than M. Macrobe. He had M. Gerold to dinner with him last night; and being a most loyal Imperialist, deeply attached to your Excellency, I can vouch that he would completely enter into your views with regard to watching the young man and reporting all he saw."

A belief in M. Macrobe—that is, in the man whose financial science was so profound, and whose hints were such a godsend to those on whom he deigned to bestow them—was one of the articles of M. Louchard's creed. He therefore turned completely sallow when in a short tone M. Gribaud replied:—"M. Macrobe is coming here presently, and possibly I may have to give you some instructions concerning *him*, M. Louchard. I have sent for him to explain his conduct in overtly taking part against a Government writer in a public restaurant, and in assisting this M. Gerold as second. M. Macrobe is a gentleman who had best mind his *p*'s and *q*'s. He has been tolerated because he was useful; but if he thinks himself strong enough to indulge in vagaries, he must be shown he is mistaken."

M. Louchard dug his right hand deep into one of the hind pockets of his coat, and drew from it a yellow bandanna handkerchief, of which he proceeded to make a sudden and noisy use. Had any of the familiars of the commissary been present, they would have recognized in this behaviour the infallible portent of extreme bewilderment, such as could only have arisen from the violence of internal emotion. M. Louchard, indeed, would as soon have expected to hear M. Gribaud attack his Majesty the Emperor as the powerful Director of the Crédit Parisien. M. Gribaud, who could not be supposed to know this, added sharply: "Have you anything further to say, M. Louchard; time is scarce and I've none to waste?"

"I—I—had one or two other observations to suggest," stammered M. Louchard, making an effort to rally; "but another occasion will do—when your Excellency is less engaged."

"I am not likely to be less engaged until I am out of office," rejoined the Minister with dryness. "If you have anything to say, out with it at once."

Just then there was a knock, and the venerable Bernard glided into the room. He whispered a few words to the statesman, and withdrew.

"Here is M. Macrobe just come," remarked the latter, addressing M. Louchard. "So make haste, please."

Perhaps it was the timely reflection that after all, M. Macrobe was very well able to take care of himself, and would, in all probability, not fail to do so when necessary, or perhaps it was simply the long-acquired habit of never letting himself be long troubled by a care about others, that caused M. Louchard abruptly to shake off his momentary stupefaction, and to discharge in a business-like manner the remainder of the errand on which he had come.

"I desire to recommend to your Excellency's indulgence, a journalist at present undergoing imprisonment," said he. "It is M. de Tirecruchon, the editor of the *Gazette des Boulevards*."

"I know him well," responded his Excellency: "as troublesome a scribbler as any in France. His paper is always turning me into ridicule."

"He is certainly troublesome," assented M. Louchard. "But he often rendered us small services, and would do more if coaxed and humoured a little. He is not a penman who could be bought with cash, like several other of the Opposition writers in our pay; but small favours would go a long way with him; they would be a profitable investment."

"Humph!" grumbled his Excellency.

"Besides," insinuated the commissary, "he has already been in prison some time, and we should only be remitting two months of his sentence. Your Excellency knows the *Gazette des Boulevards* is a paper with which it is politic, so far as is possible, to keep on good terms. Everybody reads it, and, though professing to be independent, it gives us valuable assistance in discrediting the Republicans, whom it jeers at, and unmasks most praiseworthily. Since its editor has been in prison, however, it has been dead against us, and most biting in its sarcasms. I think if we were to free M. de Tirecruchon, and offer him some small facilities in the way of sale, such as allowing his paper to be sent into the provinces by the parcels'-delivery, which would give him a start of the other journals, who are obliged to send theirs by post, we should find ourselves the better for it."

"Well, well, I'll see," growled the great M. Gribaud. "I don't like your M. de Tirecruchon. He's one of your confounded, sneering Parisians who respect nothing and nobody. I don't see that he can be better than where he is, and I wish we had all the other journalists in Paris under the same lock with him, and could keep them there to all eternity—that I do. But I'll tell you what, M. Louchard: If we release this man and throw him a bone, it must be an understood thing that his paper leaves off poking fun at me. It may laugh at my colleagues if it pleases—it's not my business to defend them—but it must respect me—and—and the Emperor," added M. Gribaud, after a moment's pause. "Do you understand, M. Louchard? If it doesn't, mind you, I'll make it unpleasant for M. de Tirecruchon.—Is that all you've got to say?"

"I wished to speak to your Excellency about Monsieur Drydust," rejoined the commissary.

"Ah! Monsieur Drydust," echoed the Minister, whose countenance at once changed and lost its stiffness. "We must be civil to him, M. Louchard. He is an ally. He writes in a paper read by a hundred thousand English shopkeepers, who'll believe what he tells them, as if it were in the Bible. We send him invitations to all the ministerial parties, and he inserts everything we ask him. Such a man must be encouraged. If he makes any request of you, that is, within the bounds of feasibility, you must accede to it."

"He often comes to the Prefecture for information," answered M. Louchard; "and so I've been thinking we could serve him and ourselves at the same time, by furnishing him with a daily bulletin, summarizing all the intelligence the Government might desire to see propagated. We would have this bulletin drawn up in English by one of our British employés, who would add such comments as we dictated to him. Gradually, Monsieur Drydust would find it the shortest way to forward our bulletin, purely and simply, to his paper: so that it will be like having a daily column in that journal at our disposal. One can insert a great deal in a column," added M. Louchard, by way of parenthesis.

M. Gribaud never fell into the bad habit of praising his subalterns, but, with a keen glance, he nodded approval.

"That reminds me I've Monsieur Drydust waiting in an ante-room all this while," said he. "Look in upon him as you go out, M. Louchard. Tell him that you will have a packet of special information ready for him every day. Mind you say *special information*. And, stay, I am so busy this morning I am really afraid I shan't have time to talk to him. Put him off politely—very politely; and give him some bit of confidential news. What shall it be? . . . Ay, this will do —and it's a good idea: Hint to him that you are on the scent of a conspiracy against the Emperor's life: mention it mysteriously, and he will be sure to make it public. Designate the chiefs of the Republican party as implicated; hint clearly at M. Horace Gerold, though don't specify him by name. Monsieur Drydust's imagination will do the rest, and his remarks will prepare the public mind, should we decide upon arresting and indicting these two Gerolds. Do that adroitly, M. Louchard; and now, good morning."

The commissary made a respectful obeisance, his

eyes quavering half with admiration, half with awe at the subtle spirit of the politician facing him. Then, his business being over, he departed.

It was now the turn of the other postulants. A few days before, on learning that M. Macrobe, of the Crédit Parisien, was in attendance, M. Gribaud would have had him introduced without a moment's delay. M. Macrobe was in favour then; but the part taken by him in the duel had entirely reversed the good dispositions of M. Gribaud—who, to mark his displeasure, resolved to let the financier wait until the whole list of visitors was exhausted—that is, possibly two hours. And no doubt he would have done so but for a circumstance altogether without precedent in ante-chamber annals: for scarcely had M. Louchard retired, than the venerable Bernard entered, and, with the look of a man hopelessly flustered by the audacity of the message he is commissioned to deliver, said: "Your Excellency, M. Macrobe has desired me to say that, having numerous calls on his time this day, he would be thankful if your Excellency could either see him immediately, or grant him an audience for some appointed hour on another day."

The venerable Bernard stood still, expecting, but prepared for a thunderclap.

The great M. Gribaud answered calmly: "Show him in."

M. Macrobe was ushered in. He was attired in the black kid-gloves which constituted his gala costume; his brass-clasped note-book was peeping out of his breast-pocket; and at his button-hole glared, scarlet as a poppy, the ribbon of his Order. He was collected and impenetrable.

With perfect composure he made his bow, and, in a tone that struck surprise into the Minister, from its firmness, said: "Your Excellency must excuse me: my hours are not my own, but my shareholders'. Time was when I could have afforded to wait two hours in an ante-room, but this is so no longer."

There was something very significant in this phrase. Thought the Minister to himself: "If this man is so impertinent, it is that he feels himself strong, and has allies with him more powerful than myself. Don't let us commit any blunder." And, like a prudent statesman as he was, instead of apostrophizing the financier in the hectoring tone he would certainly have adopted had the latter displayed any humility, he began quietly: "I desired to see you, M. Macrobe, to ask whether I had not been misinformed respecting the part you are said to have taken in the fatal duel of yesterday. It cannot surely be true that you, a man of order—a man on whom we rely—openly sided with a dangerous democrat against a gentleman known to be a trusted partisan of ours?"

"I sided with M. Gerold because he was my friend," responded M. Macrobe calmly. "As for M. de Cosaque, or Panier, I am sorry he was a trusted partisan of your Excellency's, for it seems to me that the fewer of such hangers-on a respectable government tolerates, the better for its reputation in the eyes of honest people."

M. Gribaud's blood rose to his face, and he was on the point of giving a rough rejoinder; but, at the sight of M. Macrobe's impassive countenance, he controlled himself, and answered between his teeth: "I did not say a trusted partisan of *mine*, but of *ours*, by which I meant of the Government's and the Emperor's.

You will probably allow that if his Majesty set store by M. de Cosaque, he had his reasons."

"I think we shall do better, perhaps to come to an understanding, your Excellency," replied M. Macrobe, fixing his sharp eyes on the Minister's. "Whether his Majesty set store or not by M. de Cosaque, I am unaware; but in any case partisans of M. de Cosaque's kidney are not scarce in the market: the Government can find as many of them as it pleases by offering them their price. There are other men, however, whose support it is not so easy to obtain—men of talent, rank, means, and popularity, whose co-operation would be an element of strength to the Government. I presume your Excellency would not object if I enlisted such a recruit as that for our ranks?"

"To whom are you alluding?" inquired the Minister, wondering, but still sullen.

"Your Excellency has doubtless heard that M. Horace Gerold, whom you have termed a dangerous democrat, is heir to the ancient dukedom of Hautbourg, to a splendid estate conferring immense territorial influence, and to a moneyed fortune, which, by all accounts, must be considerable. M. Gerold is, besides, a man of talent, much esteemed by his party, and a little dreaded, if I mistake not, in Imperialist circles. What would your Excellency say if I brought this young man completely over to our party, if I induced him to assume his title, and to put both his landed influence and his own personal talents at the service of the Second Empire?"

It was now the turn of M. Gribaud to fix his eyes on his interlocutor.

"You think you shall be able to manage that, M. Macrobe?" he asked.

"I promise nothing," replied the financier; "but if the Government does not thwart me by heaping petty vexations on M. Gerold, I am confident of success."

"And you will bring Manuel Gerold and young Emile Gerold over too?" continued the Minister with a keen look.

"I cannot vouch for the younger brother; and to bring Manuel Gerold over would be impossible," answered M. Macrobe; "but Manuel Gerold is an old man, and in the course of nature must soon die. As to Emile Gerold, he is obstinate; but he will cease to be dangerous when his brother is with us—his party will never trust him."

"And of course for doing this you will require a reward?" observed the Minister, with more pungency than good taste.

"Naturally," rejoined the financier, with something of a sneer at the simplicity of the remark. "But I will ask for my reward at the fitting time and place. For the present, all I have to beg is, that your Excellency will see that M. Gerold is spared those fleabite annoyances which would be likely to sour him without doing the Government any good—I mean domiciliary visits, frivolous prosecutions, personal attacks in the semi-official press, and such like. Then again, I would make so bold as to request that judicial authorities be enjoined to evince more civility than they do at present. We have been before the Public Prosecutor this morning, and I assure your Excellency his tone was such as I was obliged to resent. He talked of the duel as a murder, which was at once ill-bred and unwise. A little civility never does any harm. It is a good saying that more flies have been caught with honey than with vinegar."

"Well, hark you, M. Macrobe," returned M. Gribaud, in the quick, matter-of-fact tone which was habitual to that statesman when he was striking a bargain with a person whose head he perceived to be as long as his own—"if you are working to bring young Gerold over to us, you shall not be meddled with—I promise you that much. Only, before disarming completely, we must have some sort of guarantee that you are not deluding yourself with false hopes. On what do you ground your expectations of success?"

"On the simple fact, that it is my interest to succeed," rejoined the financier, curtly; and this answer was so pregnant of confidence that it carried conviction with it. The Minister found nothing to reply, and the audience terminated. M. Macrobe, who had been kept standing all the while, retreated as he had come, with a slight bow, in which a little deference was mingled with a good deal of self-possession and no small dose of independence. M. Gribaud watched him go, and when the door had closed behind him, fell to rubbing one of his thick ears, thoughtfully, with a knotty forefinger, and muttered: "That fellow is a rogue to beware of. I wonder what his game is?" And, probably, speculations on this horny subject continued to harass the great Minister for the rest of the day: for M. de Beaufeuillet, the secretary, and the score of ambitious supplicants in the ante-rooms, soon had occasion to observe that his Excellency was in no better humour after his interview with M. Macrobe than he had been before it.

CHAPTER XVI.

Mademoiselle Angélique.

IN proportion as the shares of the Crédit Parisien rose and the position of its Chairman became more brilliant, the world began to ask itself, with some curiosity, who the daughter of that gentleman would marry. The question was not altogether without interest, for it was reported that Mdlle. Angélique Macrobe would have ten million francs to her portion; and there were rumours that no less a person than the Prince of Arcola sought the honour of obtaining her hand.

However that might be, the young lady herself was to be seen every day in the Bois de Boulogne, surrounded by a glittering cavalcade of suitors, who pranced on various qualities of hacks round her showy barouche, bowed down to their saddle-bows in offering her their homage, and sometimes went the length of pressing extremely tender billet-doux into her hand when they thought there was nobody looking. Of course Mdlle. Angélique's aunt sat by to act as chaperon, but that excellent lady, who could never forget the time when she had cooked the boiled beef which formed the staple article of M. Macrobe's daily banquets in the days when he was a struggling man, thinking a good deal more about the pence than he did now about the pounds—Mdlle. Dorothée was too much overawed by the dazzling presence of dukes and marquises to have any discernment left as to whether what these brilliant pretenders said and did was proper or not. When a handsome, lisping sprig of nobility bent over the carriage-door, she would muse in bewilderment how much that young man could spend a year for his yellow kid-gloves; and when some enterprising *roué*, seeing her mild inquiring glance fixed on him, fancied she was watching to see whether he pushed things too far with her niece, he would be completely out of his reckoning. The poor lady was simply wondering what his Sunday clothes could be like since those he wore of a week-day were so fine.

As for Mademoiselle Angélique, she delighted, in her own inanimate way, in the life she was leading. To be dressed in light-blue silk and soft clouds of Valenciennes lace; to drive about in the barouche and see people stare at her; to have a box at the Opera, another at the "Italiens," another at every theatre when there was a new performance on: all this was better than being at school under those provoking nuns, who taught one when Clovis the First ascended the throne and when Clovis the Second descended from it. Then the gentlemen with the yellow gloves were amusing. They said funny things to make her laugh. That M. Gousset, for instance, called going to church the "baptism of new bonnets," and confession "clearing the conscience of its past sins in order to make room for those to come." The Prince of Arcola, to be sure, was a little grave: he didn't laugh so much. One of her school-friends had asked her whether it was true she was going to marry him. She didn't know; papa hadn't spoken to her about it. If papa wished it, she should not mind. The Prince was always very kind to her, but she should like him to laugh a little more; it was more pleasant.

MADEMOISELLE ANGÉLIQUE. 273

Every morning the butler of the Hôtel Macrobe brought in on a silver tray a whole pyramid of letters, burning acrostics, bouquets, and novels inscribed "with the author's compliments," all intended for Mademoiselle Angélique. The letters and acrostics were generally opened by M. Macrobe, and with the acrostics he seldom failed to light his cigar. The nosegays were stuck in vases, and the novels were handed over to Mademoiselle Angélique to read, if she cared to do so, which she never did. There were dozens of them ranged very neatly on the bookshelves of her boudoir, with the leaves cut of course (by a footman), so that an author, if he should chance to call and take up his own work for curiosity's sake, should never discover that it had not been perused. Mademoiselle Angélique did not like reading. "You have no idea how much they made us read at school," she would tell you, with a pretty, rueful expression on her bewitching face. She preferred drawing thatched cottages on a piece of white paper with a blue pencil; and when she was tired of that, she had a large red and green macaw on a gilt perch, whom she could tease with a silver bodkin.

She was precisely engaged in this last amusing occupation, when M. Macrobe invaded her bower one fine autumn morning some weeks after Horace Gerold's duel. M. Macrobe was always brisk, whether he had anything to say or not; but this time he *had* something to say.

At sight of her father Mademoiselle Angélique abandoned the bird of gay plumage and put up her face to be kissed.

"My pet, I have pleasant news for you," began

the financier. "I mean to give a fancy dress and masked *déjeûner* in the country next month. I have hired a large villa and gardens for the express purpose. M. Girth, the *costumier*, will be here in an hour to show you designs for a costume—it must be a rich one: M. Gousset, whose taste is faultless, promised me to come and help me choose it. And—ahem! where is your aunt Dorothée?—Ha, there you are, sister. You will have to choose yourself a costume too. Blanche de Castille, I should think, or Catherine de Medicis would do very well."

"Oh, dear me, Prosper, you can't be thinking of putting me into fancy dress?" was aunt Dorothée's scared exclamation.

"Why not? Stuff and nonsense! Everybody must be travestied. You'll wear a mask too,—a velvet one with lace."

"Holy Virgin!" cried the poor lady, piteously. "And shall I be obliged to show my legs like those women at the play?"

"Your legs? No; what are you talking about? And don't say the play—it's provincial; say the theatre. Angélique, my pet, there will be no time to lose. As soon as you have chosen your dress, you must have it made up. I have called at Pochemolle's, and they'll send somebody over this morning to take orders for all the satin and velvet you may want. Girth will supply the needlewomen. Ah, and he'll have plenty to do, preparing dresses for this breakfast. I intend it shall be a fête such as has never been seen within living memory. There'll be a ball after it; and fireworks—a twenty thousand francs' worth. But we'll have only two thousand invitations—people shall go down on their knees for tickets. I have my reasons for all this. Eh, eh, it will be a magic sight!"

"Oh, papa, how nice!" exclaimed Angélique, in obedient ecstasy; and she began to wonder whether her costume would be pink or blue.

"Twenty thousand francs of fireworks—two thousand invitations! Gracious mercy! where's all that money to come from?" ejaculated aunt Dorothée, feebly staring at the chimney-piece.

But at that moment the butler opened the door and announced: "Monsieur Girth."

And the celebrated *costumier* was introduced.

He entered with grace, composed in his mien, irreproachable in his attire, easy in his salutation without being familiar. Behind him a satellite, with two immense folios, which were placed on the table. The strangest thing about Mr. Girth was that, holding the sceptre of fashion in the capital of fashion, he himself was a Briton born. You could pretty well guess this from his broad shoulders, light hair, and correctly-cut sandy whiskers.

"You keep good time, I see, M. Girth," said M. Macrobe, cheerfully.

"Punctuality is the politeness of tradesmen as of kings, sir," answered Mr. Girth, with a slightly foreign accent; "but I feared I was a few minutes behind my time, from having been delayed by the Duchess of Argenteuil—a wedding-dress for her Grace's daughter. I am also afraid I must hurry away in half-an-hour, to remit three dresses to a courier specially sent by the Empress of Austria."

Mr. Girth threw out these distinguished names without embarrassment, as if he had plenty more of the same grain ready to produce as occasion should serve him.

"Dear me," rejoined M. Macrobe. "I was in hopes you could have stayed until M. Arsène Gousset arrived to guide us in our choice. I expected him here by this time."

"Here *is* M. Gousset, papa," exclaimed Angélique.

And effectively that gentleman appeared, smiling and irreproachably dressed, coming up through the conservatory of camelias and ferns that adjoined Mademoiselle Angélique's boudoir.

He bowed to the two ladies, and shook hands with the financier. Mr. Girth made obeisance to him with a respectful inclination of the head.

"Well, Monsieur Girth, armed with your two manuals of elegance, I see. I have come to take a lesson in taste."

"Nay, sir. It is for M. Arsène Gousset to give, not to receive such lessons," answered the *costumier*, amiably.

"H'm! I don't know. I gave a description of a lady's dress in my last novel, and Madame de Masseline, one of your customers, told me I was at least six years behindhand with the fashions. I think she was right, for I lately saw, at one of the Embassies, a dress in which there was blue, green, yellow, and red, all mixed up together, somehow like in a Neapolitan ice. But they told me it was quite correct."

"May I ask at which of the Embassies, sir?"

"Your own: the English."

"Ah, yes: at the English Embassy they will do these kind of things," replied Mr. Girth, with a deprecatory shrug. "My countrywomen do not understand dressing, which is a pity, with their beauty. In England we have no middle class between those who don't dress and those who over-dress. Yet the science of costume is not difficult. Harmonize—there is the whole pith of it."

"Some pretty dresses here," murmured M. Gousset, turning over the leaves of the first album—"this one especially."

"Yes: a Francesca di Rimini, originally made for the Princess of Cleves. Her Serene Highness had been reading some Swedish romances, and desired to be costumed as "Margaret Waldemar." I had to use much diplomacy to persuade her Highness that she had neither the Northern complexion, nor the warrior-look necessary for the part. She had dark hair, and was sentimental. As 'Francesca di Rimini' she looked perfect. But that is the historical album. This is the fancy one, which will, perhaps, suit Mademoiselle better."

So the leaves of the fancy-book were turned over, and nymphs, goddesses, water-fairies, and cardinal virtues appeared in fascinating succession. At every page Angélique languidly exclaimed, "Oh!" and "Beautiful!" Aunt Dorothée, from hearing the prices called out, was quickly reduced to a state of intellectual coma, from which M. Gousset's suggested amendments —all of an expensive character—were not calculated to revive her.

The financier nodded his approval now and then, but deferred all practical decision to the novelist.

At last, by common consent, the choice was made to rest between a costume of Hebe and one of The Rising Morn.

"Something rich," hinted M. Macrobe.

"The Hebe would be simple," remarked the artistic Mr. Girth: "pearls, white silk and tulle, a little blue to give relief—perhaps a few flower-buds. The dress would not be more than twelve hundred francs. But I think the Hebe a little trite: I made three Hebes last winter season. The Rising Morn would be a much more imposing conception, and would harmonize exactly with Mademoiselle's rare beauty. Pale blue and white silk, with tulle as before, but arranged differently in diaphanous clouds, and the body much more *décolleté;* diamonds in profusion, to simulate dewdrops; gold powder in the hair—though, really, Mademoiselle scarcely needs it—and a tiara, with a rising sun in topazes and brilliants. To come up to my full idea in point of splendour, there should be a ten thousand guineas' worth of diamonds with this costume."

"Nothing to prevent it—nothing," answered M. Macrobe, enthusiastically.

"Well, if Mademoiselle decides on this costume, I think I can predict a success, especially by gaslight. It will be the finest thing seen since the 'Night' of the Duchess of Alba, though that was not finer."

Needless to say that Mademoiselle did decide upon that costume, and, hearing that the "person from M. Pochemolle's" had arrived, retired to give orders for all the quantities of silk and tulle which Mr. Girth was good enough to jot down on a paper.

The "person" had been shown into Mademoiselle's dressing-room.

Angélique hastened there, and found Georgette.

It should be mentioned that the two girls had been

at school—or, rather, at convent—together some years before.

Angélique's father was then less than nobody; Georgette's was a respectable well-to-do tradesman: it was, therefore, Georgette who held the upper rank. The parts were now reversed, and perhaps, even in Angélique's naïvely serene temperament, lurked a spark of that good feeling which makes us so dearly love to patronize those who once have seen us lowly.

Anyhow she said, with a sweetly friendly smile: "Oh, Georgette, they never told me it was you: I wonder why they didn't. Do you know, I've been choosing a dress—at least, M. Gousset did for me—which is to have ten thousand guineas' worth of diamonds on it? It's a great deal, ten thousand guineas, don't you think so? How much is a guinea, I forget?"

Georgette smiled—a little sad smile it was, for the poor child did not look in mirthful mood—and said: "Are these the orders on the paper, Mademoiselle Angélique?"

"Yes, those are the orders, dear Georgette. Monsieur Girth wrote them; and he's going to send two needlewomen to work every day; but I am to try on before him, and the last touches are to be made by his foreman. Yes, I think that's what he said. But it seems odd—doesn't it?—for a fore*man* to be sewing ladies' dresses? Ah, but I'm forgetting you—you'll take a glass of Madeira and some cake to please me. I am going to ring for it. Then I'll show you over the house: I think you've never seen it. It's very big: I don't fancy I know my way all over it by myself."

"No, Mademoiselle Angélique, thank you. Please

don't ring," said Georgette. "I must be home soon; but thank you very much, all the same."

"Oh, dear, but you must take something," exclaimed Angélique.

Then stopping, and gazing with a perplexed, rather astonished air at her friend, she said: "But, Georgette, you don't look as you used to—you've been ill, haven't you? You're quite pale; why didn't you tell me?"

And with an impulsive movement not common with her, she seated herself on an ottoman, drew Georgette to her, and kissed her.

"Tell me what it is, dear?" she said.

Georgette's heart was in that full state when the least drop of sympathy caused it to overflow. She burst into tears.

Angélique was much astonished and distressed.

"Dear me, I wish aunt Dorothée were here," she exclaimed. "I always go to her when I cry. But tell me, is it anything we can do for you? You were always good to me, you know, and you would never be sad if I could help it. I wish my head were better than it is; perhaps I might guess then without needing to ask you."

"No, no, it's nothing, Mdlle. Angélique: it will pass away soon."

And Georgette made an effort to dry her eyes.

But it was only an effort, and it failed: so that when aunt Dorothée came up a few minutes afterwards to rejoin her niece she found the two young girls sobbing by each other's side—Georgette violently, Angélique helplessly and silently, from being unable to console her friend. The excellent woman was not long in adding her own tears to the group. But it was her mission in this life, poor soul, to boil beef and comfort the sorrowful: so after crying she gently pressed the afflicted girl to unburden her heart; and by degrees, by gentle questions, by dint of the confidence her kind worthy face inspired, she got at the truth. And that truth was the old, old story of a first love crossed. Georgette's father was bent upon marrying her against her will to a man she had never loved. He insisted upon it. Her mother, too, at first on her side, had ended by taking her father's, and they were importuning her so much that she knew she could not hold out longer. Besides, of what use was it to resist —she could never marry the man she loved? He would not have her; he was too high in the world, too much a gentleman to marry a poor girl like her. Yet she had once thought he loved her a little: it was an error. No, she would rather not tell his name. He had done nothing for which she could blame him. She would dry her tears and try to forget him. Well-meaning Georgette! this attempt was no more successful than the other. After drying her eyes she faltered again, and in this new gush of grief revealed that it was Horace Gerold she loved. . . . .

An hour later, when she was gone, Angélique, her eyes still red, stole downstairs to look for her father. She had a scheme on her mind. The financier was alone in her boudoir examining a landscape he had bought the day before, for about a third of its value, of a jaded artist. He was deliberating where he should hang this, for the walls were pretty well covered as it was with good pictures purchased adroitly. His back was turned to the door.

She touched his arm.

"Oh, papa, I am so miserable, and I have come to ask you to do me a favour."

He laid down the picture a little surprised. This was the first time his daughter had ever asked him to do anything.

"It's not for myself, papa,—at least, if you do it, it will please me quite as much as if it were for me. It's for Georgette, you know, who was at school with me. She's been here this morning, and she says they want to marry her to a man she doesn't like. I think she said a commercial traveller. So I thought I'd come to you, though she told me not to do it, and ask you if something couldn't be done? If you spoke to her father, he would listen to you; and you might tell him —what she hasn't the courage to—that she loves a gentleman. I am not sure whether I ought to tell you his name;—I mean this gentleman's—but I will: it's M. Horace Gerold, the same whom you know....."

M. Macrobe, whose face had remained at first impassive, underwent a sudden elongation of countenance at the mention of Horace Gerold. He kissed his daughter on the forehead and turned abruptly on his heel.

"That's queer," muttered he to himself. "I wonder what it means. I suppose there's no new unpleasantness under these cards. H'm! Horace Gerold is not the man to marry a girl of that rank, even if he were twenty times in love with her; I know that much of him; still it's curious. Perhaps, there may be a way of turning this new affair to account. I must think about it?"

CHAPTER XVII.

"The Future Madame Filoselle."

"HA, Gerold, how do you do? You have become quite a stranger here; but not for long, I hope?"

"Well, sir, my six months of disbarring will be over soon; perhaps I shall practise again then."

"Quite right. The Bar is the true career for talents fresh and vigorous like yours. By the way, how about your trial for that duel affair; are you committed?"

"I have just come from the *juge d'instruction's* closet; that is what brought me here this morning; but it seems I am to hear no more about the matter. I am discharged, as they say."*

"You owe that to your second, M. Macrobe, I suppose?"

"I think so. Perhaps a little, too, to the strength of my case. My antagonist was the aggressor; I acted in self-defence, and the jury could not but have acquitted me. The trial, however, would have afforded our counsel an opportunity for attacking the system of official journalism, and that I fancy would scarcely have suited the Government. They had more interest in hushing up the affair than we had."

Horace was replying to the barrister Claude Febvre, in the great hall of the Palace of Justice, where, as his interlocutor observed, he had for some time past become a stranger. He was still on the staff of the *Sentinelle*, but only waiting for the occasion to sever a connection which had ceased to be cordial, and which

---

* It is scarcely necessary to remind the reader that preliminary examinations are, in France, conducted *secretly;* and that the examining magistrate has unlimited discretionary powers.

there appeared little likelihood of ever re-establishing on its old footing. Indeed the breach with Nestor Roche was widening rather than otherwise. The editor's confidence in his contributor was shaken. He tried not to show it, but the fact was patent, revealing itself in a host of small symptoms, not the least significant of which was the unusual latitude he allowed Horace as regards his articles. He never altered these articles now, never ran his pen through this or that sentence, pointing out with his gruff voice and friendly look, why he thought it wise to do so. The articles were printed as they came; and it is only fair to add, that if the editor had ever been troubled with apprehensions lest his headstrong young friend should drag the paper into trouble, all fears on this account were now definitely appeased. The duel, or rather the gathering intimacy with M. Macrobe which followed that event, appeared to have marked a new era in Horace's opinions, or at least in his style. He now wrote temperately, with an absence of all acrimony, sometimes even with a courtesy of expression which made the rougher republicans amongst his fellow-contributors quiver with astonishment. Not that he was less liberal: on the contrary, he was perhaps more so; but it was the easy, philosophical liberalism of the gentleman— the liberalism of the fortunate man who sees things through pink glasses, and begins to think that after all the world is not so black as it has been painted.

And how, indeed, could it be otherwise? Every day added some new sweets to Horace's life. His walks along the Boulevards resembled triumphal processions. Distinguished men saluted him, great novelists and journalists nodded amicably to him as one of their

own set; Bonapartist writers gave him a wide berth.
When he went to the Opera, he must have been blind
not to notice that women turned their opera-glasses in
his direction—often kept them so turned a long time
—and then M. Arsène Gousset, or the Prince of Arcola,
would come down and claim to introduce him to Madame la Comtesse This or That, who desired to make
his acquaintance. As Mr. Drydust remarked, it was
flattering; he knew what it was from having gone
through it himself.

"Ah, *mon cher*," would add that eminent person,
who was beginning to give him a good deal of his
company, "take my word for it, extreme republicanism
won't do. I've seen it act—went to America on purpose
to study it. The Americans have no opera of their own,
no theatre, no novels worth mentioning, no pictures.
And depend upon it these are the essentials of life."

"What are, novels or the opera?"

"Both. Liberty should be not an end, but a means.
You don't come into the world to put your vote into
a ballot-box; you come to enjoy yourself. If you can't
get the enjoyment without the vote, then agitate for
the vote; but if you have the enjoyment, where is the
use of voting?"

"You mean that despotism which gives you operas
and museums is the *ne plus ultra* of good government?"

"Well, nearly. I adore despotism. Nothing great
has ever been done without it. See this new Boulevard
Malesherbes they are building; look at the Bois de
Boulogne—two hundred million francs spent upon it
within two years. Parliamentary government would
never have done that for you."

"Then you must be very anxious to see the form of government in your own country changed."

"No; with England it is different. Freedom is necessary to the English temperament. We must have a great deal of freedom. But we are the exception."

Horace smiled; but these conversations, and a good many others of the kind, conducted by choice spirits like M. Gousset', were insensibly operating upon him. He laughed at the paradoxes he heard; would now and then take the trouble of refuting them; but like a man who has got into the habit of sipping absinthe, and, after finding his first glasses bitter, grows to like the acrid flavour: so now it rather amused him to hear the cynical witticisms of his new friends; and he more than once caught himself admitting—not aloud, but internally—that these agreeable fellows were much more genial company than the republicans pure he occasionally met. This was especially his train of thought on the morning he exchanged the few words in passing with the barrister, Claude Febvre. It was a clear, sunny day, his blood flowed prosperously in his veins, and the balminess of the air came as a welcome relief after an unusually gloomy hour or two passed the evening before in the society of some fervid Radicals. Never had these men—journalists and ex-politicians for the most part—shown themselves more iconoclastic and rabid. "Upon my word!" muttered Horace, as he descended the staircase of the Palace of Justice. "That may be liberalism, but if so, liberalism, like most other human inventions, would seem to be perfectible."

The streets were alive with that animation which buoyant weather begets. Cabs flitting by crossed each other with rapidity; on the tops of the omnibuses passengers talked and laughed; and the pink and yellow playbills on the kiosks gleamed singularly fresh and new. It was a day to be out and walking. Horace sauntered down the quays, stopping now and then to examine the curious collections of old prints and books exposed at the open-air stalls, which encumber the left bank of the Seine; but pausing more often to consider those wonderful pieces of rusty armour, those cracked plates of three-century-old china, and the japanned bowls of rare antique coins exposed in the windows of the bric-a-brac shops. He had just spent a minute thus profitably, and was turning to resume his stroll, when a small active pedestrian, in a showy waistcoat and loaded with a carpet-bag, ran almost into him, apologizing in the same breath for his awkwardness, and laying the blame on the narrow pavement. Horace bowed and was passing on; but the other, as if struck by his face, stopped, reddened a little, raised his hat suddenly, and said: "I beg your pardon. I believe I have the honour of addressing the Marquis of Clairefontaine— M. Horace Gerold? Pardon the liberty," he resumed immediately, "but I feel myself under an obligation: I owe you a debt of thanks, and I am thankful to have the opportunity of repaying it. My name is Filoselle— Hector Filoselle, at your service."

"M. Filoselle—yes, perfectly; I remember;" and Horace began to contemplate this gentleman with some interest.

"Yes, I owe you a debt of gratitude, Monsieur le Marquis—that is, Monsieur," said M. Filoselle, who was quickly regaining his self-possession, "I am told you were good enough to employ your eloquence on my behalf. M. Pochemolle, my future father-in-law, has informed me of the circumstance. My future mother-in-law, you are aware, was at first opposed to the match. I have seen many mothers-in-law both in France and abroad, and have had occasion to notice that they are always opposed to something. Marriage, Monsieur le Marquis, would be a sacred institution but for mothers-in-law; when I am wedded I propose to keep mine at a distance. Mdlle. Georgette, my future wife, will, I have no doubt, subscribe to these views. Meanwhile, reciprocating my tender passion as she does, I am convinced that she entertains the same grateful feelings towards Monsieur as I myself."

Horace slightly bent his head without answering.

"I should have sought the opportunity of saying all this to Monsieur before; but the pursuit of business is engrossing; it has kept me away from Paris these last six weeks and will take me again into the country by the early train to-morrow. To amass money, M. le Marquis, with the intention of bestowing it on the object of one's worship, is an occupation which has always seemed to me the noblest of all; and this reminds me that if Monsieur should want a few dozen of champagne, light and dry, vintage of '49; or a flute—rosewood, with double silver stops, and a case to match, portable and convenient—he would find a profit in dealing with me preferably to with a retail house. I have another favour to ask, but this demand ought, perhaps, to be proffered by the future Madame Filoselle. However, if M. le Marquis would so far honour us as to be present at the ceremony, the date of which is not yet fixed, but shall be made known to M. le Marquis, he would be doing a gracious thing, for which he would be entitled to our sincerest thanks. Indeed,

I may say, that by his presence M. le Marquis would be giving the final sanction to his own work; for if Hymen has happy days in store for me, I shall never be able to forget that it is to the Marquis of Clairefontaine that I owe it."

Was this true? Did Monsieur Filoselle owe his prospective connubial bliss to M. le Marquis? One might have doubted it on seeing the preoccupied and not over-pleased look on Horace Gerold's features as he moved away after this chance encounter. Why did things turn up in this way? Horace had resolved that he would think no more about Georgette, and he had really tried not to do so. He had even done more: he had avoided all occasions of meeting her; and once, when he was certain that she was not in the shop, he had entered, and resolutely undertaken a furiously long eulogy of M. Filoselle, whom he didn't know—all this with 'the view to mollifying Mdme. Pochemolle: in which object he had ended by succeeding. It is true that after this achievement he had retired, not particularly satisfied that what he had done was feeling, or even honest. But he wished to put away temptation, and the end in such cases generally appears to justify the means. One thing, however, he had neglected to do, and that the simplest of all: Why had he not removed? He did not know himself. He reasoned that the thing was not necessary, since Georgette herself would soon be married and gone. But, now, hearing M. Filoselle talk, it occurred to him that he had been unwise. It would have certainly been better to remove. He could not stand this commercial fellow coming many times and thanking him like that.

He walked home out of humour. A regret that M.

Filoselle's employers had not sent that gentleman to sell their wares in the antipodes floated uppermost in his mind. Then he anathematized M. Pochemolle and all French fathers collectively who made a traffic of marriage. He wondered how Georgette looked now? It was a long time since he had seen her. Yes, weeks. What had she been thinking of him during all this while? She was indignant, of course; that must inevitably be, for women never view these things in the proper light. Still, he should be sorry that she should retain a lastingly bad opinion of him. He had acted for the best. Where would be the harm if he stepped in just to say a few kind words and make peace? She was definitely another's now; the attention could not be misconstrued.

He had reached the Rue Ste. Geneviève. He entered.

Mdme. Pochemolle was at her habitual place behind the counter. M. Pochemolle stood in the centre of the shop, receiving with respect a financial hint or two from M. Macrobe.

The latter accosted Horace, extending his hand.

"My dear young friend, I had called to tell you about this fancy fête of mine. It's got up mainly for you, you know."

Horace's eye roamed round the shop in search of Georgette. She was seated in a corner, and over the counter, talking to her and smiling, leaned a gentleman, fashionably dressed. They seemed tolerably engrossed in their conversation. "And," thought Horace, with a sudden and sharp pang at the heart, "their heads are very close together." This pang was not lessened when the stranger, turning round, showed his face. It was the Prince of Arcola.

CHAPTER XVIII.

M. Macrobe "at Home."

M. MACROBE had determined that his fête should be a success; and, in so far as the preliminaries could augur, his wish appeared likely to be realized. M. de Tirecruchon, released from captivity, heralded the event in the *Gazette des Boulevards*. Mr. Drydust talked of it to his British readers, giving them full statistics as to the number of wax-candles that would be burned, the *menu* of the supper, and the price of the champagne— nothing inferior to Cliquot, twelve shillings a bottle. Suburban Clapham rejoiced over the feast as if it were going to be present there; the semi-detached villas in Camberwell, Battersea, Islington, and Chelsea, conversed anxiously about the entertainment during a fortnight beforehand.

But it was naturally in Paris that the coming revelry caused most sensation. The windows of the draper's shops along the whole length of the Boulevards and the Rue de la Paix bloomed out with flashing satins and rich-hued velvets, festoons of gold and silver lace, superb plumes, and countless stage accessories, amongst which, skilfully interspersed to catch the eye, shone gaudy designs of fancy dresses—mediæval queens, and Hungarian peasant girls, legendary amazons, and modern *vivandières*. Monsieur Louis, "Artiste Capillaire to the Court" (hairdresser, as we say in English), had got his "list" full—which meant that on the day of the fête he would start on his artistico-capillary rounds at six sharp in the morning, and terminate his labours towards midnight. Lucky the ladies who for a hundred francs' fee could obtain a quarter-of-an-hour of this gifted being's time! He drove up to the door in his brougham, raced up to Madame's dressing-room three steps at a time, expected to find Madame ready-seated before her toilette-glass, the maids in attendance, the combs, brushes, curling-tongs, and pots of *bandoline*, all in a row within hand-reach; and even then he would glare like a gladiator and stamp his autocratic foot if the maid was stupid—took a quarter of a minute, for instance, getting Madame's tiara out of the jewel-case, or in her hurry dropped a hair-pin. As for Mr. Girth, he was, of course, run off his legs.

There were no bounds, he would say, to the exigencies of ladies. If he called upon all who wrote to him he should never have a spare minute at his command. So he was really obliged to establish a rule. He would be at home at stated hours; other stated hours he would confine to calls; but his patronesses must please to understand that on no account could he ever devote more than half-an-hour to one consultation. It is not certain whether his patronesses understood this or not. Anyhow, their broughams extended in a three hundred yards' *queue* outside his door, and ladies who would not have waited five minutes to please their lawful husbands, sat, with the patience of saints, their two and four hours at a time to bide the good pleasure of Mr. Girth. Perhaps the only lady who, previous to the fête, was not called upon to undergo some ordeal of the kind was Mademoiselle Angélique.

As daughter of the host she was entitled to exceptional regard. Mr. Girth did himself the honour of waiting upon her personally once or twice a week, and she, apprised beforehand of his coming, awaited it with meditative anxiety, as we do the Doctor, or an R.A. who is coming to paint us. It was a scene not devoid of grandeur. Mademoiselle Angélique, attired in the as yet unfinished costume, stood motionless, with a cheval-glass to the right, another to the left, and a third in the background. Behind, but out of the line of sight, two attendant needle-women and a maid, silent and awe-struck. On a sofa, Mademoiselle Dorothée casting glances of resignation at the ceiling; and in the foreground, Mr. Girth, gloved, meditating, and impassive: throwing out curt orders to an aide-de-camp foreman, who deferentially consigned them to a note-book. Michael Angelo superintending the works of the cupola of St. Peter's; Lenôtre, planning the royal gardens of Versailles, were not more great and admirable.

To say that Angélique took pleasure in all this would be true, and yet her joy was not quite unalloyed. Her rich dress and the approaching fête were perplexing her a little. No doubt it was satisfactory to be informed that she would be queen of a pageant unsurpassed in splendour and unsurpassable; and to see the pretty eyes of her lady friends twinkle jealously as they examined her costume, and the ten thousand guineas' worth of diamonds to be tacked thereon, was a sensation of which any lady, however good at heart, will easily understand the sweets. But underlying these gratifying impressions, lurked a vague presentiment that this unusually brilliant festival had not been projected without some object in view—M. Macrobe, she knew, was not the man to invest twenty thousand francs in fireworks for the pleasure of watching coloured sparks fall—and somehow Angélique began to fancy that with her father's object, whatever it was, she herself might not be altogether dissociated. It must be confessed that her perspicacity scarcely went deeper than this. She thought, indeed, a little of the Prince of Arcola, wondered why, if he really intended marrying her, he did not propose sooner; but she was at a long way from guessing the truth, when the financier repeated to her for the fourth or fifth time:

"My pet, you must mind and be very civil to M. Horace Gerold, who will be present at the fête. You will find him a most amiable young man."

"Certainly," thought she, "I will be civil to M. Gerold," and she was very glad at having the opportunity of meeting him. As to his being an amiable young man, her father knew best, but it was not exceedingly amiable to act as he had done by Georgette. It is true that he was a rich and high-born gentleman, so they pretended, and that Georgette was a tradesman's daughter; but after all what did that matter? Had she not heard M. Gousset say often that a woman's rank was her beauty, that King Coph—Cophetsomething had married a beggar-maid and that he had done quite right, for that the party honoured by this transaction was not the beggar-maid, but King Coph—himself—why then should not M. Gerold do as much? Georgette was not a beggar-maid: at school she used to carry off prizes which she—Angélique—could never manage to do; and she was pretty—oh yes, prettier far than any girl she had ever seen. Everybody declared so; even the Prince of Arcola, who had been to

Pochemolle's the other day with her father, had come back quite enthusiastic about the young girl's beauty.

She wondered, in her mild, meek way, whether she could not try something to soften M. Gerold—he did not look like a very hard young man, and she was truly anxious to befriend Georgette. If her father had done what she wanted, the whole thing might no doubt have been settled by this time; but her father did not seem pleased at her interfering in the matter. He had kissed her quite abruptly and gone away, and the next time she had appealed to him, he had answered, impatiently: "Tut, tut, my pet, Georgette is a little goose, and you too."

She could not see why Georgette was a goose, though she had deliberated upon the matter gravely. It was not being a goose to cry because one had been jilted. Aunt Dorothée said it was a shame for gentlemen to steal away the hearts of young girls, that it was much more cruel and dishonourable than robbing money. Then Georgette was so gentle too! "Yes," thought Angélique, "I will try whether I cannot work upon M. Gerold's good feelings. I will take advantage of his presence at the fête to speak to him." This wise idea, which occurred to her after many days of reflection, she kept to herself; but every day the idea twined itself more tightly, like a strong shoot of ivy, round her usually inert imagination. Meanwhile, on the prettiest sheet of toned paper in the world, and with the tiniest gold pen extracted from a liliputian desk, she wrote to her friend *"not to be miserable,"* drawing three lines under the word miserable, which, as connoisseurs in ladies' calligraphy are aware, means that there are three excellent reasons, if not more, why one should not be *miserable*. She added that she had got a plan for "*setting everything right*"— words underlined as before.

It is probable that if M. Macrobe had intercepted this affectionate communication on its way to the post and taken cognizance of its contents, he would have frowned, and with considerable vexation. But he was too busy now to see much of his daughter. Every spare hour he could snatch from business he spent at Marly in the villa he had hired, a noble residence with a beauteous park, in which a whole army of workmen were employed, erecting marquees, extemporizing terraces, and laying out parterres of costly flowers. Nothing was to be wanting to the completeness of the fête. In case of rain there were arrangements for covering in the entire grounds. Châlets, bright with paint and gilding, verdant with creeping foliage, had been run up here and there, and furnished with a luxury that could not have been excelled, had these ephemeral dwellings been destined to last permanently. To keep the grounds and line the approaches to the ball-rooms, a hundred men, attired as halberdiers, had been retained; and two hundred boys, dressed as pages of Francis the First, and selected for their comely looks, were to officiate as waiters. This part of the arrangements had been effected by a celebrated theatrical manager, expert in *mise en scène;* and the same enterprising genius had suggested that a hundred of the prettiest girls amongst the metropolitan *corps-de-ballet* should be recruited to act as *bouquetières*, and distribute to the guests flowers and bonbons. The programme might be altered according to circumstance, but for the present it was as follows: At four, the *déjeûner;* at six, the drawing of a tombola with valuable prizes; at ten, fireworks; after which the grounds were to be illuminated with an invention, then in its infancy, called "electric light;" masks were to be put on; and there was to be a ball, with supper and cotillon, lasting—until it pleased heaven to make the sun rise.

Small wonder that M. Macrobe was busy. He had long ago been obliged to relent from his original decision of only issuing two thousand invitations. No half-dozen post-bags could have contained all the letters he received cajoling, begging, entreating, raving for tickets. What made it difficult to refuse, too, was that there were a good many shareholders of the Crédit Parisien amongst the supplicants. These honest and importunate persons claimed the favour of an invitation as a sort of right, and they were delighted to hear of the fête, for it is evident that a chairman who has so much money to spend must be looking very closely after the interests of his shareholders. In fine, M. Macrobe had been obliged to increase the tickets to four thousand, without thereby greatly diminishing the number of those who in private declared they were being shamefully ill-used, and in public that they had never solicited invitations, not they, and that they certainly should not have gone to the party even if they had been asked. But M. Macrobe could afford to make light of these fox and grapes rancours. The essential point in his eyes was that all the personages of importance whom he had invited had accepted with alacrity, and that Horace Gerold—the most important of any—had, with perfect good-nature, entered into the spirit of the thing, and promised to come in costume. "So that's all right," muttered the financier;

"and I think this seed-corn we are scattering will soon begin to fructify—barring accidents," added this prudent gentleman, who, in his calculations, always left a wide margin for contingencies.

At last the long-looked-for day of the fête arrived.

The evening before, Horace had attempted, without success, to induce his brother to accompany him. Emile had refused firmly but gently; alleging no reason, however, save the somewhat indefinite one, that he should probably be busy. Horace had hired for three hundred francs a magnificent costume in the fashion prevailing under Henry II. (of France). It was white satin slashed with cerise; a short mantle of white velvet profusely embroidered with silver fell over the shoulders, a silver-hilted sword in cerise velvet sheath hung by his side, and a flat bonnet with white plumes fastened with an aigrette of diamonds adorned the head. Now, it may be weakness, but when we have attired ourselves in a garb of this sort, and are surprised by a friend contemplating ourselves in a glass, we expect to be complimented on our appearance, otherwise we look foolish. Horace felt so when Emile, entering unexpectedly, just as he had put on a pair of red-heeled shoes and was watching the effect of them, said gravely: "Oh! I beg your pardon, I see you are engaged."

"Engaged! no," exclaimed Horace, reddening with some confusion. "Come in, man, what is it you want to say?"

"I was going to write to Brussels to-day. Have you any message I can send?"

"My love, of course. But what are you going to write about?" asked Horace, wishing he had got his black coat and trowsers on instead of these silk stockings and this sword.

"Well, you know, I received a letter yesterday:— and, by the way, what am I to answer about the passage that concerns you?"

Horace sat down on his bed and played moodily with his bonnet.

"How am I to say?" answered he in a vexed tone. "The whole thing is absurd and calumnious. Some of those Republicans of Brussels have been telling my father that they hear I am keeping loose company, and am turning renegade; and he feels pained. Tell him it is not true; and you might add that it is only Republicans who would be capable of inventing such trash; for I am sure I begin to think with Jean Kerjou, that we shouldn't be happy in our party if we didn't perpetually accuse one another of treachery."

"And what am I to say about M. Macrobe?" proceeded Emile quietly.

"M. Macrobe is my friend," replied Horace in an impatient voice. "I've told you so already, and think you might spare me the trouble of repeating it. Write to my father that he is misinformed about the man. Thank God, our father is not cut out of the same wood as his brother Republicans; he has the soul of a gentleman, is just and generous. He can require nothing more when I say that I answer for M. Macrobe's honour on my own."

"On your own honour, brother?" answered Emile doubtfully. "You are not surely in earnest; for if you really went bail for this man's honour, Horace, how could *I* hold out any longer? You cannot think that

I would continue to suspect the man if I thought you convinced of his honesty."

"But why *do* you suspect him?" rejoined Horace with irritation. "What is the meaning of this mania of yours for suspecting people, you who used to be such a good fellow, and never spoke ill of a fly? It seems to me that it is you who are being spoiled by bad company—that of these envious, bilious demagogues whom they tell me you frequent. What has M. Macrobe done to you, come, tell me that; and what has he done to me? Why, since I have come across his path he has done nothing but repay me good for evil—had he been Job himself he could not have evinced more longanimity. I begin by vilifying him in a court of justice—he holds out his hand to me and asks me to dinner; I cut him—he takes my part when I am publicly insulted, and risks imprisonment by abetting me in a duel; he knows I am a Republican, that is a foe to his party, and he good-naturedly asks my advice about distributing twenty thousand francs to the people of our clique who may have suffered during the revolutions. Frankly, what can be his object? I am no great man that he should have any interest in currying favour with me. I am a poor devil without fortune or title, with only a rag of popularity at my back, which a day has made and which a day may take away. M. Macrobe, on the contrary, is a millionaire with more power than a cabinet minister. It would be both presumptuous and arrogant to pretend that there can be anything else but condescension on his part in treating me in the way he does."

The blood rose to Emile's habitually pale face.

"Well, Horace, this is the last time I shall ever

speak about M. Macróbe, then," said he, with the slight hectic cough which excitement of any kind generally brought on. "I will not promise to like the man," added he with an effort. "But your good word is a passport—to, at least, my respect. For your sake I will try to forget what I had heard and believed about M. Macrobe."

And he held out his hand—a white, thin hand it was, and feverish.

"Why won't you go to this fête with me?" asked Horace, still dogged.

"No: don't ask me to do that," pleaded Emile, shaking his head. "To begin with, I should not make a very lively guest; and I hardly think I could afford the expense. Besides, you see it is too late now. I fancy this is the concierge come to tell you that your carriage is waiting."

It was no longer Georgette who ran up on these sorts of errands now. The concierge, cap in hand, informed "Monsieur" that a gentleman in a landau with postilions was down below, "dressed like in carnival time." The person meant was the Prince of Arcola, who had arranged to call for Horace and give him a lift. Horace put on his glittering bonnet, wrapped himself in a flowing cloak of white cashmere and descended.

Never since the days of the Grand Monarque, when high court and revelry were held there, had the shady groves of Marly resounded with the echoes of such a festival. It was an event to be remembered evermore by the inhabitants, and to be narrated some eighty years hence by the youngest of them as a reminiscence of how men lived and caroused under the notorious

Second Empire. A troop of mounted municipal guards, their steel helmets and breastplates flashing in the sun of a cloudless sky, had been lent by the Prefect of the Seine to act as guard of honour. Picked men, with flowing moustaches, slung carbines, and clinking sabres, they swept up the Grand Avenue at a fast trot half-an-hour in advance of the first carriages; then, having reached their destination, turned and separated—half forming themselves into a glittering semi-circle round the park gates, the others starting off by twos to occupy strategical points down the road, and silently point the way to doubting coachmen. Simultaneously a hundred members of the Parisian police took up their position at equidistant spaces of twenty yards on either footway to keep back the curious, and see that the stream of vehicles flowed by uninterrupted. Magnificent policemen these, with cocked hats, straight swords, white gloves, folded arms—men you would have taken for officers in any other country. Then the carriages began to appear, first singly, then two or three almost abreast, as if racing; then one after another, settling gradually into a gorgeous slow-moving procession that seemed never to end, tapering and glimmering far into the distance, out of the reach of sight, like the trail of a starry meteor. The harness of the horses jingled, the hoofs of the noble animals pawed the ground impatiently, large flakes of foam dropped from the furbished bits, coronet after coronet, 'scutcheon after 'scutcheon flashed by on shining panels, and, every now and then, down the whole line there would be that ten minutes' dead stop, which acts on the nerves of fair occupants of broughams, and evokes from the powdered gentlemen on the box such doleful replies as this: "Impossible to move faster, Madame la Marquise; there are more than two hundred carriages ahead of us."

But if the scene without was sufficiently imposing, what language can be used to paint the spectacle within the grounds? Such a sight needs more than a pen. Tents of purple vellum and gold, gilt awnings ablaze with silken streamers; squads of radiant girls with pyramids of flowers piled up in vase-like baskets. On plats of emerald grass, and under the spreading shade of giant oaks, rich carpets and velvet cushions spread out to invite repose; and trenching on the marble whiteness of terraces, the drooping folds of blue, scarlet, and orange draperies. If anything, the eye had too much of colour, and turned with relief to the cool fountains, which threw up their waters in columns of spray, and splashed so musically in the round deep basins. Fair forms leaned over these basins, dipped their hands in, and filled the air with tinkling laughter. And these silvery sounds formed a melodious interlude to the strains that issued from the open orchestra pavilions, around which, eddied and flowed a festive crowd revelling in garbs of every variety of fashion, richness, and tint.

"Upon my word it seems to be a success," said the Prince of Arcola to his companion as they passed together into a sumptuous reception-marquee where a master of the ceremonies, who looked cut out of a picture by Titian, took their cards.

The master of the ceremonies bowed low before them and two pages in green and gold stepping forward, relieved the one of his white cashmere cloak, the other of a blue roquelaure that concealed a costume in violet velvet, of the time of Henri IV.

CHAPTER XIX.

Young Candour, Old Subtlety.

"Now here you are, that's right, and I am going to tell you who all the people are," cried Mr. Drydust, laying hold of Horace's arm as soon as he caught sight of him.

Mr. Drydust figured as a Scottish chieftain, presumably Rob Roy, and his intelligent brow disappeared under a bonnet of warlike dimensions. But he was none the less affable. Slightly embarrassed by a giant claymore from the hilt of which he was afraid to trust his left hand very far, his pace was perhaps less rapid than usual, but he still made excellent play with the hand remaining to him, and waved it about gracefully and easily to give effect to all he said: "Now see," said he; "this is true ease—the ease of an age when men understood costume, and fashioned it so as to give free play to all the limbs. I always feel fettered when I wear a frock coat—pardon, Madame" (Mr. Drydust had tripped up over his claymore), "but in this, one is at home. Aha, there is my friend Catfeesh Pasha; I'll introduce you. I declare this is like the Corso of Rome in Easter week; one meets everybody one knows."

So one did. All Paris was present. Not in truth the Paris which eminent foreigners would have comprehended in that title. One might have searched the whole grounds through without finding a single one of the men whose presence here below will be remembered a hundred years hence. But the Paris of the Second Empire was there, a throng of senators, ministers, deputies, stock-jobbers, patchouli-novelists, eau-de-rose journalists, and the gayer spirits of the Corps Diplomatique, all in short who would consent to clothe themselves in the garb of departed centuries and stalk about thus clothed for the amusement of the community. M. Macrobe had allowed of no exceptions in this respect: modern attire had been pitilessly excluded, and Horace met, within a space of five minutes, a cabinet minister dressed as a Turk, a councillor of state habited as a Jew pedler, and an envoy extraordinary and minister plenipotentiary disporting himself very successfully as a Cochin-China fowl.

In these sorts of things it is highly essential that the guests should not be thrown too much upon their own resources, but that there should be a few sportive minds, to leaven the lump, play the fool a little, and keep the merriment from flagging. M. Arsène Gousset had undertaken this part. He was the presiding genius of the fête. Assisted by M. de Tirecruchon, some young journalists, and three or four artists, he darted about from group to group organizing quadrille parties, introducing people one to another, and seeing that there was an endless flow of champagne. He had also composed a jocular *Gazette des Masques*, which, printed in gold on white satin, was distributed broadcast by him and his acolytes with piping cries such as newsvendors utter.

Horace would have been glad to sit down somewhere, whence he could have seen without being himself observed; but this would not have tallied with the plan of his host, which was to make him an actor in, not a mere spectator of, the pageant. M. Macrobe had instructed swift messengers to bring him immediate intelligence of Horace's arrival, and the latter had scarcely had time to accustom his eyes to the novel show around him, when the financier, transformed into a Jacques Ango, (famous merchant of Dieppe who threatened to make war upon Portugal at his own cost, in the reign of Francis I.) accosted, welcomed, and drew him away with Mr. Drydust to the *déjeûner* tent.

There Mademoiselle Angélique was holding her court, amidst a dense circle of worshippers, transfixed with admiration. Flattering murmurs circulated on all hands: Horace himself was fairly dazzled. Certès, the great M. Girth had triumphed. Nothing could have been more beautiful, more enchanting than this young girl of angelic loveliness, dressed in the graceful disguise of the Rising Sun. Her round white arms were bare, except where glittering bands of jewels encircled them, her rich hair fell in golden cascades over her snowy shoulders, the sun of brilliants that crowned her fair brow blazed like the fiery orb it represented, and the child herself, intoxicated by the incense of praise, enlivened by the music, the wine, the festivity, the compliments, glowed with an animation which heightened her beauty a hundred-fold.

"You must cater for my daughter," said M. Macrobe, leading Horace forward, and introducing him.

And, noting the ill-concealed look of envy on the countenances of some of the suitors he was then ousting, Horace could not avoid the reflection that, perhaps, indeed he was a man to be envied.

The tent was rapidly filling, for the signal had gone forth that the *déjeûner* was served, and fancy costume is no deterrent to appetite.

Horace led Angélique to one of the numerous tables spread in view of this tardy luncheon or early dinner. He was more or less the cynosure of a group of ladies, not indisposed to flirt with him on the strength of his reputation as a "lion"; but his matchless partner engrossed him, and she, to reward his assiduities, smiled, talked, and occasionally fixed her eyes upon his with a curious expression at once pleased and confiding, which, devoid of fatuity as he was, sent the blood to his head, and caused his heart to palpitate.

M. Macrobe, from whose watchful glance none of these signs, however slight, escaped, smiled to himself with contentment. He was standing with the Prince of Arcola.

"Well, mon prince," he said, "have you forgiven me for taking you to see that pearl of price—that bewitching Mademoiselle Georgette—the other day? I remember you said it was doing an ill-service to show you a face that would inevitably remain fixed in your memory, and, perhaps, trouble your peace."

"Did I say that?" replied the Prince, with an embarrassed laugh. "One says those things, you know, without meaning them. A handsome statue, a striking picture, creates an impression which one at first thinks lasting, but which wears off."

"To be sure. But Mademoiselle Georgette is a very striking picture;—at least, I know of some one who was considerably smitten in that quarter."

"Who?" asked the Prince, quickly; not noticing

that, at this vivacity, which somewhat belied his previous difference, M. Macrobe's eyelids slightly twinkled.

"That would be telling tales out of school," laughed the financier. "Still, mon prince, as a secret between you and me, the admirer was young Gerold. You know he lives in the same house as this handsome statue."

The Prince changed colour a little. It did not look as though the news much pleased him.

M. Macrobe, to repair matters, took his arm, and presented him to the fascinating daughter of an American citizen, Cincinnatus Jickling, Esq., whose ambition was to crown a long career of democracy and drysalting by allying himself to some one with a title. Mr. Jickling was stirred to the depths of his republican heart on seeing Miss Jickling escorted to the breakfast-table by an authentic prince.

Amidst the popping of champagne-corks, the clattering of plate, the running to and fro of sprightly pages, carrying silver trays loaded with choice viands or eccentric-shaped flagons, Horace pursued his attentions to Angélique. When the banqueting was at length over, she accepted his arm, and they issued on to the lawn.

"How refreshing the air is," she said. "But we must sit down—or shall we go to one of those châlets? They look so nice and cool."

So they turned their steps towards the châlets, which were deserted—the stream of wassailers being directed towards another part of the grounds, where the Tombola was to be drawn.

M. Macrobe, who saw them walk alone, was careful

not to disturb them. He had now mated himself with an English dowager—the Lady Margate—who had seen the Eglinton tournament, and was regaling him with her recollections of that historic event. He led off her ladyship, and charmed her with his good-humour, his perfect manners, and admirably-genial deference. "A most becoming Frenchman," was her ladyship's unuttered verdict.

Yet, if M. Macrobe could have divined the motives of his daughter for enticing Horace to the châlet, it is not so sure that Lady Margate would have been captivated by his demeanour. It is probable that he might have earned the reputation of being a very distraught and ill-tempered Frenchman.

As we have said, Angélique had come to the resolution that she would help Georgette. This was the first time in her life that the idea of helping any one —or even the possibility of doing so—had ever occurred to her; but, from the very fact of its novelty, the determination had taken firm hold of all her faculties, absorbing her energies, and monopolizing her thoughts. There are no resolutions so deep as those which have been a long time taking root. She had turned the matter over waking, dreamed of it sleeping, and ultimately had resolved that, cost what it might, she would do such and such a thing on a certain day.

As we must never make men and women braver than they are, perhaps one ought to own that, at the moment of putting her scheme into execution, she was not a little emboldened by the two or three glasses of Madame Veuve Cliquot's vintage which she had sipped. Anyhow, they were no sooner seated than, with the amazing courage of innocence and inexperience, looking up into Horace's face, she said:

"I am sure you must be very good."

"Good?" replied he, disconcerted. "Are men ever good?"

"Yes, I think you are. I have heard gentlemen speak about you: they said that, though rich, you were a friend of the poor, and gave all your money to them. It seems to me that if I were a man I should like to be like that. I see many gentlemen who pass their lives in trying to amuse themselves; they do not appear to me so happy as you. Only, if I were a man, and anybody loved me I think I should perceive it, and I should not despise the love; for, you see, we women have nothing to give but our hearts, and when we have bestowed that, if we do not get another heart in return, our lives are dark and miserable ever after."

Horace sat not knowing what could be the meaning of this. Was it a declaration? He felt what is called queer. The incomparable beauty of the girl who was addressing him, the solitude, the strangeness of the situation, all combined to form one of those passes in which precipitate men do foolish things. Luckily his emotion deprived him for the moment of utterance, and thus saved him from ridicule.

"You look astonished," pursued Angélique artlessly; "but what I say is true. Men are strong, and should have pity on the weak. A woman's love may not be much in the estimation of a man, but if they only knew what tears and suffering it costs, I think they would be too generous to leave it unrequited. I know people say that marriages should be between persons of the same rank and having like fortunes: but do you really think this is the only way to become happy? Is affection quite worthless, unless it have armorial bearings on it like one's dinner-spoons?"

Altogether on the wrong tack, and growing much more excited than was prudent, Horace seized Angélique's hand.

"Can you suppose," he said gallantly, "that any sordid considerations would stand in the way of my marrying a woman who gave me her heart?"

She abandoned her hand to him without mistrust; but in a tone of wondering remonstrance: "Then why do you not marry Georgette?" she asked.

"Georgette!" he exclaimed, suddenly releasing her hand.

"Why, yes: of whom else could I be speaking?" replied she simply. "I learned your secret,—at least, it would be truer to say that my aunt and I wrung it from poor Georgette, for she would never have told it us of her own accord. But she is very unhappy, Monsieur Gerold, believe me—so unhappy that I thought I would tell you this, for I said to myself: 'It is impossible M. Gerold can be aware of the pain he is causing.' Georgette is my old school-friend, you know; we were at the convent together; and she was a much better and cleverer girl than I;—oh yes—and there is not a nobleman in the world but might marry her without derogating."

The position was perplexing. A man always plays a rather silly part if he has been supposing without reason that a woman is making love to him. Horace felt neither more nor less abashed than most men feel under such circumstances. Yet Angélique, in pleading for her friend, was so naïvely eloquent, her voice bore the accent of so much womanly kindness, that he was touched. Had her design been to win him to herself, by a comedy adroitly played, she could not have succeeded more completely. Perceiving that she had not been thinking in the least about him, he began, with man's unfailing instinct, to think about her.

He hesitated a moment; then, drinking in her truly uncommon beauty with his eyes, he said, "Mademoiselle, my conduct has been misrepresented if you have been told that I have trifled with the affections of the young lady you mention. Had I loved, there are no considerations of rank or fortune that would have dissuaded me from marriage. But to marry without love, or with love existing only on one side, would be folly; and I assure you that until this day my heart was free. Yes," added he, becoming quite serious, whilst his voice grew more impassioned, "until I came here two hours ago I never knew what love was. The aims of my life were selfish: they tended to my own advancement only, and I had never contemplated associating any woman with my destiny. But from this day"—and he fixed his eyes with an intent gaze on her—"I have a new ambition,—one that will blend itself with and sanctify all my other aspirations—and this ambition it is you alone that will have the power to fulfil it."

He rose, looking at her with a new glance full of love and meaning; and before she, in her surprise and distress, had found a word to say, he was gone.

Whilst this was taking place in the châlet, the world was enjoying itself at the drawing of the tombola, and Mr. Drydust was explaining to the Austrian ambassadress wherein this tombola, which was a plain lottery, differed from the Italian tombolas—an exposition to which her Excellency listened with as much good-nature as though her husband had never been civil governor of Milan, and specially occupied during ten years of his life in superintending the Austro-Lombard lotteries. At every moment there was enthusiasm and clapping of hands, as a spirited lady, perched aloft on a platform and turning a wheel-of-fortune, drew out a ticket and proclaimed a prize; which M. Gousset (capital make-up as a court-buffoon), or one of his staff, instantly fetched from behind a curtain and handed, with compliments, to the owner of the winning number. As a general rule, these lotteries are not a boon. One gets pen-wipers which one doesn't want, or paper-cutters which embarrass one the whole evening; but M. Macrobe had ordained this on the same grand scale as the other arrangements. He had simply invested five thousand guineas in jewellery, and not the least pleasing feature of his triumph was the amazement of his lady-guests, who, examining the lockets or brooches they had drawn, discovered them to be real gold! The sharpest of money-men find it difficult to steer clear of snobbishness.

But amidst this riot and jubilation a slinking somebody, draped in a Venetian cloak and wearing a black mask, was wandering about looking for the host. As the day was waning, and it was part of the programme that masks should be assumed at dusk, the Venetian-cloak gentleman soon found his example followed, which appeared to make his researches more difficult, for he more than once stopped and fixed on the wrong man, interrogating him first, and then apologizing. At last he lit upon M. Macrobe, who had just watched his daughter and Horace leave the châlet at a few minutes' interval, both flushed and pensive, and was quietly radiant.

"M. Macrobe," said the mask. "I thought I should never find you."

M. Macrobe started at the voice.

"Is it possible—can it be your Excellency?" he exclaimed. "This is an honour I dared not have counted on."

"Well, well," muttered M. Gribaud—for it was he —"my wife and my daughter were here: you had been good enough—hem—to send them an invitation, so I thought I would just come in like this:" he glanced deprecatingly at the cloak that covered his legs and gave a slight shrug.

"Your Excellency could not have conferred a greater favour—but let me lead you to the refreshment tent— you must be exhausted."

"No, no, thank you! By the way, if you have a mask, too, it might be as well to put it on; we shall be the less noticed."

M. Macrobe was not sorry to cover his face. Interviews with Monsieur the Minister Gribaud were often severe tests to physiognomical impassiveness. He knew his Excellency well enough to be certain that this unexpected visit was no mere act of amiability, but must have some business motive at the bottom of it.

"I have come because I had something to say on a matter that concerns us both," began the statesman, leading the way to a retired avenue. "You are still getting on well with young Gerold?"

"Your Excellency can see him yonder," answered

M. Macrobe, turning. "There to the left, in the cerise and white, talking to a lady—Mdme. de Margauld."

"Yes, I see him. Humph! how the boy has grown since I knew him. Well, M. Macrobe, you remember the conversation we had some time ago about this young man . . . . ?"

"Assuredly; and your Excellency must have noticed that the confidence I then expressed was not unfounded. Compare the political attitude of M. Horace Gerold now, and his attitude six months ago."

"He still gives us a great deal of trouble with those newspaper articles of his."

"I did not guarantee immediate results. Your Excellency will recollect my stating that the conversion would need a certain time; yet even in these newspaper articles, you must have remarked a daily increasing moderation."

"Moderate criticisms, M. Macrobe, are not those which give least annoyance," answered the Minister phlegmatically. "Still, I grant there is a change; what I have now to propose is an arrangement that may do a great deal at a single stroke. M. Chapoteau, the member for the Tenth Circumscription of Paris, died this morning."

"Which renders a seat vacant."

"Yes, and one it will be difficult to fill as we should like. That poor Chapoteau was a fool, but he made an excellent member. He was elected immediately after the *coup-d'état*, when people were still frightened, and he never gave us a minute's bother. But it would be nonsense hoping to get such a one elected again. People have got over their fright now, and they will be for electing some Radical just to spite us; it's always the same story with these Parisians. However, if you can answer that young Gerold will come over to our side by-and-by, it might be worth while putting him forward and letting him carry the seat, which he might do, popular as he has become."

"But how could the Government help him? Horace Gerold would not accept an official candidateship; neither, did he accept it, could he hope to win the seat, for his popularity would collapse on the spot."

"You don't quite follow me," answered M. Gribaud, with some impatience. "My suggestion is that you should induce young Gerold to stand as opposition candidate. We, of course, shall have our official candidate, and we will do our utmost to get him through; but failing the possibility of that—and I repeat, I don't think it is possible—our agents will receive instructions to give Gerold all the occult assistance they can. And supposing there should be several opposition candidates, and that a *ballotage* should be necessary by reason of the division of votes; then, on the second day's polling, our candidate shall withdraw in Gerold's favour, and so make the seat safe for him. All you will have to do is to prevent the young fellow from entering into any league with his brother opposition candidates."

There was a silence. M. Macrobe mused a moment.

"I will be frank with your Excellency," he said, at last. "I am rather afraid to adopt this plan. If it were certain that within a given time of his entering the house, Horace Gerold would cross over to the Government benches, the scheme would be a good one; but I greatly fear that if once elected as an opposition candidate, he would remain faithful to his party ever after. Gratitude in the first place, and in the next the pride of occupying an absolutely unique position—that of sole liberal member in a house full of Bonapartists—would combine to revive his republican sympathies, and so undo all the work we have been so patiently pursuing of late. But there is another way in which it strikes me this election can be turned to account in bringing young Gerold over more rapidly to our camp." M. Macrobe paused, and threw his eyes round him to make sure there were no eavesdroppers. "We will prevail upon Gerold to stand as opposition candidate, your Excellency; but we must contrive to get his election defeated by the Radicals. Let the Government press have orders to combat him, courteously; on the other hand, let there be stirred up against him a few of those Radicals who have affinity with the Préfecture de Police, and let these fellows be incited to assail him with all the ranting violence and calumnious abuse with which their pleasant vocabulary is stored. They might be licensed to start a paper on purpose to attack him, and furnished with the necessary funds. This would disgust Gerold. He is extremely sensitive; he shrinks from black guardism, and the more signal the courtesy shown him by his Bonapartist opponents, so much the more would he writhe under the low insults of his own party. If he lost his election through their doings, it would be all up with the connection. I should not be surprised to see him snap it there and then, and desert over to us in a dudgeon with arms and baggage."

His Excellency M. Gribaud passed his knotty hand over his chin. The project of M. Macrobe evidently tallied completely with his own ideas as to how an election ought to be carried on under the reign of Universal Suffrage. He saw no flaw in it. He approved.

"The only thing is about the vacant seat," muttered he. "Who will have it?"

"Not unlikely your official candidate," answered M. Macrobe, smiling. "If Gerold breaks with the radicals he will, probably, resign in favour of the Bonapartists to mark his utter contempt for the party he abandons. Then by this election your Excellency will have killed two birds with one stone—kept the seat in the Corps Législatif for the Bonapartists, and won over a dangerous adversary."

It was some time before these two pillars of the political and financial worlds separated. As their mutual esteem for each other increased by the disclosure of kindred sentiments, they continued to converse, broaching a variety of topics, and taking one another's moral measure. When M. Macrobe was again free, night had set in. Signor Scintilli, the pyrotechnician, had discharged his twenty thousand francs' worth of fire-works—the most goodly blaze ever seen—and the maskers had all retreated from the night-air into the brilliantly-illuminated saloons where the ball was to take place. The financier hurried across terraces and up staircases in his sable-gown and gold chain. He was bent upon finding Horace at once, and obtaining from him a promise to stand at the election. Wine, music, and the revelry aiding, it was presumable the young man would be more accessible to the counsels of ambition, more inclined to view his chances with a sanguine eye, than in a soberer mood to-morrow. But first M. Macrobe wished to see Angélique for a single moment, and discover by a passing question whether Horace had committed himself to any proposal. The ball had commenced, and the financier stood regarding it from the threshold of the room. Everybody was masked, and, as a consequence, everybody was behaving as he or she would not have done had their features been unveiled. The distinguished plenipotentiary, dressed as a fowl, was kicking his legs in the air in a style that would have secured his immediate ejection from Mabille. A quadrille composed of official deputies and senators' wives, figuring the devil, a monk or two, some historical dames, and a clown, were going through evolutions, which excited shrieks of interminable laughter from a surrounding ring of noble and illustrious spectators. Mr. Drydust, long ago severed from his claymore, and with his arm encircling the waist of a Russian princess, was performing all his steps Scotch-reel wise, and flinging his manly limbs about him like the branches of a tree, tempest-tossed. M. Gousset had so thoroughly entered into the spirit of his part that one would have taken him purely and simply for one of the loose characters of his own novels. M. Macrobe caught sight of Angélique seated and fanning herself. She had just been dancing with the Prince of Arcola, and, on account of the heat, had for a moment taken off her mask. Her aunt Dorothée, utterly unrecognisable and weird to witness as Catherine de' Medici, was beside her. Poor woman, she looked like a worthy soul from the upper world fallen by accident into pandemonium.

"Well, my pet, is your card pretty full?"

"Oh, papa, look!" she said. "I don't know how I shall ever keep all these engagements."

In truth, the card was full from the first dance to the twenty-second inclusive. An instant's survey showed M. Macrobe that Horace's name was not down.

"Have you danced with M. Gerold?" he asked carelessly.

Angélique blushed scarlet.

"M. Gerold never asked me," she said, fanning herself more rapidly and speaking shyly.

M. Macrobe knew all he cared to know.

"The courtship has begun," he muttered gaily; and he made for a corner of the room where Horace, easily discernible, though masked, was handing the fascinating daughter of Cincinnatus Jickling, Esq.; back to her seat after—as she prettily termed it—"going the pace" with her.

Five minutes later there were two happy men in the room—M. Prosper Macrobe, who had obtained his promise and been thanked into the bargain with a sudden and earnest effusion of gratitude that had surprised him; and Horace himself, who, animated with the whole day's proceedings, the wine, the lights, the dance, was saying, with beating pulse and glistening eye: "Deputy at twenty-five! I shall not have a fortune to offer her, but I can make myself a name: and then, perhaps, her father will not refuse his consent. That man seems to be my guardian angel."

END OF VOL. I.

www.ingramcontent.com/pod-product-compliance
Lightning Source LLC
Chambersburg PA
CBHW030117240426
43673CB00041B/1314